First Love

Discovering our Design of Love and Unity with God

Geoff Woodcock

onewith**christ**.org

Jesus—with all my heart and soul, I love you.

Thanks to Brian Upsher for editorial support, Nikki Miller and Donna Nichol for proofing, and to Silas Kemp for cover art concept design. And thanks of course, to my wife Melanie, without whom this book would not have been possible.

First Love by Geoff Woodcock

Book One of the *One with Christ Series*

Revision 1, April 2020

ISBN: 978-0-9951207-4-7

ISSN: 2624-411x

Published by Acacia Media - www.acacia.media

This book is available free online at www.onewithchrist.org

Contents

Introduction .... *i*

DESIGN OF LIFE

1 . Revelation and Reality....................................1

2 . By Design 7

3 . First Things First..12

4 . Love in Union..18

5 . A Movement into Union 24

6 . What is Life?..30

7 . What is Love? 35

8 . Love and Life 40

9 . Circumcision of the Heart...........................46

10 . One Spirit...51

11 . Higher Ways..56

12 . The Source of Thoughts................................62

13 . Testing Thoughts...68

14 . Making Agreements 74

IDENTITY IN CHRIST

15 . A New Identity...80

16 . Identity in Love..86

17 . Prevailing Grace..91

18 . Relationship and Religion............................97

19 . Life in Love 103

20 . Breaking the Cycle......................................111

21 . Crime and Punishment 116

22 . Sin and Deception 122

23 . Teaching Grace..129

LOVE IN UNITY

24 . Love in Eternity 135

25 . Multiplying Love 142

26 . Love Like This...148

27 . Loving and Giving..155

28 . Giving in Unity..162

29 . Love Discerns..169

30 . Will of God..175

31 . Founded in Love...181

32 . All of You 187

33 . Infinite Love..194

34 . The Simple Gospel 200

35 . Revival Fire...206

36 . Freely Give..213

Study Guide... 219

Reference Notes 257

Introduction

"If you turn off the lights, do the walls change color?"

A few weeks earlier I had started to wonder if my children were losing the natural instinct to think. So at dinner one night I asked a simple question: "If you turn off the lights, do the walls change color?"[1] The response was immediate: three yes, one no. After a short pause the no became yes and a yes became no, and a "not sure" entered the mix. I listened and waited for the lights to come on.

The speed of their responses told me that my children were no longer thinking about questions in a meaningful way. They were developing the belief that most of the questions in life have clear and simple answers that we should already know. Like the children, we can be tempted to dismiss questions with surface-level answers, never taking the time to come to meaningful conclusions. When we fail to give real thought to the questions of life, we let go of something really special. Not only do we deny ourselves new knowledge, but we forfeit some of our own potential to grow and mature.

As people we are designed to grow in both body and in character. And by definition, *growth is change*. It is the transformation that comes as we mature. In the course of life, our bodies reach full maturity relatively early. Yet our character never needs to stop growing. If we have the desire, we can keep changing inwardly for our entire lives. We can learn new things that change the way we think about life, other people and ourselves. We can discover truth and gain wisdom. We can find healing through forgiveness. We can forge a vision that changes the entire direction of our lives. But first we need to ask ourselves: do we really want to change?

There are many ways that we can change and grow spiritually, but there is one thing that brings about lasting transformation like no other: love. Love is not a theory that we learn, but a reality that we experience as we encounter the God who is love. He can change us more in a single encounter than we could ever change ourselves with years of learning. God's love heals a broken heart faster than any amount of counseling. His love brings freedom from the bondage of selfishness and addiction; it energizes, refreshes, renews and restores us. His love imparts vision for a new life and then releases the power of God to make that vision a reality.

It is wonderfully freeing to know that God is not asking us to change ourselves by our own efforts. He is simply asking us to open our hearts and let His love do the work. With this in mind, at the end of the book is a Study Guide that contains some exercises to help you process each chapter, connect with God, and open your heart to His love. I would like to encourage you to do these reflections, giving the questions some real thought and taking time to explore your answers. You do not have to do all the questions and you may like to write your own. Know that the time you invest with God will bring a very real return.[2]

This book is split into three sections. The first section, "Design of Life," looks at how God defines life in relationship with Him. This provides the foundation for "Identity in Christ," where we look at how the presence of the Spirit of Jesus within us changes our sense of identity. In the third section, "Love in Unity," we look at how God's love flows through us to one another.

If you find that what you read does not make sense, is dry or hard to read, simply leave it. It may not be quite right for this stage of your journey. Instead find something else that speaks to you where you are, conveys a sense of life and inspires you to keep growing in God. If the timing is right, then may God deeply bless and enrich your life as you read this book. May your heart be flooded with His presence and transformed by His grace. May the Spirit of God bring you into a life of abundant love, intimacy, and unity with Jesus. And may it all be to His great glory and your great joy.

– Geoff (Jeff) Woodcock

1 | Revelation and Reality

1 John 4:7-8
Beloved, let us love one another, for love is from God, and whoever loves has been born of God and knows God. Anyone who does not love does not know God, because God is love.

I remember meeting up with a friend one day. She seemed unusually happy.

"God gave me a revelation last night," she said. "God is love."

"Yes, I know," I replied. It seemed like the logical response. Scripture is crystal clear on this.

"No, you don't know. *God is love.*"

I looked at her, not sure if I should be offended or not. She repeated it again with a wide smile. "You don't know! God is love!"

Somehow, something had happened to her that night. The Spirit of God took her beyond an intellectual knowledge of this truth and into a profound revelation. The truth that "God is love" was now real for her. As a result, all the implications of God being love were now flooding her life. She now knew that God was only ever going to be good to her. She could trust Him. She knew that God really liked her. She could be honest with Him. She no longer needed to fear failure. She felt secure. She could draw close to Him. Her entire life was being changed by God with the gift of one simple revelation: God is love.

This revelation gave my friend a new sense of identity in God's love. She knew God loved her, and the joy it brought was uncontainable. I thought I knew that God is love and I was comfortable in that knowledge. But on that day, I realized that what I believed in my head was not what I knew in my heart. In my mind, I believed that God is love, but my heart was yet to be convinced. I needed a revelation. I needed reality.

An Unimaginable Inheritance

John 16:13

When the Spirit of truth comes, he will guide you into all the truth, for he will not speak on his own authority, but whatever he hears he will speak, and he will declare to you the things that are to come.

The word *truth* here is the Greek word *aletheia,* which means "true to fact; reality."[1] The truth of God is not merely a theory to be taught, but a reality to be experienced. God is so good and He does not intend for us to work our own way into reality. Instead, He gives us the gift of His Spirit to make it easy for us. The Holy Spirit is here to teach us the truth of God and to make it our reality by bringing us into the actual experience of the truth.

1 Corinthians 2:9-12 (BSB)

Rather, as it is written:

"No eye has seen,

no ear has heard,

no heart has imagined,

what God has prepared for those who love Him."

But God has revealed it to us by the Spirit. The Spirit searches all things, even the deep things of God. For who among men knows the thoughts of man except his own spirit within him? So too, no one knows the thoughts of God except the Spirit of God. We have not received the spirit of the world, but the Spirit who is from God, that we may understand what God has freely given us.

What no eye has seen, nor ear heard... What no one envisioned; what no one ever preached; what no one ever dared to imagine or dream of—this is what God has prepared for us because we love Him.

When Jesus died, He gave us an inheritance beyond all comprehension. Because our minds are so limited, no amount of learning can empower us to take hold of what God has prepared for us. The only way we can get a vision for our inheritance is through the Holy Spirit. It is His work to enable us to understand and receive the gifts that God has so freely given us. And He does this through revelation.

Ephesians 1:18-19a

I pray that the eyes of your heart may be enlightened, so that you may know what is the hope of His calling, what are the riches of the glory of His inheritance in the saints, and what is the surpassing greatness of His power toward us who believe.

Revelation is not about God teaching us something new, but about God making something real for us. Through revelation, the Spirit of God opens our eyes to see the gifts He so longs to give us. At one time, the Spirit may give us a revelation of God's love; at another time He may reveal God's joy or peace or His presence or power. When the Holy Spirit reveals what He is freely giving us, His revelation speaks directly to our hearts. In our own strength, we so often strive to declare the truth of God in our lives, hoping that what we know to be true in our minds might become a reality in our hearts. Yet what no amount of human effort can ever achieve, the Spirit of God can do in a moment of time. Through revelation, the Holy Spirit gives us faith, understanding and vision, and together these create a platform in our lives for reality.

Deuteronomy 11:18 (NASB)

"You shall therefore impress these words of mine on your heart and on your soul..."

Joshua 1:8 (NASB)

"This book of the law shall not depart from your mouth, but you shall meditate on it day and night, so that you may be careful to do according to all that is written in it; for then you will make your way prosperous, and then you will have success."

Revelation is not a gift that we passively receive from the Spirit. It requires our willing participation and obedience to produce the fruit that God has purposed for it. Like the soil in the parable of the Sower, we need to prepare our hearts for revelation so that the seed of truth can be nurtured through to reality. When the Spirit shares His word with us, our call is to impress His truth on our heart and soul through meditation. This is not the emptying of our minds through New Age or Eastern meditation but the infilling of our hearts with the truth through Biblical meditation. This is a discipline that engages both the heart and mind. We start by reading a Scripture slowly, memorizing it, repeating it, and thinking it over. We then ask the Spirit of Jesus to inspire our imagination and turn faith into vision.

Imagination bridges the gap between the mind and the heart. This is why Jesus speaks in so many parables. The word-pictures He uses inspire the imagination, which brings together both the heart and mind of the hearers. When something we hear or read inspires our imagination, our brains become active as if they are processing real-world senses. We can picture ourselves in a situation and imagine what it would be like to smell, hear, taste and feel within that situation. As we use our imagination to meditate on a truth of Scripture, we pass beyond the borders of logical thought and engage our senses and our emotions in the truth.

People in the world embrace imagination as a tool for creativity and innovation. Yet in many religious circles, imagination is considered to be self-inspired fantasy and therefore something to be avoided. However, imagination is simply thought that is expressed in pictures and explored with the senses and emotions. And Scripture *never* calls us to avoid thinking. Instead we are called to take our thoughts captive and only nurture godly thoughts. In the same way, Scripture never calls us to avoid our imagination. On the contrary, the word of God encourages us to use our imagination in a positive way.[2]

When used negatively, our imagination leads us out of reality and brings us into the fantasy of lustful, proud, religious or self-serving thoughts. However, when the Holy Spirit inspires our imagination, instead of immersing us in an inner fantasy, our imagination brings the truth to life for us. We can imagine what it would feel like to humble ourselves under the hand of God.

We can imagine what it would be like for God's joy to become our strength. We can imagine being filled with boldness and confidence through the Spirit. Every time we engage our imagination with the Scriptures, we create space for the Holy Spirit to bring revelation and make His truth a reality in our lives.

I Shall Lack Nothing

I remember the first time I took time to dwell on a single verse of Scripture. For 15 minutes I focused only on Psalm 23:1, "The LORD is my Shepherd, I shall not want [or I shall lack nothing]." I repeated it slowly over and over, allowing the weight of that truth to sink in. *Jesus is my Shepherd; I shall lack nothing.* I imagined Jesus providing for me. I imagined never having to worry about provision ever again. As I meditated on this verse, the Spirit burned His word into my heart. It was like God Himself was speaking and promising me that He would provide everything I would ever need in life. This revelation produced an unshakeable confidence within me. I knew in my heart that Jesus was truly my Shepherd and He would always look after me.

It was not long before this promise was tested. I started my fourth year at university with only two dollars to last me for five days. I knew that God would provide for my needs, so I reasoned that if I needed food, He would give it to me, otherwise I would fast. I resolved not to share my need with anyone but just to trust God to determine what I truly needed.

On the first day I helped a friend who was a chef and was having technical issues with her computer. I walked in the door and she looked up and spoke.

"I am so glad to see you. The kitchen over-catered for a conference last night and we have all this food left over. Can you take some?"

I smiled. "I think I can help you out with that." She gave me croissants, fruit and a large three-layer chocolate gateau that would last for several days. The next day a friend invited me to have dinner with his family. On another day, a friend shared some French baking that his sister saved from being thrown out at a local bakery.[3] Every day God provided me with better food than I would have bought myself if I had the money. He was keeping His promise and taking care of me. Jesus was my Shepherd and I did not want.

Revelation leads to reality. The revelation of God as my provider started with a time of meditation and imagination. The truth of God's promise to provide my needs was impressed on my heart and then experienced in my life. This truth set me free and set me and my family up for life. Since that time, I have never felt any stress over where we would sleep, what we would eat, or the clothes we would wear. Jesus promised to care for me and for my family, and He has always kept His promise.

We are called to be a people of the truth; a people who not only know the theory but live in the reality of our inheritance in Christ. If we are to answer this call, we need to learn to treat our times of meditation on the truth of God as sacred, holy and deeply precious. As we create space for revelation, the Holy Spirit will be faithful to inspire our imagination, to increase our faith, to clarify our vision, and to transform our lives.

Pray
Father, please inspire my imagination and help me to impress your words on my heart.

2 | By Design

Our experience of life is shaped by the way we think. All the thoughts that we have about life and the outside world combine to form our *worldview*. As children we go through the wonder of having a blank canvas for a worldview. Our first years are a discovery of the world and our place in life. Through our experiences we paint our picture of what we think the world is like. The worldview we create then helps us to make sense of life as we grow and mature.

> **Matthew 18:2-4**
> And calling to him a child, he [Jesus] put him in the midst of them and said, "Truly, I say to you, unless you turn and become like children, you will never enter the kingdom of heaven. Whoever humbles himself like this child is the greatest in the kingdom of heaven."

In order to possess the kingdom of God, we need to be willing to become like little children again. We need to be prepared to start over and let Jesus paint a new picture of life for us. As He teaches us, we will begin to see life as He sees it: a sacred gift of great wonder, power and blessing.

> **Proverbs 23:7a**
> For as he thinks in his heart, so is he.

Just as we have thoughts about the outside world, we have thoughts about the inner world of who we are in our heart and soul. These thoughts combine to form our *identity*. Our identity is simply our unique perspective on our own unique personality. When we look at the person in the mirror, all the thoughts that run through our mind are insights into the identity we have created for ourselves.

We start creating our identity from birth. I have a friend who has been fostering a young girl since she was three. From birth, this girl was tragically neglected by her parents. She shared her room with a number of cats and rarely saw her parents. As a result, she spent the first three years of her life believing she was a cat. She ate cat-food, meowed instead of talked, moved like a cat, and licked her arms to mimic the way cats would clean their fur. In the absence of a healthy human model, this beautiful young girl developed her sense of identity by watching the cats around her. When she was taken into her new home, she had to unlearn everything that she previously believed about her life. Instead she had to learn what it truly means to be human.

This is one of the basic problems with identity. It is part of our human nature to create our identity from what we see around us. Even though the human design is biologically encoded within all people, it is only by studying and interacting with our parents that we learn what it means to be human. We know that we are designed to walk on two legs, but unless a child sees people walking, they will not learn to walk by themselves. We need a model to impart vision and the desire to change.

This process is known as *imprinting* and it works well when the parents are healthy. However, in our infancy, we have no way of knowing whether the people who raise us are accurately modelling true humanity to us. In fact, as infants, we lack the ability to question if our models are even human at all. As a result, there have been children who have been raised by dogs or monkeys or cats and have grown up living and acting exactly like the animals who raised them.

This principle is exactly the same in the spiritual realm. As we grow spiritually, we imprint on those around us and we build a spiritual identity for ourselves which is based largely on what we see in other people. But what if everyone has been living in something less than God's design? How do we know if the people we copy are getting life right?

Imprinting on the World

2 Corinthians 10:12

But when they measure themselves by one another and compare themselves with one another, they are without understanding.

Comparing or measuring ourselves to others is deeply unwise. Like my friend's foster daughter, we can look at those around us and think we are doing well, yet live in a reality far below God's design for our lives. Instead of forming our sense of identity by looking at the people around us, we need to measure ourselves according to God's specific design for our lives.

Romans 12:1-2

I appeal to you therefore, brothers, by the mercies of God, to present your bodies as a living sacrifice, holy and acceptable to God, which is your spiritual worship. Do not be conformed to this world, but be transformed by the renewal of your mind, that by testing you may discern what is the will of God, what is good and acceptable and perfect.

Do not be conformed to the world... In other words, do not imprint on the world. Do not let the world define you. Do not let it shape your identity. Why? Because the world has a deeply distorted image of what it means to be human. The world tells us that we exist for our own benefit.[1] It raises us in a culture of selfishness and strips us of our sense of purpose. And in our infancy, we simply accept what we see as true. The world tells us we exist to work, play, buy and die. We believe the lie and grow up expecting to get a job so we can make enough money to entertain ourselves and build our material wealth before we die. We have no reason to question the call of the world to live for ourselves. *Indulge yourself. Secure your own future. Do what is best for you.* The message of selfishness so permeates our culture that it influences the way almost every person thinks. Because of this, as we form our sense of spiritual identity, it can be easy to mix the selfish with the spiritual.

*Be transformed by the renewal of your mind...*Like little children, we need to ask the Spirit of God to transform us by renewing our worldview and our identity. A key part of this renewing is exploring the reason why God created us and the world we dwell in.

When we create something, we always design our creation to serve a specific purpose. Clocks are designed to tell the time. Cars are designed to transport us places. Houses are made to give us shelter and provide a space for us to live. Every created thing has a purpose and design that is defined solely by its creator.

So what is God's design for us? What does a life as God intended look like? If God's goal was that we would spend eternity with Him in heaven, then why did He not simply create us in heaven? There must be a reason why we are here on the earth. These questions can be rolled into two basic questions that we all need to find the answers to:

1. Why did God create us?
2. Who are we?

The first question deals with our design and purpose, the second with our identity. We cannot answer the second question before the first because identity always stems from design. We can see this in the natural realm. A lion does not get to choose its identity. It is a hunter because from tooth to claw, a lion's whole body is designed to hunt. Because of this, no healthy lion defies their design and stops eating meat. On the contrary, like us, a lion can only find its ultimate satisfaction by living according to its design. Sheep are not hunters. Sheep are designed to mill around and eat grass. If a lamb was to grow up thinking it was a lion, it would experience a frustrating, confusing and short life. In the same way, if we are to come to a true sense of identity, we need to firstly discover God's design and purpose for our lives. Only when we know why God created us, will we be able to look into the mirror and see who we truly are.

10

God has created everything for a purpose beyond itself. Therefore, the more we focus on self, the more we lose sight of our purpose in life. I wanted to explore this with my children, so one day I asked: "Can you think of anything that has been created only for its own benefit?" My younger children thought about the question for a few moments and then lost interest. However, my eldest son Jacob spent the day thinking about it. At the end of the day, he had no answer. Everything he could think of was created for a reason outside itself.

"So if everything has a purpose, imagine that one day you found a strange machine that someone had invented. How could you figure out what it was created for?" Jacob paused and then answered simply: "Ask the person who made it."

Like the strange machine, when we look at our lives, it can be a puzzle trying to learn why God has created us. Yet in the search for identity, we cannot discover who we are by getting to know ourselves better. We cannot find our identity in the people around us or in the things we do. We cannot find our identity in our age, in our beauty, in the color of our skin, in our sexuality, in the country we live in, the media we watch, in the religion we follow, or in the language we speak. The only way we can form a true sense of identity is by discovering our design.

And this is what makes this adventure so simple. If we want to learn about our design and find out why we were created, there is only one thing we need to do. We simply need to ask the One who made us.

Pray
Lord, please show me who I really am and why you created me.

3 | First Things First

Identity starts with design and design happens at the very beginning of creation, before anything is made. Our journey into life therefore starts with the beginning—our genesis.

Genesis 1:1
In the beginning God created the heavens and the earth.

In the beginning, before anything spiritual or physical was ever created, was God. He is the source of all life and so the Bible starts by telling us that God created the entire universe.

Genesis 1:26-27
Then God said, "Let Us make man in Our image, according to Our likeness; and let them rule over the fish of the sea and over the birds of the sky and over the cattle and over all the earth, and over every creeping thing that creeps on the earth." God created man in His own image, in the image of God He created him; male and female He created them.

Psalm 139:13-14
For You formed my inward parts;
You wove me in my mother's womb.
I will give thanks to You, for I am fearfully and wonderfully made;
Wonderful are Your works,
And my soul knows it very well.

In the beginning God created everything, including us. As people, we are not a consequence of chance. Not a single feature of the awesome complexity that is found in every part of our bodies came about because of chance or random changes in nature. Every part of us: body, soul and spirit has been deliberately designed and wonderfully made by God. And if we are deliberately designed by God, it is because He has a clear purpose for us. As our Creator, He alone holds the answers. He alone can tell us who we are and why He has created us.

Looking into the Mirror

In the natural realm, mirrors show us how we look physically. They are so much a part of our life that it is hard to imagine being raised without mirrors and not being able to recognize our own face. Yet that is exactly how so many people live spiritually. Too many people drift through life, never stopping to look into a spiritual mirror to see who they really are.

> **James 1:23-25** (emphasis added)
> But prove yourselves doers of the word, and not merely hearers who delude themselves. For if anyone is a hearer of the word and not a doer, he is like a man who **looks at his natural face in a mirror**; for once he has looked at himself and gone away, he has immediately forgotten what kind of person he was. But one who looks intently at the perfect law, the law of liberty, and abides by it, not having become a forgetful hearer but an effectual doer, this man will be blessed in what he does.

In this passage, James says that the word of God is like a mirror. In the same way that our glass mirrors show us our physical image, the Bible is a spiritual mirror that shows us our natural face. The word translated as *natural* here is the Greek word *genesis,* meaning "source, origin, or birth."[1] Our natural face is our *genesis* face. It is our identity as God originally designed.[2]

This makes the Bible so much more than a collection of historical books. It is a living revelation of God and of His original design for our lives. Like a person staring at their reflection, if we look intently into the word of God, we will be able to see our true purpose and identity in Christ. However, if we fail to act on what we see, we become like people who look at a mirror only to turn away and forget who we truly are. It is therefore essential that we learn how to move from reading to reality. Every time God speaks to us through the Scriptures and reveals who we are in Christ, we need to act on that word and let the Holy Spirit make it real for us.

The Greatest Command

As our Creator, God has made us with a specific design in mind and so our identity is forever set. It can never be changed because it can never be improved. No matter what kind of identity we try to develop for ourselves, it will never be as good as God's design. And because God is so good, He has shared His design with us. It is not meant to be a mystery—every living person is supposed to know what it really means to be human.

It took me some time to come to this knowledge. Even though I grew up in a church, I knew little of why God created me. Then I heard a person teach the Bible with a spirit of wisdom and revelation. It was awe-inspiring and humbling to hear. To listen to someone speak of the word as a reality left me feeling like a complete novice. I realized that despite my knowledge of Scripture, I was still far from knowing the truth. One day, I threw my Bible on the bed and stared at it. I turned my thoughts to God.

"I know nothing about this book. If I'm going to learn to understand the Scriptures, you're going to need to teach me."

A short time later, I began reading the Bible and quietly came to a point of revelation. As I opened the Scriptures, the Holy Spirit opened my mind and showed me a truth that would alter the course of my life. He showed me what it meant to be human.

Matthew 22:34-40 (BSB)
And when the Pharisees heard that Jesus had silenced the Sadducees, they themselves gathered together. One of them, an expert in the law, tested Him with a question: "Teacher, which commandment is the greatest in the Law?"

Jesus declared, "'Love the Lord your God with all your heart and with all your soul and with all your mind.' This is the first and greatest commandment. And the second is like it: 'Love your neighbor as yourself.' All the Law and the Prophets depend on these two commandments.'"

If I was a clockmaker who made living clocks, I would not give my clocks the freedom to define themselves. If I did, one of my clocks could spend all day on a wall looking at a toaster and start to think that it too was a toaster. Instead, I would make their design and purpose clear. To do this, I could write a long instruction manual containing everything a clock must do to function. But if I was to write only one command for the clock, I would simply say: *Tell the time*. Within that one command I would communicate the whole design of my creation and its very reason for being.

Jesus does exactly the same thing here.

By revealing His greatest command, Jesus shows us why He created us. Every single one of us has been expertly designed to love God with all our heart, all our soul, all our mind, and all our strength. Our entire being is created for love.

Though I had read this passage many times, I had never read it as a revelation of my purpose or identity in Christ. I had also never paused long enough to realize what Jesus was doing by making this command *first*. It is first, not in the sense of being the initial command given to humanity, but first in terms of priority and importance. This is God's number one priority for our lives. Why? Because it is the very reason for our creation.

Deuteronomy 6:1-5 (emphasis added)
"Now **this is the commandment**, and these are the statutes and judgments which the LORD your God has commanded to teach you, that you may observe them in the land which you are crossing over to possess, that you may fear the LORD your God, to keep all His statutes and His commandments which I command you, you and your son and your grandson, all the days of your life, and that your days may be prolonged. Therefore hear, O Israel, and **be careful to observe it**, that

it may be well with you, and that you may multiply greatly as the LORD God of your fathers has promised you—'a land flowing with milk and honey.'

"Hear, O Israel: The LORD our God, the LORD is one! You shall love the LORD your God with all your heart, with all your soul, and with all your strength."

The most important command of God is first found in Deuteronomy. Like the rest of Scripture, the Mosaic Law contains many statutes and judgments, but they are all based on *one single* command: to love the LORD our God with all our heart, soul, and strength. This first command exists as the foundation and context for all the rest of Scripture.

1 John 2:7 (NASB)
Beloved, I am not writing a new commandment to you, but an old commandment which you have had from the beginning; the old commandment is the word which you have heard.

God does not change and neither does His design for humanity. There is no Plan B. Therefore, Scripture has always been unwavering in the call of love. From the very beginning where God first breathes life into Adam through to the very end where Christ reigns with His bride in awesome glory, the message of love resounds throughout all of Scripture. Within its pages we see an undeniable picture: We were all created by love, through love, and for love. Each one of us is a custom creation, specifically designed and perfectly built to love.

A Glorious Ideal
The greatest command expresses God's unchangeable design for humanity, and it is worded in such a way that it leaves no room for partial obedience or half-hearted devotion. We are called to love God with our entire being and nothing less.

On the surface this seems like an out-of-reach ideal, disconnected from the reality of a fallen life. It is strangely comforting to think of the commands of Scripture as ideals that we strive for rather than realities that we attain. After all, who can be perfect as our heavenly Father is perfect, or completely humble and gentle?[3] Who can fervently love others from a pure heart or pray without ceasing?[4] Surely the commands of the Bible represent a collection of divine principles that we are to use as we strive to become more like Jesus. And because we are unable to meet the ideals of Scripture then surely our striving to keep God's commands will be counted as obedience and rewarded by God. Or could we be wrong? Could there be a way to live in wholehearted obedience to God? Are we in fact capable of loving God with all our heart, soul, mind and strength?

Because all the commands of Scripture hinge on the greatest command, there is one question that we must be able to answer with absolute certainty. Concerning the greatest command, it is essential that we all—every single believer—settle this question in our hearts: Is it possible?

Pray

Father, I need to know: is it truly possible for me to love you with all my being? If it is possible and this really is your highest will for my life, then please show me.

4 | Love in Union

Is it possible to love God with all our heart, soul, mind and strength? A modern parable may help as we begin to explore the answer to this question.[1]

As He walked, Jesus came to a village. A crowd soon gathered, and out of the crowd, a man came to Jesus and asked, "Teacher, what must I do to have eternal life?"

Jesus answered him saying, "If you want eternal life, you must be at least eight feet tall."

The crowd stirred. The man turned to the people and asked, "How can this be?" No one knew. So the people returned to their homes and began to think of ways they could make themselves eight feet tall. Some of the people made stretching machines and others invented height-enhancing diets. One man crafted a pair of stilts. Although the stilts were uncomfortable to wear, difficult to use, and leased for an expensive fee, people loved them. Using the stilts meant that people could avoid dieting or stretching, and still be eight feet tall.

Many months later, Jesus returned to the village. He looked around at the people all walking on stilts and sighed. The people were trying so hard to stay balanced on their stilts that few noticed His arrival. However, a little girl saw Jesus and came to Him.

"Jesus, I want eternal life, but I am only three feet tall. I am too young to wear stilts. How can I become eight feet tall?" she asked.

Jesus smiled and said, "Come. Let me lift you up on my shoulders. Together we will be eight feet tall."

A light started to grow in the young girl's eyes but there was some fear as well.

"But Jesus, I am a bit scared. What if I fall?"

Jesus replied, "I will be holding you the whole time. And if you lose your balance, I will always catch you. I promise."

The little girl climbed onto Jesus' shoulders. A sense of joy filled her heart as Jesus lifted her high into the air. Her whole world changed.

Some of the people wearing stilts saw the girl and Jesus. One man, who had always had difficulty stilt-walking, stared at the sight. He saw the joy in the girl's face and the same joy in Jesus. He looked down at the bruises on his body. He had fallen from the stilts more times than he could remember. Tears filled his eyes as he unstrapped the stilts and stepped down onto the ground. Some of the people around him were concerned for the man.

"Are you turning your back on eternal life?!" they called. "Don't you want to go to heaven?" But the man ignored the voices and walked shakily over to Jesus. He fought back his tears as he spoke.

"Jesus—are you able to take adults on your shoulders as well?"

Jesus looked him in the eyes, smiled and said...

As adults, we often complicate the words of Scripture and even life itself. We are so often tempted to strap on our stilts and put all our strength into living a good Christian life. We believe that if we try really hard to keep God's commands that He will be pleased with our efforts and sincerity. However, no matter how hard we try, we cannot escape the fact that we are all incapable of keeping the commands of God in their fullness. We simply cannot make ourselves eight-feet tall.

Matthew 18:2-3

And calling to him a child, he put him in the midst of them and said, "Truly, I say to you, unless you turn and become like children, you will never enter the kingdom of heaven."

Unlike adults, little children view life with a humble honesty. We need to rediscover this childlike simplicity if we are going to make sense of our call to wholehearted love. This starts with acknowledging our helplessness. Adam could not breathe until God gave him breath and we cannot love unless God gives us love. So instead of striving to love, we simply need to surrender and join ourselves to the One who is Love.

Abide in Me

John 15:5 (NASB)
"I am the vine, you are the branches; he who abides in Me and I in him, he bears much fruit, for apart from Me you can do nothing."

When the Holy Spirit revealed that I was designed by God for wholehearted love, He helped me to see how impossible it was. I could hardly tell my heart what to feel let alone demand that it love God. The pride, lust and selfishness that raged within me were often entirely overpowering. I knew there was no way I could ever possibly fulfil the first command apart from Jesus. Apart from Him I could do absolutely nothing. With this realization came a sense of relief. Like the man who took off his stilts, I finally accepted that there was no point in pretending that I could do it by myself. If God had commanded me to love Him with all my heart and soul, then He would need to make it a reality. Jesus would have to lift me up and set me on His shoulders.

Matthew 11:28-30 (NASB)
"Come to Me, all who are weary and heavy-laden, and I will give you rest. Take My yoke upon you and learn from Me, for I am gentle and humble in heart, and you will find rest for your souls. For My yoke is easy and My burden is light."

In the natural realm, a yoke unites two animals to allow them to work together as one. When Jesus calls us to take His yoke upon us, He calls us to come into union with Him and let Him bear the burden of our obedience. His yoke is easy because Jesus uses His own strength to obey the Father's will through us. Jesus bears the full weight of all God's commands, especially the greatest command to love. Our part is simply to learn how to live in unity with Jesus and let Him love through us.[2]

Jesus originally spoke these words of compassion to people who were collapsing under the weight of the law. For years, the teachers of Scripture had been piling the burden of obedience on the backs of the people without offering a single finger to help lift the load.[3] These teachers saw righteousness as the perfection of behavior and so they taught enough principles and commands to govern even the smallest details of life. The result was that their teaching left the people broken, exhausted, isolated, condemned and empty. In their zeal for righteousness, the teachers had failed to understand a crucial principle: God does not expect us to obey a single command of Scripture on our own. In fact, the standards of Scripture are presented as impossibly high as to remove any thought of obeying in our own strength. Instead, our entire obedience to the will of God is only made possible through our unity with Jesus.

Obey in Union

Deuteronomy 11:22-23

"For if you are careful to keep all this commandment which I am commanding you to do, to love the LORD your God, to walk in all His ways and hold fast [*davaq*] to Him, then the LORD will drive out all these nations from before you, and you will dispossess nations greater and mightier than you."

In this passage we see the beautiful simplicity of our call to love. The word translated as *hold fast* in this passage is the Hebrew word *davaq* (pronounced da-vak) meaning "to join together; to glue or bond; to become one."[4] It is first used in Genesis 2 where it speaks of a man being joined (*davaq*) to his wife and the two becoming one flesh.

The command to love God and walk in all His ways is inseparably connected to the call to become bound together as one with Christ. Why? Because God is love and He is the only source of love. Apart from Jesus we cannot love God nor walk in His ways. Our obedience to the first and greatest command is only possible through our union with the God who is Love.

Earlier we learned that the first command defines God's highest will and purpose for our lives. God designed us for a life of love and yet now we learn that we can only keep the first command in union with Jesus. What this shows us is that God did not just create us to love Him with all our heart and soul; He created us to live in union with Him.

Christ in You

2 Corinthians 13:5
Examine yourselves, to see whether you are in the faith. Test yourselves. Or do you not realize this about yourselves, that Jesus Christ is in you?—unless indeed you fail to meet the test!

Unity with the Spirit of Jesus is woven into the very fabric of our design. And we only come into this design through faith. The test of faith is therefore not a question of intellectual belief but of spiritual possession. Is the Spirit of Jesus living within us? Are we one with Him? How can we know for sure?

The spirit within a person shapes their thoughts, emotions, words and actions. For example, if a person is possessed by a spirit of rage, they will internally experience thoughts and feelings of rage, which are then expressed externally in their words and actions. In the same way, if the Spirit of Jesus is alive within us, His presence can be seen through His love. We can therefore test ourselves by asking: Are we increasingly thinking about love? Are our hearts growing in compassion? Are we learning to speak more words of love and to act more often in love? The more we grow in our unity with Jesus, the more His love will be seen in our lives.

Philippians 4:13
I can do all things through him who strengthens me.

Apart from Christ a life of wholehearted love is an absolute impossibility. But we were never designed to be apart from Christ. We were created to be one with Jesus, and in unity with Him we can do all things—*especially* love. When we let the Spirit of Jesus take possession of our lives, we will find that the greatest command is more than possible; it is easy.

So let us accept the truth that apart from Christ we can do nothing. Let us step down from our stilts and humble ourselves. Let us come to Jesus and find rest for our souls in the arms of Love. Let us be one with Christ.

Pray

Lord Jesus, thank you that you do not expect me to keep the greatest command by myself. Thank you that you want to be one with me. Please share your hunger for unity with me.

5 | A Movement into Union

John 3:16 is probably one of the best known and most memorized verses in the Bible. It is used all over the world as a one-sentence summary of the Christian gospel. It is an awesome statement of truth when taken at face value. However, if we venture beneath the surface of this verse, we will find that the gospel speaks of a life that is beautifully united with Christ through faith and love.

Into Jesus

John 3:16

For God so loved the world, that he gave his only Son, that whoever believes in [*eis*] him should not perish but have eternal life.

Eis (ice): *Into*

The Greek word eis means literally 'motion into which', implying penetration ('unto,' 'union') to a particular purpose or result. The word eis roots to the literal meaning 'one.' TDNT (2:434) notes that 1519(eis) was once used for the digit 'one' indicating union for a purpose or result.

The Greek word *eis* literally means *into* and stands in contrast to the Greek word *en* which means *in*. Just as a river flows *into* the sea and the waters become one, the word *eis* conveys the idea of an active movement that results in a union.[1]

John 3:16 tells us that God has shown His limitless love for us by giving His only Son so that we might have eternal life as we believe *into* Jesus. "Believing into Jesus" is an awkward phrase both in Greek and in English, and yet John uses it intentionally and often. He tolerates the awkwardness in order to communicate a major point of the gospel: Real faith takes us beyond just believing in Jesus and actively moves us into union with Him.

We can think of it like this: it is one thing to believe in marriage as a covenant relationship, but it is something else entirely to believe *into* marriage. To believe *in* marriage is to be confident that such a relationship exists. To believe *into* marriage implies that our belief has actively led us to get married.

Like a single person who believes in marriage, we can believe in Jesus without being changed or moved towards unity with Him. However, when we begin to believe *into* Jesus everything changes.

Love and Unity

John 17:20-23

"I do not ask for these only, but also for those who will believe in me through their word, that they may all be one, just as you, Father, are in me, and I in you, that they also may be in us, so that the world may believe that you have sent me. The glory that you have given me I have given to them, that they may be one even as we are one, I in them and you in me, that they may become perfectly one, so that the world may know that you sent me and loved them even as you loved me."

The Scriptures constantly compel us towards a union with God. When God called Israel to hold fast (*davaq*) to Him, He was calling them into unity. When Jesus called the people to take His yoke upon them, He was calling them into unity. Before Jesus embraced the cross, His final prayer for us was that we would be one with Him. Jesus knew there was simply no other way for us to fulfil our design. We were always created to live in love and unity with Him, and so Jesus came to restore His design by making us one with Him.

Galatians 3:24a
Therefore the Law has become our tutor to lead us to [*eis:* into] Christ...

1 Timothy 1:5 (NKJV)
Now the purpose of the commandment is love from a pure heart, from a good conscience, and from sincere faith...

The theme of love and unity with God runs through the entire body of Scripture. The purpose of the commandment is love—wholehearted, selfless, relentless love. To this end, the Law of Scripture acts as a tutor that compels us *into* union with Jesus through faith.[2] The Bible does this by commanding us to be righteous but then teaching us that no one can become righteous apart from Christ. Scripture tells us that Jesus alone is righteousness and so the only we become righteous is by believing *into* Jesus.[3] As we become one with Christ, Jesus shares His righteousness with us and we become righteous in Him.

Be Holy

We can see how Jesus makes our obedience possible in the command to be holy.

1 Peter 1:15-16
But as he who called you is holy, you also be holy in all your conduct, since it is written, 'You shall be holy, for I am holy.'

For a long time, I saw this verse as an impossible ideal, so I would read it as *Try your best to be holy.* Only the harder I tried the less holy I became. When I finally accepted that striving in my own strength only led to failure, I began see this command in a new light.

Hebrews 12:10
For they disciplined us for a short time as it seemed best to them, but he [God] disciplines us for our good, that we may share his holiness.

God never intended for us to try to be holy apart from Jesus. Instead His intention was always to share his holiness with us. The command to be holy is therefore not a command to try to be like God in our outward behavior. It is a call to let Jesus share His holiness with us. Like little children, we simply rest on His shoulders while Jesus lives a holy life through us.

Ephesians 3:14-19

For this reason I bow my knees before the Father, from whom every family in heaven and on earth is named, that according to the riches of his glory he may grant you to be strengthened with power through his Spirit in your inner being, so that Christ may dwell in your hearts through faith—that you, being rooted and grounded in love, may have strength to comprehend with all the saints what is the breadth and length and height and depth, and to know the love of Christ that surpasses knowledge, that you may be filled with all the fullness of God.

Each command of Scripture reveals what life looks like when Jesus dwells in our heart. The Bible calls us to love God with our entire being only because Jesus loves the Father with His entire being and we are designed to be one with Him. God calls us to make the first command our first priority in life only because it is Jesus' first priority. Scripture calls us to be humble and gentle because Jesus is humble and gentle in heart, and He shares His heart with us. Through the commands of Scripture, the Holy Spirit is inviting us to become more one with Christ and to let Him live through us.

The unity we share with Jesus not only affects how we live out our lives but also how we relate to the Father. Jesus loves the Father with His entire being and the Father loves Jesus in exactly the same way—without reserve, in unlimited, eternal, perfect love. The awesome reality is that when we live in union with Jesus, the Father loves Jesus where He lives: *in us*. The Father's entire heart, soul, mind, and every ounce of His limitless energy is focused on loving Jesus *in us*. This deserves repeating: When we live in union with Jesus, the Father's entire heart, soul, mind, and strength is focused on loving

Jesus *in us*. Our unity with the Spirit of Christ exalts us to be flooded with the infinite love of God and then empowers us to return the Father's love in wholehearted affection.

Learning Unity

1 Corinthians 6:17
But he who is joined to the Lord becomes one spirit with Him.

Our unity with Jesus is a unity of spirit. However, because unity is spiritual, it can seem like an abstract concept, removed from our daily experience of life. What does "union with God" really mean? Does sharing one spirit with Jesus affect our day-to-day life now or is it something that we only fully appreciate after we die?

Earlier we saw how believing into Jesus is like believing into marriage. It is a movement into union. In the natural realm, when we are married, we share our life with our spouse. We share our home, our food, our income, and we share ourselves. We no longer live as single people but as a married couple and this changes the way we think and feel about life.

In the same way, when we are in relationship with Jesus, we share our interior life with Jesus. Our hearts become a shared space with the Spirit of God; Jesus shares His heart with us and we share ours with Him. Our minds also become a shared space as Jesus shares His thoughts with us and we share ours with Him.[4] The more we grow our unity with Jesus, the more we share His love as it flows into our heart, soul, and mind. The presence of God's love within us then begins to shape more of our thoughts and feelings. It flows through to our words and actions, and ends up affecting every aspect of our daily lives.

Through our ongoing union with Jesus, all the elements of our inner person are taken out of the realm of self and into the realm of love. With this change of heart comes a change of identity. Just as a man and woman leave their families and become one couple in marriage, so we are called to come out of our independence and forge a new identity in union with Jesus. There is no option in this. If we are to love God with our entire being, then we must become one with Christ and that means learning how to live again.

Our only work in this is to yield to the desire of God; to cease striving and simply surrender. When we try to move in our own strength, we lose our balance and fall from Jesus' shoulders into His arms. He will always restore us back, but it is important that we learn to not try so hard. Instead we need to let Him balance us so we can move as one with Him. Some call this living in a place of rest. It is the sense of security that comes from knowing that Jesus is good, He loves us, and we are safe when we say *Yes* to Him. It is the rest that comes from no longer needing to strive on our own. It is the peace that comes from abandoning ourselves to God and allowing Jesus to be Jesus in us.

Pray

Lord Jesus, please live in me and share your love for the Father with me. Let your highest priority be my highest priority. I want to share my life with you, so I invite you now: please share my heart, soul, mind and life. I am yours.

6 | What is Life?

Becoming one with Christ involves an ongoing process of renewal. In this process, the Spirit of Jesus changes the way we think and transforms our sense of identity. He redefines how we see the world and even life itself.

We are raised in a material world and so we tend to view life through a material lens and see life and death as physical states. If someone is breathing, they are alive; if they are no longer breathing, then they are dead. However, Scripture considers a person as more than just a body. In the Bible, a person is a being with a body, mind and spirit all united in one unique soul or identity.[1] From this perspective, life itself is not limited to a physical reality. It is defined as something else entirely.

> **Deuteronomy 30:6** (NASB, emphasis added)
> Moreover the LORD your God will circumcise your heart and the heart of your descendants, to love the LORD your God with all your heart and with all your soul, **in order that you may live.**

In this verse, God promises to enable us to love Him with all our heart and soul, *so that we may live.* Here we find that there is more to life than just being physically alive. According to Scripture, **life is only found in the wholehearted love of God.** Until we learn to love God with all our heart and soul, we are not truly alive.

> **Luke 10:25-28**
> And behold, a lawyer stood up to put him [Jesus] to the test, saying, "Teacher, what shall I do to inherit eternal life?"
> He said to him, "What is written in the Law? How do you read it?"
> And he answered, "You shall love the LORD your God with all your heart and with all your soul and with all your strength and with all your mind, and your neighbor as yourself."

And he said to him, "You have answered correctly; do this, and you will live."

In this passage, a lawyer asks Jesus "what shall I do to inherit eternal life?" Jesus directs the lawyer back to the Scriptures, which give us the true definition of *life*. The answer is obvious: love God with your entire being and love others. Jesus then responds simply: *Do this and you will live*. In other words: *If you love God and love others, you will be truly living*. Life is defined by love and that love is eternal.

John 3:16
For God so loved the world, that he gave his only Son, that whoever believes in [into] him should not perish but have eternal life.

1 John 5:11-12
And this is the testimony, that God gave us eternal life, and this life is in his Son. Whoever has the Son has life; whoever does not have the Son of God does not have life.

Often when we read the words *eternal life*, we think of life in heaven after we die. Yet Scripture says that eternal life is found right now in union with Jesus. We can see this in John 3:16. Those who believe *into* Jesus have eternal life. The word *have* is written in the Greek present tense, which speaks of a present, ongoing experience. This means that eternal life starts right now and extends into all eternity.[2] So when we read about eternal life, instead of thinking about our future in heaven, we need to focus on our present life here on earth.

The word of God abides forever, which means that God's definition of life cannot change. Life will always be the state of wholehearted love for God, even in heaven. The first command will forever remain first and so our call in heaven will be the same as it is here: to love God with our entire being and to live in unity with Him. And this all starts now. Eternal life is a whole new way of living that begins with embracing our First Love and then never ends.[3]

The Gift of Life

Romans 6:23b

...the free gift of God is eternal life in Christ Jesus our Lord.

It is important to note that when Jesus talks with the lawyer about eternal life, He is not saying that eternal life can be earned by acts of love. Eternal life is a free gift that God gives us as we believe into Jesus through faith. From the very beginning, no one has ever been able to earn life. Adam did not earn his breath and neither do we. It has always been and always will be a free gift of God's grace.

Instead when Jesus says that we need to love to inherit eternal life, He is saying that life is defined by love. It is like someone asking, "What shall I do to have a successful marriage?" To respond, "Love God with your entire being and let Him love your spouse through you," does not mean that love is a work that earns you a successful marriage. Rather love is the definition of a successful marriage. If two people continually set their hearts on the love of God, their marriage cannot fail. In the same way, love is not a series of works through which we can earn life. Love is life.

Are We Alive?

So are we alive? Remember back to the foster girl who believed she was a cat. When she lived as a cat, she was physically alive, but she was not truly living. As part of coming into her new home, she had to leave behind her old identity as a cat and come into her true identity and learn a whole new way of life. We too have formed our identity by looking at the lives of those around us. But what if the people around us are not loving God with all their heart? What if they are alive in the eyes of the world but not truly alive with love? Like the foster girl, we can compare ourselves to those around us and think we have life. Yet the truth remains: **Real life is only found in the wholehearted love of God.**

This is Your Life

Deuteronomy 30:19-20a (NASB, emphasis added)

I call heaven and earth to witness against you today, that I have set before you life and death, the blessing and the curse. So choose life in order that you may live, you and your descendants, by loving the LORD your God, by obeying His voice, and by holding fast to Him [*davaq, becoming one with Him*]; **for this is your life**...

In these verses, Moses gives us some more detail about what it means to truly live. Again we find the word *davaq*, meaning to fuse together and make one. In this passage we find that we choose life by:

1. loving God (with all our heart, mind, soul and strength),
2. hearing and obeying His voice,
3. being one with Him.

Here we find the beauty and simplicity of life as God designed. We love God by hearing His voice and acting in union with Him. No other life can ever be as love-filled, joyful, satisfying, selfless, or powerful. In union with the Spirit, we find life as children of God and lovers of Christ, spending each day talking and acting with our awesome God of love.

Because true life is so simple, it is available to anyone and everyone. There are no qualifications required except a childlike faith. All we need to do is surrender to the will of God and focus on loving God, obeying His voice and living in union with Him. If we set our hearts on these three things, God will do everything that is required to bring us into our design of wholehearted love. If we need healing, He will heal us. If we need deliverance, He will deliver us. He will be faithful to keep His word and bring us into life as He designed.

A Life of Love

John 10:10

"The thief comes only to steal and kill and destroy. I came that they may have life and have it abundantly."

In this passage Jesus says that He came to give us life *in abundance*. Jesus did not come just to give us a little life and to save us for another life in heaven. He came to save us to the uttermost and give us life in its fullest. And because love is life, Jesus came not just to give us a little love but to give us a life of overwhelming, overflowing, excessive, abundant love.

Applying the Scriptural definition of life, this verse gives us a promise that God will work to empower us to love Him abundantly—with all our heart, soul, mind and strength. Jesus longs to give us His life in abundance. However, He cannot do this without our permission. We need to decide: are we satisfied with the life we have or do we hunger for more? Do we want to love God with all our entire being? Do we share God's heart for life and love in abundance?

Pray

Jesus, I thank you for the gift of eternal life. I want to honor you by not being casual or lukewarm or reserved in my response. Please help me to receive the gift of eternal life with humility, thankfulness, and wholehearted devotion.

7 | What is Love?

John 18:38a
Pilate said to him, "What is truth?"

When Pilate talked to Jesus, he asked a simple yet profound question: *What is truth?* The irony here is that Pilate was speaking with the only person to ever call himself *The Truth*. Pilate asked the question and Jesus was the answer. Yet Pilate looked Jesus in the eyes and failed to recognize Him as the Truth. Why? Because Pilate expected truth to look like something entirely different.

Often we try to fit God into our own ideas of what He should be like and we do the same with His love. We think we know what love is like and then we expect God to act according to our assumptions. But what if God's idea of love is different from our own? What if the thing we call love is not truly love? Until we let God define love and show us what it truly means to love, we will never be able to love Him with all our heart and soul. We therefore need to ask: *What is love?*

1 Corinthians 13:4-8a (BSB)
Love is patient, love is kind. It does not envy, it does not boast, it is not proud. It is not rude, it is not self-seeking, it is not easily angered, it keeps no account of wrongs. Love takes no pleasure in evil, but rejoices in the truth. It bears all things, believes all things, hopes all things, endures all things. Love never fails.

Scripture reveals much about love. Love is patient, kind, secure and humble. Love is quick to forgive and slow to anger. It does not seek its own. Love always hopes, even in the midst of pain and delay. And love never, ever fails.

God is love and so as we study love, we learn of the character of God. God is patient and kind, secure and humble. He is not self-seeking and is not easily angered. He never gives up on us and He never fails.

Agape Love

Mark 12:29-30

Jesus answered, "The most important is, 'Hear, O Israel: The LORD our God, the LORD is one. And you shall love [*agapáo*] the Lord your God with all your heart and with all your soul and with all your mind and with all your strength.'"

There are many books and articles written about the Greek words for love that are used in the Bible. There is the love between friends (*phileo*), the protective love within family (*storge*), romantic or sexual love (*eros*), and then there is the highest form of love: *agape*.

Different scholars have differing views on the word *agape*, which says something of the richness of love. Combining some of these perspectives we find that for the believer, agape love involves acting in resonance with God, actively doing what God prefers.[1] It is love based on evaluation and choice; a force of the will in action.[2] Agape love conveys a sense of admiration, approval and adoration, borne out of a recognition of the inherent worth in the object of love.[3] The one who has agape love acts vehemently or intensely and yet is completely at rest and supremely contented in God.[4] To love God with this kind of love is to take pleasure in Him and prize Him above all things.[5]

With a focus on the unity in love, one lexical author writes of agape love as "a pleasing surrender of friendship to a friend; an identity or sameness of soul."[6] This sameness of soul comes as God shares His heart with us and makes us one with Him.

The Holy Spirit enables this unity of soul by connecting us like branches to the Vine of Christ so that we can draw our love and life from His presence. Like branches, we do not generate our own love but rather we simply let the love of God flow through us. Because of this, the Scriptures that speak about love give us the clearest picture of who we really are in union with Jesus. The more His love flows into us, the more patient, kind and secure we become. As love grows, we become faster to forgive and slower to anger, our faith increases, we can endure greater hardship, and we become more hopeful and optimistic. And best of all, when we act in love, we never, ever fail. Love eliminates the possibility of failure from our lives. From a worldly perspective, we may lose everything and be called a failure over and over. But from an eternal perspective, it is impossible to act in true love and fail. Love always succeeds. It always overcomes. Love always wins.

The Depths of Love

The picture that Scripture paints of agape love is one of incredible depths and dimensions to explore with Jesus. On the surface of love, we find an emotional love, full of pleasure and delight. However, if we would dare to look below the surface, we would find a greater aspect to love—one that has little to do with emotion.

> **1 John 4:10** (NLT)
> This is real love—not that we loved God, but that he loved us and sent his Son as a sacrifice to take away our sins.

This is real love. The incredible depth of God's love was revealed at the cross for all creation to see. When the Father allowed us to sacrifice Jesus, He allowed us to break His very heart. At the cross, the Father displayed His limitless love for the world by giving up His one and only Son, Jesus Christ.

At the same time, Jesus also showed us the depth of His love by willingly giving His life to fulfil the will of the Father. Because of His great love, the King of All Creation humbled Himself at the feet of the humanity He came to save. And we crushed Him.

In the darkest hour of human history, the light of love shone its brightest. In that moment of time, both the Father and Son defined real love. Together they revealed to all creation that the depths of love are not found in emotion but in selfless sacrifice.

Love Does Not Seek Its Own

Deuteronomy 32:9-12

But the LORD'S portion is his people,
 Jacob his allotted heritage.
He found him in a desert land,
 and in the howling waste of the wilderness;
 he encircled him, he cared for him,
 he kept him as the apple of his eye.
Like an eagle that stirs up its nest,
 that flutters over its young,
 spreading out its wings, catching them,
 bearing them on its pinions,
 the LORD alone guided him,
 no foreign god was with him.

The Lord's inheritance is His people and as He did for Jacob, so He will do for us. Here we find that God likens Himself to a mother eagle. When it came time to learn to fly, the mother eagle would often stir up her nest. She would rip away the warm and soft lining of the nest and make it uncomfortable for the chicks. She knew that if the chicks were to survive, they had to leave the comfort of the nest, spread their wings, and fall until they flew.

Like the mother eagle, God carefully cares for us in His nest while we are young. This nest is a place of ultimate safety, warmth and nurturing. However, the nest is also a place of infancy. As we grow in Christ, God calls us to a deeper, greater love. He calls us into our true design. And so He stirs up the nest and makes life uncomfortable.

We respond as most infants do: we resist. We believe in a life of comfort, so when God stirs up the nest, we try our best to make it comfortable again. We want to remain enjoying the emotional rewards of love without paying the cost and so we fight the call to selfless sacrifice. We love at a safe distance and avoid risking hurt or failure or rejection. In our infancy, we do not want to get too involved and we definitely want to keep what we have for ourselves. However, God knows that we will never reach our design of love while we remain in our infancy. So He keeps on stirring up the nest and calling us to a life of selfless, wholehearted love, and intimate union with Him. He keeps pushing us to the edge, waiting for us to take a leap of faith into an unknown life.

We cannot choose this life of love and hope to retain control over our lives. This is why spiritual growth often starts with a fall. Letting go brings us into deep dependence on God and that dependence gives God permission to move in our lives. While we stay in control, we are like people with clenched fists, unable to receive the blessings that God has for us. Yet, if we find the faith to fall into love, we will quickly learn that God will always catch us. He will never let us down. He may stir up the nest and make life uncomfortable, but it is all for a reason. Just as the eagle pushes her chicks to learn to fly, so God keeps pushing us to take the risk and embrace His design for our lives. When we finally accept God's design of love and His relentless commitment to it; then we will learn how to give in, spread our wings and truly soar.

Pray

Father, I invite you to push me into my design of love. Please overcome every resistance within me. Make my life uncomfortable if you must. I just ask that you would do whatever it takes to enable me to love you with all my heart and soul.

8 | Love and Life

Romans 12:1-2

I appeal to you therefore, brothers, by the mercies of God, to present your bodies as a living sacrifice, holy and acceptable to God, which is your spiritual worship. Do not be conformed to this world, but be transformed by the renewal of your mind, that by testing you may discern what is the will of God, what is good and acceptable and perfect.

Do not be conformed to this world. We looked at this passage earlier in terms of design, but it is useful to look at it again in the context of love. We have all grown up in the world and to differing degrees the world has shaped what we believe about love.

In the world, love is conditional. As adults the world gives us a list of all the things we need to do to earn love. We need to be thinner, taller, smarter, more beautiful, wealthier, stronger or more successful to make ourselves worthy of other people's attention and affection. We believe the lie and so we spend our time and money trying to qualify for love. Like everyone else, we believe that love is earned because the world has been telling us the same lie for our entire lives.

Without transformation, it is natural for a worldly perspective of love to shape our relationship with God. In the natural realm, we make mental lists of what we want to see in a potential friend, husband, or wife—what would qualify someone for our love. We then naturally believe that Jesus also has a list of requirements that we must meet to be worthy of His love. Like a woman who beautifies herself so that she can attract men, or like a man who feels he has to earn approval through accomplishment, in our worldly thinking, we can believe that we need to earn God's love by the things we do.

Romans 5:8
But God shows his love for us in that while we were still sinners, Christ died for us.

The reality is that God already loves us now as much as He ever could. He poured out His love to its greatest degree at the cross, *while we were yet sinners*, long before we had done a single thing for God. Just as we could never do any work that would make us deserving of Christ's death, so there is nothing we could ever do that would make us deserving of His love. God's love is and always will be a free gift of His extravagant goodness.

God longs to share His love with us and to show us our true value in His love. If we stop striving for a moment, He will tell us how much He already loves us, regardless of what we do or have done. He will help us to wash off our makeup, to take down our trophies, and to simply be still and know that He is God, He is love, and He loves us. He truly, deeply, passionately loves us.

Worthy of Love
Matthew 10:31
Fear not, therefore; you are of more value than many sparrows.

God has forever established our value in love and our worthiness to be loved. The world would say that we need to earn love; the reality is that God designed every one of us for love. Love is encoded in our very creation.

We can see this design in the way that our bodies respond to love. Like breathing, love is a source of life to our bodies and it is essential not only to our health but to our survival. In the early years of life, affection stimulates the brain to produce growth hormone, which is vital to our development. In the absence of loving affection, babies are often unable to draw energy from their food. Though they eat the same amount as others, unloved babies lack the same levels of growth hormone and so fail to gain as much weight. Stress sets in and the immune system slowly begins to shut down. Even though these babies may have food, shelter and warmth, without love they often simply die.[1]

Science confirms our need of love, which continues all through life. If we compare brain scans from a three-year who has been loved to one that has not, the brain of the unloved child appears diseased. In our youth and middle age, love dramatically improves our spiritual, physical and mental health. Even into old age, a lack of love significantly reduces life-expectancy.[2] In other words, people are dying from loneliness and isolation. Throughout every stage of life, we are designed to need love.

We all know that our bodies are designed to breathe air and so we never question our worthiness to breathe. But if we also know that we are designed to love, why would we ever question our worthiness both to love and be loved? It is because the world keeps telling us the same lie over and over and a part of us believes it. This has to change.

A Matter of Life and Death

Scripture defines life as the wholehearted love of God. But if life is love then what is death?

> **1 John 3:14**
> We know that we have passed out of death into life, because we love the brothers. Whoever does not love abides in death.

In his first letter, John assures believers of their salvation through faith in Christ. He writes that because life is found only in love, we can be confident that we have passed out of death and into life because we love one another. Love is the evidence of life.

Whoever does not love abides in death. We could not study light without learning about the darkness that comes from the absence of light. In the same way, we cannot learn about love without looking at its opposite.

In the emotional shallows, love is a display of affection or compassion. At this level, we could say that the opposite of love is hate or indifference. However, as we go deeper, we discover the selfless and sacrificial nature of love. In these depths of love, we find that its opposite is not hate, nor fear, indifference. The opposite of love is *selfishness*.

Scripture therefore presents life as an ongoing state of love and death as an ongoing state of selfishness. No matter what we say, which church we go to, or which doctrines we believe—if we do not actively love others then our selfishness reveals that we are living in a place of spiritual death.

We can see the reality of love as life and selfishness as death at work in our physical design. On a biological level, our physical bodies respond entirely differently to love and selfishness. When we are selfish, a chemical called dopamine triggers the reward center of the brain, which causes us to experience a short-lived but addictive high.[3] We enjoy buying something new but the high soon fades and we are left thinking about our next purchase. Our desire for the selfish high then compels us to buy more. It is not so much the purchases that we really want—it is the feeling of a dopamine high. The same principle works for all selfish and addictive behaviors. We take another drink, click another link, work another hour, eat another sweet, and enjoy the high then hit the low and then go back for more.

The irony of selfishness is that in our minds we think we are doing what is best for us, but our bodies prove otherwise. While we may gain greater wealth and pleasure through our selfish actions, it all comes at a cost. Selfishness impacts our whole being, leading to an increase in stress, anxiety, insecurity, fear, indifference and social isolation.[4] Every selfish action numbs us emotionally and reduces our ability to feel true joy. Finding lasting fulfilment through selfish behavior is biochemically, psychologically, and spiritually impossible. No matter how much we feed it, the selfish nature can never be satisfied. In fact, the more we gratify our selfish desires, the greater they become, and the deeper we fall into spiritual poverty.

God did not design us for selfishness. From His perspective, **selfishness is not normal**. He never intended for us to live with the stress, anxiety or addiction of self. Physically, it is a slow death for our bodies.[5] Therefore Jesus says: *Do not worry. Cast all your cares on Me because I care for you.* He comes to take our selfishness and stress and exchange them for His healing love .

Unlike the body's response to selfishness, when we act in love our bodies come to life. Instead of producing a fleeting high, our bodies release a chemical called oxytocin which gives us a deep sense of fulfilment that can last *for days*. Oxytocin increases our sense of trust, empathy and connection, while reducing fear, stress, anxiety and depression.[6] It boosts our overall feeling of well-being, which even allows our bodies to heal faster.[7] Oxytocin also creates a strong sense of unity between people—mother and baby; husband and wife; between friends, family and even strangers. For these reasons, oxytocin is also known as the "bonding chemical" or "love hormone." Scripture says that love is the perfect bond of unity and the biochemistry of love confirms it.[8]

It is oxytocin that creates a sense of deep resonance in us when we are exposed to love. When we see someone do something loving or selfless, we feel the "warm fuzzy" feeling of oxytocin. In situations like this, we do not even have to give or receive love to feel its effects. We simply need to see love in action.[9]

What this shows us is that **God designed us to love and to be inspired by love**. If our bodies could talk, they would tell us: *We were not created for selfishness. Selfishness is not normal! We were created for love—so love! Enjoy love! Give love! Find healing as you love. Let love satisfy your soul. Let the love you see inspire you to love and let that love inspire the world!*

Finding Ourselves in Love

Every living thing in creation finds its greatest fulfilment by living according to its design. Because we are designed for love and union with Jesus, when we love others, we experience an oxytocin-based feeling of fulfilment in life. This feeling of fulfilment naturally creates a sense of identity and purpose within us. Like an eagle when it first feels the thrill of flying, when we love others, our thoughts and feelings unite in the realization: *This is who I am.*[10]

This sense of identity is the natural result of love because love binds us more and more to Jesus. Love brings us home to the place of union where we find our real identity *in* Christ. This is the place of His presence, where love reigns supreme. As we create a habit of living in His presence, we find better highs than anything that our selfish nature could ever offer. When we experience God's presence, our brains often respond by releasing both oxytocin and dopamine. This gives us both a temporal high and a long-lasting sense of wellness, love and unity with God. For those who have taken the time to learn to abide in the presence of God, His presence is both deeply satisfying and positively addictive. In His presence, they are completely fulfilled by His love and yet left longing for more. In His presence, they find themselves in the love of God.

Because our experience of love forms our sense of identity far more than our learning, we need to be sure to act on what we learn. We must not settle for knowledge without experience. Instead we need to join ourselves to God, listen for His voice, and take every opportunity to love others.

More often than not, this will feel great. However, if we have trained our brain to reward selfishness, it may take a little time for it to find a deep sense of fulfilment in love. If this is the case, we can be encouraged by the knowledge that God has pre-wired our brains and bodies to reward love. It may take some time to be restored to that design, but it will happen. If we persist in our call to love then we will experience an ever-increasing sense of life, fulfilment, and identity in Christ.

Pray

Father, I thank you that you love me and that you created me to love. Thank you that I am perfectly designed to love. Please help me to feel more of the joy, peace and fulfilment of love. Free me from my selfishness, renew my mind, and transform my soul so that I may love with you.

9 | Circumcision of the Heart

Regardless of background or belief, everyone knows deep in their hearts that we are designed for love. Experience proves it. If people are truly honest, almost everyone will admit that selfishness is a short-lived thrill and that it is love alone that truly satisfies us. But if our design of love is so obvious, why is the world not full of love?

At the center of humanity is a broken heart that has long forgotten how to live. While most people know that we are designed for love, when we look inside our hearts, instead of finding a fire of love, we find a black hole of selfishness—a consuming darkness that denies love and seeks only to feed its own insatiable desires.

On a corporate scale, the heart of humanity has created a culture that is oriented around selfishness, which it proudly calls *the love of self*.[1] Like a cornered animal, this selfish world rages against the threat of love. It lies about love. It steals love. It redefines love as lust and then disqualifies people from love based on their appearance. The world replaces the pursuit of love with the pursuit of wealth and offers us entertainment instead of joy. Capitalism thrives on covetousness rather than generosity and so sex sells. Lust for stuff sells. Pleasure sells. *Selfishness* sells.

The world does everything it can to keep people from realizing their design of love. But ultimately, love will win. Love always wins. The question is not a matter of if but when. When will love win in you?

Lovelessness

Growing up in a selfish world usually taints the way we view ourselves and others. In a world that sees love as the exception and selfishness as the rule, we are constantly told the lie that selfishness is normal. However, deep down we know that it is not true. Selfishness is not a part of God's design. All through life, our bodies cry out for us to abandon our selfish ways so that we might truly live.

In many Christian circles, people have twisted the gospel to make room for selfishness. Many even try to appeal to people's selfishness to bring them to God. *Come to Jesus and you will not go to hell when you die; have faith and God will make you rich.* However, the reality is that we cannot hope to be both Christ-centered and self-centered at the same time. The first command allows no place for selfishness in a believer's life. Because love is selfless, to be selfish is to be loveless. Even if it is only for short periods of time, whenever we act selfishly, we define ourselves as loveless.[2]

Many Christians go through life fitting moments of love into a lifestyle of selfishness. They reason that a little love will outweigh a lot of selfishness. This may make sense outside of covenant with God, but it cannot exist within the bounds of the first command. Our call is to selflessly love God with all our heart, soul, mind and time.[3] Love is not reserved for emergencies or special occasions, nor does a little love redeem a life of selfishness. Love is life. It is an ongoing state of the heart that constantly flows in action and affection. If we are to live in the love of God then we must turn against our own selfishness, calling it what it really is: lovelessness.

The Circumcised Heart

As long as selfishness occupies space within our heart, we cannot love God with *all* our heart. Therefore, if we are going to devote our lives to the first command, we need to know: can God take the selfishness out of our hearts? Does He want to?

God gives us the answer in the form of a promise:

Deuteronomy 30:6 (NASB)
"Moreover the LORD your God will circumcise your heart and the heart of your descendants, to love the LORD your God with all your heart and with all your soul, in order that you may live."

The God of Creation is all-powerful and all-loving. Nothing is too difficult for Him. In this verse, we see the Almighty God promising to circumcise our hearts and so empower us to love Him with all our heart and with all our soul.[4] The only way to experience wholehearted love for God is to let Him cut away our selfishness. But is it really possible?

Not Too Difficult

Deuteronomy 30:11-14 (NASB)

"For this commandment which I command you today is not too difficult for you, nor is it out of reach. It is not in heaven, that you should say, 'Who will go up to heaven for us to get it for us and make us hear it, that we may observe it?' Nor is it beyond the sea, that you should say, 'Who will cross the sea for us to get it for us and make us hear it, that we may observe it?' But the word is very near you, in your mouth and in your heart, that you may observe it."

God has spoken and He cannot lie. Having commanded us to love Him with all our heart and soul, God then promises us that He is able to make it a reality. What is impossible for man is possible for God. If we let Him, God will change our hearts and enable us to love Him with our entire being. The voice of fear and doubt would say: *This is too difficult. I could never love God with all my heart and soul.* But the voice of the Spirit of God would say: *This is not too difficult, nor is it out of reach. It is possible and within reach. I can do this. We can do this. Don't be afraid. Just believe.*

Because God makes it His work to enable us to love wholeheartedly, every single person alive can do it. No one is disqualified. Are we materialistic? God can free us from our love of money. Are we bound by religion? God's grace is greater. Are we addicted to drugs, alcohol, work, pornography, news, gaming, shopping or entertainment? God can overcome our addiction. Do we feel that our culture, history, or sexuality disqualifies us? No! God has commanded us to love Him with our entire being and so the burden of our obedience rests with Him. If we have the faith and are truly willing to let God change our hearts, He will do whatever it takes within us to enable us to love.

Our part is simply to devote ourselves to the love of God and call on Him to keep His promise. And He will—it is a promise He cannot possibly break.

Choose Life

> Deuteronomy 30:19-20 (NASB)
>
> I call heaven and earth to witness against you today, that I have set before you life and death, blessing and curse. Therefore choose life, that you and your offspring may live, loving the LORD your God, obeying his voice and holding fast [*davaq,* becoming one] to him, for he is your life and length of days, that you may dwell in the land that the LORD swore to your fathers, to Abraham, to Isaac, and to Jacob, to give them.

Life and death are present states of being. As we learned earlier, life is found in loving God with all our heart and soul, obeying His voice, and being one with Him. This is the place of union, intimacy, and identity. In this place, Jesus is our life.

The curse of death is a spiritual reality that we experience when we live for ourselves rather than for the love of God. Today we have a choice. God has commanded us to love but He will not force us to love. It must be a free choice otherwise it is not love at all.

Choose life so that you may live. Life starts with a choice, which requires a lifelong commitment. When we choose life, we bind ourselves in covenant to love God with our entire being, to obey His voice, and to live in union with Him. Before we make this choice, we need to really consider what God is asking of us. To love God with all our heart is to let the Holy Spirit share the heart of Christ with us so that His love comes to completely define our identity and character. To love Him with all our soul is to let Him transform our every emotion, feeling and motive into love. To love God with all our mind means that every thought, attitude and action flows from love. And to love Him with all our strength, means that we devote all our energy, resources, wealth and effort to doing God's perfect will of love. Choosing life means depending on God to make all this a reality and to be the source of our love forever.

When we bind ourselves to God, He binds Himself to us and promises to make our covenant a reality. He commits Himself to circumcising our hearts and removing everything from our lives that stands against His love. He devotes Himself to bringing us into union with His Spirit and sharing His love with us. Because of the depth of this commitment, we cannot make this choice casually. The choice to love will cost us our selfishness and will completely redefine what it means for us to live. This choice will bring us into a new depth of covenant love with Jesus that will last our entire lives and beyond. It will be a choice that will affect the generations that follow us. The reward outweighs the cost far more than can ever be described, but still we must consider the cost.

Even if there was not a single person in the world who loved God with all their heart and soul, it would not diminish the promise and call of God in this verse. The Spirit of God asks: *Will you allow Me to circumcise your heart? Will you let me free you from yourself? Will you choose a life of love and come into union with Me? Will you let me become your very life?*

Each of us must choose whether or not we will surrender to the will of God and let Him circumcise our hearts. Choose today.

Pray

Father, thank you that you are willing to do anything to enable me to love you with all my heart and soul. I surrender to your will and turn from all my sin and selfishness—everything that is not love. Please open my heart and give me the faith I need to inherit this promise. Please make this a reality in my life.

10 | One Spirit

John 6:63
It is the Spirit who gives life; the flesh is no help at all. The words that I have spoken to you are spirit and life.

The life that the Spirit brings us is not only a sense of energy or spiritual vitality; it is life as God defined. It is the life that is found in loving God with all our heart and soul, hearing His voice, and living in unity with Him. This life is only possible through our relationship with the Spirit of God. He is the one who circumcises our hearts, fills us with the love of God, speaks the words of God to us, and makes us one with Christ.[1]

In this chapter, we will look at how the Holy Spirit brings us into these three different aspects of life.

1. Love

Romans 5:3-5 (NASB)
And not only this, but we also exult in our tribulations, knowing that tribulation brings about perseverance; and perseverance, proven character; and proven character, hope; and hope does not disappoint, because the love of God has been poured out within our hearts through the Holy Spirit who was given to us.

The love of God has been poured out within our hearts through the Holy Spirit. The Holy Spirit has been given to us to act as a channel for the love of God. God's love far surpasses any love we could ever find in the world. It is a divine love without fear or reserve. It is a simple, pure and profoundly passionate love. It is selfless, extravagant and secure. It is a confident, devoted, humble and enduring love. When we give Him permission, the Holy Spirit pours this love of the Father into our hearts.

We live out in our actions what we have let into our hearts. If we do not have the love of God in our hearts, then we cannot hope to keep the first command. It is impossible to generate a wholehearted love of God through our own will-power. It is a gift of God's grace and will always be a gift.

As a gift, love is like joy. We do not expect to experience true joy simply by making a choice to be joyful. If we have no joy in our hearts, we cannot fake joy or talk our way into it. Love is the same. We cannot just decide to be loving. Love can never be forced or fabricated.

Thankfully, God does not expect us to try to generate our own love. When He calls us to love Him with all our heart, He calls us to seek Him for the gift of love. He wants to fill us with His love through His Spirit and then let that love flow through us. Our response to the greatest command therefore must be one of resolve—not the resolve of stubborn obedience, but a resolve to constantly receive love from His Spirit.

2. Hearing and Obeying

John 16:13

When the Spirit of truth comes, he will guide you into all the truth, for he will not speak on his own authority, but whatever he hears he will speak, and he will declare to you the things that are to come.

The Spirit of God is the voice of God. He shares with us what he hears from the Father's heart. We then need to obey what we hear. For as Jesus said: Whoever hears His words *and acts on them* is like a wise person who builds upon a solid foundation. Anyone who hears but does not obey is spiritually foolish and will suffer loss.[2]

Philippians 2:13

...for it is God who works in you, both to will and to work for his good pleasure.

The word *will* in this passage is the Greek word *thelo,* which means "to desire...and to be ready and willing to act on it."[3] The word *work* is the Greek word *energeo,* which has the idea of energy flowing through action. In this verse we see how God is so endlessly good to us. He does not expect us to follow His voice in cold, robot-like obedience. Instead, when the Holy Spirit speaks to us, He offers to share His desires with us so that we will feel a sense of delight in doing the will of God. He then energizes us so that we can work with His strength.

> **1 Kings 3:5-9** (edited)
> At Gibeon the Lord appeared to Solomon in a dream by night; and God said, "Ask! What shall I give you?" And Solomon said… "I am but a little child…Therefore give to Your servant an understanding [*shema*] heart to judge Your people, that I may discern between good and evil. For who is able to judge this great people of Yours?"

> **Shema** (sh'ma): *Understanding*
> Properly, to hear, especially to *obey* (implement) what is heard – i.e. hearing with *follow-up.*

The word *shema* means *to hear and to act on what is heard.* For this reason, it is often translated in Scripture simply as *obey.*

In this passage Solomon asked God for the gift of a *shema* heart. He wanted a heart that would hear and obey God's voice. Solomon knew that the voice of God is the only source of true understanding and discernment.

Like Solomon, we do not need to pretend to be greater than we are. If we humble ourselves like a little child, we too can ask God for the gift of a *shema* heart. And God is always good. If we ask, He will share the heart of Christ with us—a heart that feels what He feels and delights to do His will. Then like Solomon, we will know true wisdom—not the wisdom of the world that is found in education, experience, intellect or understanding. Rather we will receive the true wisdom that comes from hearing and obeying the voice of God.

Deuteronomy 6:4

"Hear [*shema*], O Israel: The Lord our God, the Lord is one. You shall love the Lord your God with all your heart and with all your soul and with all your might."

This verse begins a passage known by Jews as *the Shema*. It is recited as a daily prayer and is a reminder of Gods' purpose for our lives. The more that the Spirit of God forms a *shema* heart within us, the more we will be drawn to the *Shema* prayer. It will become our vision and priority, and through the power of the Holy Spirit, it will become our reality.

3. Union

1 Corinthians 6:17

But he who is joined to the Lord becomes one spirit with him.

As we join ourselves to Jesus, we become one spirit with Him. This experience of being joined to Jesus is closely connected to the baptism of the Spirit.

The word *baptism* is a Greek word meaning to immerse, submerge or overwhelm. An ancient Greek recipe for making pickles explains how a vegetable is first dipped in boiling water and then baptized in vinegar.[4] As the vegetable soaks in the vinegar, its taste and texture become permanently changed. Through its baptism, the vegetable is so saturated and so transformed that it becomes known by a new name: a pickle.

Just as the vegetable is transformed into a pickle through baptism, our immersion in the Spirit of Jesus produces something entirely new. By filling us with His Spirit, Jesus makes us a new creation—no longer one by ourselves but now one spirit with Him.

It is important to understand that God alone is God and the unity that we have with the Spirit of Jesus does not turn us into God. Even though a vegetable may be preserved in vinegar, it does not become vinegar. However, because of baptism, the vegetable is now one with the vinegar and so it can claim to be a new creation. It is the same with us. Even though we are immersed in the Holy Spirit, we cannot claim to be Jesus or to be the Holy

Spirit or God. God alone is God. But because of our immersion in the Holy Spirit, we need to accept the reality that we are an entirely new creation, a people who are becoming more and more one with Christ.

A quick dip in vinegar is not enough to turn a vegetable into a pickle, and it is the same for the baptism of the Spirit. A one-off experience of the Holy Spirit or His gifts does not make for an immersion. The baptism of the Spirit is not an event but an ongoing relationship of love and unity. We can think of it like marriage. A marriage starts with a wedding, but its substance is found in the ongoing life of love. In the same way, our baptism in the Spirit is an immersion into a life of ever-growing unity with Jesus.

> **Luke 3:16**
> John answered them all, saying, "I baptize you with water, but he who is mightier than I is coming, the strap of whose sandals I am not worthy to untie. He will baptize you with the Holy Spirit and fire."

In Scripture, fire is a symbol of God's love in its awesome refining and consuming power.[5] Here we find that Jesus came to baptize us with the Holy Spirit *and* fire. Not only is Jesus wanting to make us one spirit with Him, He wants to utterly consume our lives with His love. He wants to fill our entire being with the raging fire of His love so that like Paul, we will come to say that "the love of Christ compels us."[6] Our part is to surrender to His will and become like living sacrifices, waiting for God's fire to consume us. And Jesus will be faithful. He will come to immerse us in His Spirit and fire. Then we will know that our God is a consuming fire because He lives and burns within us. Faithful is He who calls us and loves us. If we are willing, He will do it.

Pray
Lord, thank you for the grace to surrender. I give in to your will. Jesus please immerse me in your Spirit and in the fire of your divine love. I want to burn for you. Let us become more one today.

11 | Higher Ways

Romans 5:1-2
Through him [Jesus] we have also obtained access by faith into this
grace in which we stand, and we rejoice in hope of the glory of God.

Scripture speaks of life as a gift that God gives by His grace. And the only
way we can access grace is through faith. Therefore, if we are to live a life of
wholehearted love for God, we need to understand the nature of faith. What
is faith?

In modern English, the word *faith* speaks of a belief in something without
any evidence or proof. In a broader religious context, *faith* refers to a person's
beliefs about God. However, neither of these definitions matches the Biblical
meaning of faith.

The word translated as *faith* is the Greek word *pistis*. Combining different
lexicons, we find that pistis speaks of: confidence, trust, and reliance on; a
persuasion; the conviction of the truth of something.[7] Far from being a belief
without proof, biblical faith is the confidence of the heart.[8] Some people call
this kind of confidence *trust*.

We see real faith operating in our natural relationships every day. Many
times, I have had to repair things that my children have broken. It is now
natural for them to come to me in the belief that I can fix the consequences
of their latest adventure. If I say I can fix it, they simply believe me and trust
me to fix it. Their faith in me is not a belief without proof. It is a confidence
that comes from hearing my voice and is proven through experience.

Romans 10:17
So faith comes from hearing, and hearing through the word [*rhema*]
of Christ.

Rhema (ray-mah): *Word*

That which is or has been uttered by the living voice, thing spoken, word.

Faith is inseparable from the voice of God. All through Scripture we see a God who speaks to people. His voice is not always understood or recognized, but He is always speaking. The Bible shows a God who speaks to people through visions and dreams; as a voice from Heaven; through people or angels; in His written word, or through creation. Often the Holy Spirit speaks as a still, small voice or a quiet thought in a person's heart. God spoke the first words at the dawn of creation, and He will speak the final words at the end of our time. Our God is a God who speaks.

The confidence of faith is only found in a living relationship with God. When Jesus speaks personally to us, His voice produces a level of confidence in our hearts that we could never talk ourselves into. We know we can trust Him. We know that God will never let us down. He has proven His love and faithfulness over and over again. We know that God cannot lie or fail to love, and so we know that He will fulfil every word that He speaks to us. So is our faith blind or without proof? No. Our faith is a confidence Christ Himself shares with us and is proven in experience.

If we try to divorce faith from the voice of God by defining it solely as a belief in the Bible, we will quickly find ourselves believing in a philosophy rather than living in a relationship. Remember: faith brings us *into* Jesus. Faith is not just an intellectual belief about Jesus for Scripture says that "it is with the heart that a person believes."[9] Faith is the heart-based confidence that comes from hearing the Spirit of Jesus speak to us.

The Thoughts of God

1 Corinthians 2: 10b-12, 16

For the Spirit searches everything, even the depths of God. For who knows a person's thoughts except the spirit of that person, which is in him? So also no one comprehends the thoughts of God except the Spirit of God. Now we have received not the spirit of the world, but the Spirit who is from God, that we might understand the things freely given us by God…

"For who has understood the mind of the Lord so as to instruct him?" But we have the mind of Christ.

No one knows the thoughts of God apart from the Spirit of God. *And we have received His Spirit.* God has given us His Spirit so that we can know His thoughts. This does not mean that every thought that enters our mind is from God. On the contrary, Scripture calls us to take captive our thoughts, conforming every thought to the mind of Christ.[10] It simply means that the Holy Spirit will share the thoughts of God with us. He will speak from where He resides: in our hearts.

Psalm 139:17-18
How precious to me are your thoughts, O God!
   How vast is the sum of them!
If I would count them, they are more than the sand.
   I awake, and I am still with you.

This Psalm is written from experience. The Holy Spirit shared the Father's thoughts with David and David treasured every one. He discovered that the thoughts of God are countless beyond all measure. They outnumber the sands of the earth, the stars of the sky, and all the words of Scripture combined. There is simply no limit to the mind of God. He is constantly thinking about us and He wants to share those thoughts with us.

The word translated as *thoughts* in this passage is the Hebrew word *rea* which speaks not only of thoughts but also of feelings and desires. When God shares His thoughts with us, it can often simply be a feeling, impression or intuition. At times we may receive some understanding apart from words like a dawning revelation. His voice may come to us as a dream or vision, or He may speak to us in a flow of unexpected, articulated thought. Regardless of how God speaks, every word is spirit and life and every word is precious.

Overcoming Fear

"I just wish pastors would teach people how to hear God's voice, " I shared with a national leader of a Christian organization as we drove to the airport. He replied without any hint of humor.

"Don't you think that would be dangerous?"

Isaiah 55:7-9

Let the wicked forsake his way,
>and the unrighteous man his thoughts;
>>let him return to the LORD, that he may have compassion on him,
>and to our God, for he will abundantly pardon.
For my thoughts are not your thoughts,
>neither are your ways my ways, declares the LORD.
For as the heavens are higher than the earth,
>so are my ways higher than your ways
>and my thoughts than your thoughts.

My thoughts are not your thoughts. The second half of this passage is often quoted by those who fear the idea that God would share His thoughts with us. But when we read this passage in context, we find that God is speaking to wicked and unrighteous people. *Let the wicked forsake his way, for your ways are not my ways. Let the unrighteous man forsake his thoughts, for my thoughts are not your thoughts.* Isaiah is reminding the people that God is righteous and forgiving and that they need to change the way they think so they can walk in God's ways.

Instead of being a passage that distances us from the thoughts of God, these verses give us a promise: If we turn to God, He will forgive us and restore our relationship with Him. God will teach us His ways and speak to us, and His word will not return void. As we take time to listen to the voice of God, our old way of thinking will be changed, not by a teaching or philosophy, but by every precious thought that God shares with us.

Learning to Listen

Habakkuk 2:1-3

I will take my stand at my watchpost
    and station myself on the tower,
    and look out to see what He will say to me,
    and what I will answer concerning my complaint.
And the LORD answered me:
    "Write the vision;
    make it plain on tablets,
    so he may run who reads it.
For still the vision awaits its appointed time;
    it hastens to the end—it will not lie.
If it seems slow, wait for it;
    it will surely come; it will not delay.

Like David, Habakkuk took time to wait on God and listen to His voice.

To see what He will say to me. The Hebrew here literally reads "to see what He will say *in* me."[11] Habakkuk was not expecting God to speak with an audible voice. Instead he was listening to what was happening within his own heart, waiting for God to share His thoughts. Habakkuk asked God a question and then looked for a response. God responded and told him to write down what he heard. Habakkuk obeyed God and recorded the vision.

God still longs to share His thoughts with us but most of the time His still, small voice is not heard above the noise of life. Therefore, like Habakkuk, we need to take some time to intently focus ourselves on Jesus. As we quiet the world around us, we can ask God a question and then give the Spirit space to share His mind with us. As we wait, we may experience a flow of thought in our minds or see a vision in our imagination. Like Habakkuk, if we write down what we receive then we have a record that we can test afterwards.

Hearing and Believing

I once taught about listening to God's voice at a small group. A woman there told the group about a time when God shared His thoughts with her.

"I used to teach a group of young children at Sunday school. At the end of the year, I gave them each a card. As I wrote the cards, the Lord gave me something beautiful and unique to write to each child. It was really amazing." It was clear that God wanted to share His thoughts with this woman, but she expected Him to do this only for other people or on special occasions. At the end of the night I spoke with her.

"I'd like you to do some homework over the next week. Buy seven cards. Every day for the next week, write down something special from the heart of God *for you*." She agreed. The next week came and the woman arrived with a wide smile. She showed me her seven cards.

"Every day God gave me something." Tears were welling up in her eyes. "This is what I've been wanting for the last two or three years. This is what I've been praying for." We looked over the cards and talked about how kind and wonderful and beautiful the thoughts of Jesus are towards us. He loves us.

It is easy to believe that God wants to speak through us to touch the lives of other people. With this confidence, we pray for others, prophesy, and speak out the thoughts that God shares with us. Yet for some reason it can be a struggle to believe that God wants to share His thoughts about us directly with us. However, if we would dare to believe, we would find that God is more than willing to share both His heart and His mind with us. Like David, we would find that the thoughts of God outnumber the sands of the shore. The Spirit of Jesus is always willing to share His mind with us. When we open our hearts to hear the thoughts of Christ, we open a channel of divine beauty, joy and truth into our lives.

Pray

Jesus, please share your thoughts with me and give me real faith in you.

12 | The Source of Thoughts

John 10:27
My sheep hear My voice, and I know them, and they follow Me.

Communication exists at the heart of every relationship and this is especially true of our relationship with God. Here Jesus says, "My sheep hear my voice." This is not a statement of potential, as if to say, "My sheep are able to hear my voice." It is a statement of fact.[1] Every true believer is already hearing the voice of God. His voice is already empowering us to love, creating confidence in our hearts, bringing us life, and drawing us into union with His Spirit. Hearing God is therefore not a matter of ability but of discernment.

When I first started learning to hear God, I had little discernment. I always expected that God's voice would boom with authority and would sound clearly different from my own. And there have been moments like this. At one time, I was in turmoil before God, wondering if my latest fall from grace had caused me to forfeit my future with Christ. As I prayed, a thought came into my mind with intensity and authority:

"I will NEVER give up on you."

On that occasion God's voice resounded in my heart and pierced through all the noise. It brought me into the truth of His unfailing love and required little discernment on my part. However, I have found that this kind of thought is generally the exception rather than the rule.

In the days before email was widely used, I remember having a thought to write a letter to a friend called David. I wrote about life and my spiritual journey and asked how his life was going back home. I posted the letter and thought little more about it.

When I next connected with David, he was elated. He shared how he had prayed that I would write a letter and then my letter arrived. I did not share his joy. In fact, I was offended. The experience made me feel like God was controlling me and I did not want to be His puppet. The thought that led me to write the letter did not sound like a command from heaven: *Geoff! Write David a letter!* Instead this came as a normal, everyday kind of thought. *Hmmm, I might write David a letter.* I felt like God had violated my freewill by taking away the choice to obey or disobey His voice.

After some reflection, I realized that God was not controlling me. Rather, He was simply living in unity with me. Up until that point, I had always expected God to speak to me as an external deity—a God who was seated far away in heaven and would speak to me when He wanted something done. But this experience reminded me that the Spirit of God speaks from where He is dwelling: within us.

As we learned earlier, when we choose to live in union with Christ, our lives become a shared space with the Spirit of Jesus. He shares His love with us and it feels like our own. He shares His joy with us and because it comes from within us, it too feels like our own. The same is true for the thoughts of His mind. Because God's thoughts flow from the unity that we share with Him, they often sound like our own. Everyone has a story of how they "just had a thought" to do something or go somewhere, only to find out afterwards that God was leading them and orchestrating glory. My friend Megan has one such story.

"I was out with my kids and had a thought about going down to the river. We went there and found two girls drowning. I ran in but was suddenly out of my depth. The girls were panicking and we all started going under. My oldest daughter and I managed to get one of the girls to safety, but I was struggling with the other girl. I tried but I couldn't get up for air. I thought I was going to drown, so I prayed that God would wash me down the river so my kids wouldn't see me die. Then God told me to push the girl up in the water. So I pushed. She went up in the water and I went down. I didn't know it at the time but other kids on the shore had formed a human chain into the water. They grabbed the girl as she came up and pulled her to the shore. I don't know what happened next. I just found myself on the riverbank."

Megan's thought to go to the river sounded like her own because it flowed from her unity with Jesus. Only afterwards did she really realize that the thought was from God. He was sharing His mind and acting as one with her to save two dying people.

Seeking the Source

Because all our thoughts seem like our own, we can often fail to recognize the thoughts of God. We can also end up taking ownership of thoughts that do not come from God or from our own heart at all. Such thoughts are formed as a response to the spiritual environment that we are in at the time. I remember one morning waking at 4am with a flood of thoughts about the future. *We do not own a house and the housing market is going insane. We will never be able to afford a home. How will we survive? We have no security. What will we do?* My sense of peace was gone, and I called out to God.

"Father, what's going on?" I looked to God, and He calmly spoke into my thoughts.

"The person you have staying with you is in agreement with a spirit of mammon (worldly wealth)." Our guest had set her heart on pursuing worldly security which had created space for a spirit of mammon in her life. While she was staying with us, that spirit started to feed its thoughts into my mind. I took authority and bound the spirit and my peace was instantly restored. I thanked God for His promise to provide for all our needs and I went back to sleep.

This kind of experience happens naturally to everyone, almost every day. We can think of it like spiritual weather. In the physical realm, our skin helps us to discern the weather by telling us if it is warm or cold. It is such a natural part of everyday life that we barely think of the process. It is the same in the spirit. Our thoughts and feelings are our spiritual skin, often telling us what the weather is like in the current spiritual atmosphere. When our thoughts are suddenly different than normal, it is often due to an outside influence. However, few of us recognize our thoughts as a source of discernment. So often we assume that because thoughts take place inside our own head that they all must come from our own heart. This is simply not true.

One day I had coffee with my wife Melanie at a new café. As we were sitting there, a waitress passed by our table. A thought came into my mind: *She is really attractive.* I dismissed the thought and another waitress passed by. *She's really attractive too.* Instead of ignoring the thought I took it to God.

"Lord, what's going on here?"

"There is a spirit of lust in this place." The Holy Spirit showed me that the owner of the café had allowed a spirit of lust into his life, which was affecting the spiritual atmosphere of the place. I got up to wash my hands and the Spirit spoke again.

"You'll see a picture of topless women in the restroom." I opened the door and saw a painting of Polynesian art, but without any topless women. I started to second-guess what I had heard but then turned to my right and saw a painting of two topless Polynesian women. It was a confirmation that a spirit of lust was operating in the café and feeding lustful thoughts into people's minds. Those who engaged with the spirit of lust and took ownership of the thoughts would then leave with a new level of bondage. *Can I offer you some lust with your coffee?* Knowing that such thoughts were coming from outside my own heart, it was easy to take them captive, bind the source, and then refocus my mind on better things.

Testing the Spirits

Philippians 4:8

Finally, brothers, whatever is true, whatever is honorable, whatever is just, whatever is pure, whatever is lovely, whatever is commendable, if there is any excellence, if there is anything worthy of praise, think about these things.

If we are to use our thoughts as a source of discernment, we need to let the Holy Spirit renew our minds and make us confident in our new "normal" way of thinking. Here Scripture calls us to a thought-life that is dominated by love, purity and excellence. Any impure thoughts either come from our selfish nature or an evil spirit. Rather than tolerate such thoughts, we need to ask God to show us the source of the thoughts. If they are coming from within us, then we need to let Jesus circumcise the selfishness from our hearts and renew our minds. If they are coming from a demonic spirit, then we need to bind it and take our thoughts captive to Christ.

The more Jesus shares His mind with us, the more normal it will become to think like Him. In our renewed thinking, it is relatively easy to discern the presence of a spirit like lust or greed or pride or anger. Those thoughts are so obviously different from our renewed thinking. However, there is one particular spirit that is difficult to detect. Just as Satan tempted Eve with something that looked good, this spirit tempts us with the promise of a blessing if we obey it instead of God. It quotes Scripture and uses half-truths that seem to make sense and sound righteous. This means that unlike lust, greed and pride, this spirit is much, much harder to discern. It is the religious spirit and it is one of the most attractive of all Satan's demons.

While I could discern thoughts from other spirits, for a long season I struggled to discern between a religious spirit and the Holy Spirit.

"You should fast today." The thought would enter my mind and my heart would feel weighed down, but I would obey the thought. Later that day I would hear the thought, "It is ok to eat a little. There is grace." I would then be in conflict: Do I accept God's grace and eat, or continue fasting and strive for perfect obedience? If I ate, thoughts of failure would come. If I continued the fast, I would still feel no closer to God. Why were my acts of obedience not rewarded with a sense of love or affection? Why would God call me to obey but then change His mind?

In retrospect I can see that often when God spoke, the religious spirit would also speak in order to create confusion and frustration. It would use Scripture to cause me to second-guess the voice of God. However, often it would simply impersonate God. At one time it convinced me that I was going to die within a nine-month period. I reasoned that the Holy Spirit was telling me of my approaching death to motivate me to make the most of my time. I developed speech problems and started to think that I might have a brain tumor. As it turned out, the speech problems stemmed from my fasting and poor sleeping habits. I started to eat and sleep properly and my body returned to health. The nine-month deadline came and went. I then knew for sure that it was not God who was speaking such thoughts into my life, but a counterfeit, religious spirit. This realization brought relief, but it also presented a real problem. Why could I not discern between the voice of God and the voice of a religious spirit?

Pray

Father, thank you that you always want to share your thoughts with me. Lord, I ask for the gift of discernment. Please help me to discern where my thoughts are coming from Please help me to treasure every thought that comes from your heart and to take captive all others.

13 | Testing Thoughts

Recently Dave and Anna shared the story of how their marriage nearly failed. Dave started to have thoughts about their marriage coming to an end. He prepared for the worst and prayed that the kids would be ok and that his wife would be happy. For weeks he believed that God was preparing him for an inevitable marriage split. Anna also started to have thoughts about the marriage failing. However, she questioned the source and looked ahead to where the thoughts were leading. She discerned that the thoughts were not from God and so she took them captive and carried on with life. She did not realize that the same spirit was feeding thoughts into her husband's mind in an effort to destroy the marriage. It was not until they talked honestly that they realized what was happening. Together they brought their thought-life into the light, bound the enemy, and saved their marriage.

A different couple suffered a similar attack on their marriage, but in this case the attack came from a spirit of lust. This spirit caused the husband to experience feelings of intense sexual desire, while stealing all sexual desire from the wife. This created a wedge in the relationship that allowed rejection, hurt and despair to set the stage for a spirit of adultery to attack. By His grace, the Holy Spirit exposed the strategy of the enemy. The couple then began to take their feelings captive and to restore unity in their relationship.

As we develop our two-way communication with God, we need to be prepared to battle an enemy that wants to destroy our intimacy with God. Demonic spirits are often trying to sow their thoughts and feelings into us, and some of these spirits will attempt to imitate the Holy Spirit. Great damage has been done all through history by people who thought they were hearing the voice of God but were actually following the voice of demons. Their failure to test their thoughts has led to sects, divisions and false religions, leading generations of people into spiritual bondage and death.

Though we may not be deceived on the same scale, if we fail to discern the thoughts of the enemy then we will suffer loss: the loss of relationship, loss of time, loss of resources, loss of truth, loss of faith, loss of joy, or a loss of love. It is therefore critical that we learn to take our thoughts captive and fight for our intimacy with God.

Taking Thoughts Captive

2 Corinthians 10:5

We destroy arguments and every lofty opinion raised against the knowledge of God, and take every thought captive to obey Christ...

God is always good. He does not expect us to learn to discern His voice on our own. Instead, He has given us His Holy Spirit to speak to us and to teach us how to recognize His voice. It is His job.

At first, we may feel like infants slowly learning the language of our Father. While we may make mistakes, it is important to remember that God is on our side and He never sets us up for failure. On the contrary, He wants to teach us how to hear His voice with clarity. This clarity comes by listening to His voice and then testing what we hear.

The Love of God

Luke 6:45

The good person out of the good treasure of his heart produces good, and the evil person out of his evil treasure produces evil, for out of the abundance of the heart his mouth speaks.

God speaks out of the abundance of His heart. Every thought that the Holy Spirit shares with us is an expression of His heart of love. And like His words, every thought of love brings us life.[1] With this in mind, we can test our thoughts by looking at the tone. *Is there life in the thought? Does it express the love of God? Does this thought reinforce my unity with Christ? Does it inspire me? Or is it trying to control me? If I follow this line of thought, will it lead me deeper into selfless love or into something else?*

The Word of God

If we are serious about learning to discern God's voice clearly then we will also be serious about spending time in the Scriptures. The Scriptures are His voice on paper. As we abide in the word, we become more familiar with the tone of God's voice and better able to discern His thoughts.

The word of God is truth and every thought that the Spirit shares with us will align with Scripture. However, it is important to remember that Satan used Scripture against Jesus and a religious spirit will do the same with us. Even if a thought is consistent with Scripture, it does not necessarily mean that it is a thought of God. So how can we tell the difference?

> Matthew 22:37-40
>
> And he said to him, "You shall love the LORD your God with all your heart and with all your soul and with all your mind. This is the great and first commandment. And a second is like it: You shall love your neighbor as yourself. On these two commandments depend all the Law and the Prophets."

The term Jesus has made it clear that all of Scripture depends on the first two commands.[2] Apart from love, the Scriptures can be twisted to support almost any thought. If we are to understand the Bible and use it to test our thoughts, then we need to read it through the lens of love.

Setting the Goal

In the natural realm, Olympic athletes make choices in life that support their goal of winning a gold medal. As they prepare, their intense desire for gold creates a natural filter that they use to train their thoughts. *Will this help me to be faster, stronger, or smarter?*

We do the same. All through life we filter thoughts and make decisions based on our heart's ultimate goal. If our hearts are not truly devoted to our first love, then testing our thoughts will prove to be a difficult discipline. However, when Jesus shares His passion for loving the Father with us, we will become like an elite athlete, obsessed with loving God with all our heart and soul. As His zeal grows within us, taking our thoughts captive will quickly move from being a discipline to a delight.

Discerning the Voice

Romans 12:6-7

Having gifts that differ according to the grace given to us, let us use them: if prophecy, in proportion to our faith, if service, in our serving; the one who teaches, in his teaching...

People who prophesy, speak out the thoughts of God in proportion to the faith they possess.[3] Our faith creates a context for hearing the voice of God. For example, if a person does not believe that it is possible to keep the first command, they will not call others to pursue the first command when they prophesy—even though it is the highest priority on God's heart. The same is true for teachers: they only teach according to their faith. Their faith creates boundaries on the thoughts that God can share with them and through them.

This was the main reason that I struggled to discern between a religious spirit and the Holy Spirit. I had created my own faith based on what I thought God was like. I did not truly believe in the loving nature of God and so I expected commands rather than affections. The thoughts of the religious spirit then naturally matched what I expected God to say. The result was that I was easily deceived by the voice of religion instead of being set free by the voice of Love.

To avoid this deception, we need to truly know the infinite love that God has for us. This knowledge cannot be taught; it can only come through a revelation of God's love. As we learned earlier, we can position our hearts for revelation of love by spending time meditating on the love of God. As the Spirit inspires our imagination and reveals more of God's love to us, we will naturally become better at discerning His voice. Through revelation we will realize that God is always good—better than we could possibly imagine. We will realize that the thoughts God shares with us are always loving, kind and encouraging. Even when the Spirit speaks words of correction, discipline or judgment, they remain true and deeply edifying. God constantly affirms our identity as His beloved children. He corrects us without condemnation or discouragement. He is always compassionate and yet uncompromising. His words inspire and stretch us; they both humble us and lift us up. All His words are spirit and life, and each one calls us deeper into His love to become more one with Him.

Two or Three Witnesses

2 Corinthians 13:1

This will be the third time I am coming to you. "By the mouth of two or three witnesses every word [*rhema*] shall be established."[4]

Every *rhema* is established by two or three witnesses. This verse applies on both a natural and a spiritual level. If we are unsure if what we are hearing is really God's voice, then we can ask Him for two or three witnesses or confirmations. This is not testing God but rather testing our discernment. These confirmations may come in many ways, including signs and wonders, passages of Scriptures, fleeces or lots, prophecies, divine coincidences, words from people, and so on. When God confirms His word, it then gives us a solid confidence to act on His voice.

Practice, Practice, Practice

Hebrews 5:14-6:1a

But solid food is for the mature, for those who have their powers of discernment trained by constant practice to distinguish good from evil. Therefore let us leave the elementary doctrine of Christ and go on to maturity...

Our powers of discernment are trained through constant practice. In terms of hearing God's voice, the more we practice, the easier it is to discern His thoughts. By its very nature, practice is experimental and so we need to be prepared to make mistakes and not get discouraged as we learn to discern.

"Would you like to share a milkshake?" I asked Melanie as we waited in an airport.

"Sure," she replied

"Cool. What flavor would you like? They have vanilla, chocolate, banana and strawberry," I asked.

"I don't know. Anything. Maybe strawberry," Melanie replied. I returned a few minutes later with a strawberry milkshake.

"What's this?" Melanie asked.

"It's a strawberry milkshake," I replied.

"I said, 'anything *but* strawberry.'" I had misheard Melanie, but instead of giving up on ever listening to her again, I just drank the milkshake.

In every relationship, we can mishear or misunderstand the other person and our relationship with God is no different. Mistakes will happen. Even when the enemy is not involved, at times our hearts can be distracted, or our beliefs, fears or agendas can distort the voice of God. When we mishear God, we need to resist the temptation to stop listening. We train our discernment of His voice by constant practice, not by giving up. So instead of getting discouraged, we need to continue to listen to God and test the thoughts we hear. If we are faithful to practice listening, we will find that our discernment quickly grows. This growth then sets in motion the awesome cascade effect of faith. As we train our senses to hear God's voice more clearly, our faith then grows.[5] Greater faith enables us to receive more grace and enter a greater union with Jesus. In deeper union, Jesus shares even more of His thoughts with us, which in turn leads to greater faith, greater love and a greater union. This rapid spiritual growth is available to all of us, and it starts with being willing to practice hearing God's voice. Let us begin!

Pray

Father, please share your passion for love within me. I love you and want to hear your voice more. Please help me to practice listening to you and teach me how test my thoughts.

14 | Making Agreements

Romans 10:9-10
If you confess with your mouth that Jesus is Lord and believe in your heart that God raised him from the dead, you will be saved. For with the heart one believes and is justified, and with the mouth one confesses and is saved.

1 John 4:15
Whoever confesses that Jesus is the Son of God, God abides in him, and he in God.

We confess with our mouths what we believe in our hearts. The word translated as *confess* is the Greek word *homologeo*, meaning to "voice the same conclusion...because in full agreement."[1] When we confess that Jesus Christ is the Son of God or that He was raised from the dead, we are not voicing just an intellectual belief. Instead, we are speaking from a heart-based faith that was birthed within us when we first came into agreement with God.

All our agreements are spiritually powerful. When we agree with a thought that God shares with us, we give God permission to fulfil His word in our lives. For example, when Jesus speaks to us about peace, our agreement gives the Holy Spirit permission to release His peace over us. In this sense, agreement is a form of willing surrender. It is saying: *I agree—I give in. May it be unto me according to your word.*

Agreement usually takes place in the thought realm and the principle of agreement works the same way for the enemy as it does for God. When a demonic spirit sows a thought into our minds, it wants us to agree with it. As soon as we accept a thought as our own, we give that spirit permission to affect the way we think and feel about life. If we keep on agreeing, that spirit's influence will grow, and our deception will increase. Eventually we will begin to act on those ungodly thoughts and engage in sin.

Because a simple agreement with a single thought of the enemy has the potential to open a door to long-term deception, it is essential that we learn to take our thoughts captive. When we become aware of a thought, we need to either consciously agree and accept the thought or disagree and dispose of it.

It is important that we deal with both our present thoughts and our past agreements. We do this by asking the Holy Spirit to show us where we have made agreements in the past with the enemy. It can be helpful to look at our recent patterns of thought and feelings. If we see any ungodly thoughts in operation, then we need to break our underlying agreements and cancel the permission that these spirits use to work in our lives. We can then release the blood of Christ to undo any damage that our agreement with the enemy has caused within us or through us. Once our minds are free from the source of these thoughts, we can then guard ourselves against any future threat.

A prayer that breaks an agreement can sound something like this: *In the name of Jesus, I break all agreement with _____. I renounce it and through the blood of Jesus I reject it from my life. I cancel every legal right of the enemy to influence my life through _____ and I repent of believing the lies that have been sown in my heart. I ask You, Lord God, to set me free from the lies that formed an agreement. Please undo the damage that _____ has caused in my life and through me in the lives of others. Please bring blessing in place of the curse, truth in the place of lies, and life in the place of death. I agree with You and give you permission to do whatever it takes to bring me into a wholehearted love for You. I take hold of Your grace and surrender my life to Your design of love.*

Building Strongholds

The Greek word *synergos* means co-worker. From this word we get the English word *synergy*, which speaks of the ability to create something that is greater than the sum of its parts. We experience synergy when we agree with others. Through our agreement we achieve more than we could possibly hope to achieve alone. Agreement is power.

In the story of the Tower of Babel, we find that agreement can be used powerfully for good or evil. For this reason, the world is constantly vying for our agreement. As we grow from children to adults, we are fed ideas and thoughts by people, books, media, movies, and so on. Some ideas we reject and others we accept. After we first agree with an idea or thought, it becomes natural for us to accept similar thoughts. Over time, these thoughts combine to create a whole way of thinking. Like building a fortress stone by stone, we build thought upon thought and eventually create what Scripture calls a *stronghold of the mind.*

Our strongholds influence every part of our lives. The decisions we make, the voices we listen to, the way we interpret experiences and engage with life around us; we process everything according to the strongholds of the mind. In academic circles, scientists call these strongholds *cognitive biases.*[2] They are biases because they cause us to interpret life in a way that aligns with what we already believe.[3] Because the brain is constantly looking for evidence to reinforce its existing beliefs, we rarely interpret any event of life objectively. Instead, we filter out information that challenges the way we think and reinterpret life in a way that confirms our beliefs. This is one of the reasons that the strongholds of the mind are so strong.

For example, if a person has a stronghold of self-hate or rejection, they will be sensitive to the slightest hints of rejection in their relationships. Any sign that can be twisted into evidence of rejection will be used by the brain to build up the stronghold of rejection. *He didn't acknowledge me in the street. She turned her back when I was going to speak. They laughed at me. He interrupted me when I was talking. They don't value me. All my friends hate me. No one loves me.*

The problem with biases is that the brain excels at collecting evidence but is terrible at fact checking. We are too quick to assume and too slow to question. If we only took the time to find out the truth, we would find that most of the time, our negative assumptions are wrong.[4]

I recently spoke with a friend about the lies we believe. She shared how her father left the family when she was eight years old. She carried a profound sense of rejection into adulthood, believing that she was unlovable. She shared how she got married, only to spend the first seven years trying to destroy her marriage. She thought that if she could get her husband to leave her, it would confirm what she had always believed: that she was unlovable. Thankfully, God exposed the lie, healed her heart, and restored her ability to love. What this highlights is that not only does the brain filter life to confirm its beliefs, it will often compel us to construct evidence to support the lies.

Biases about God

I was raised to relate to God as a righteous moral judge. This was my bias and so all the teachings I heard seemed to confirm the idea that we love God by obeying His commands. However, while it is true that our love for God leads us to obey His voice, it is not true that obedience equates to love. For as many employees know, it is possible to hate someone but still obey them.

> **John 14:15**
> "If you love me, you will keep my commandments."

In this passage Jesus is not saying that obedience is love. Instead He is saying that the root of love will always produce the fruit of obedience. If we set our focus on obeying God in order to please Him, we risk making obedience the root in the place of love. To believe that we can produce any good fruit from the root of our own works is to enter a subtle but profound deception.

This was a lie that I naively agreed with and built into a stronghold within my mind. Such was the strength of the lie that it skewed my understanding of God. It led me to believe that God wanted to *use* me rather than *love* me. This is why I always expected God to command me to do something when He spoke to me. Tragically, this belief led me out of agreement with God and into agreement with a religious spirit. This gave the religious spirit the right to influence my thoughts and feelings and even to impersonate the voice of God. It was always quick to command me and reward my obedience with pride and punish my failure with condemnation.

This stronghold of religion made me interpret events in a way that confirmed my beliefs about God as my moral judge. When I sinned, I believed that anything negative that followed was evidence that God was punishing me. I felt condemned and guilty and believed that God was rightly condemning me. Likewise, when I did well, I tended to interpret any blessing that I experienced as God rewarding me for my works. Through my subconscious filtering of life, I kept finding evidence that God was either judging me or rewarding me all through my life.

This stronghold was a safe place from which a religious spirit could rule over my mind and undermine my intimacy with the real Jesus. Something had to change.

2 Corinthians 10:3-5

For though we walk in the flesh, we are not waging war according to the flesh. For the weapons of our warfare are not of the flesh but have divine power to destroy strongholds. We destroy arguments and every lofty opinion raised against the knowledge of God, and take every thought captive to obey Christ...

Scripture calls us not only to take every thought captive but to destroy the strongholds of the mind that stand against the true knowledge of God. These strongholds are refuges of lies that we shelter in to protect ourselves from God's love. While the strongholds remain, we feel safe. We feel in control. We feel secure in what we know. Yet, our strongholds are expensive to maintain. Every day we pay the cost as we forfeit our design of love.

Even though we use the strongholds of the mind to lock God out of our hearts, He is relentless in His pursuit. He stands at the gate and knocks. He calls through the walls. We expect to hear the voice of the Judge but instead the Bridegroom calls us: *Come away with me!* So we stand within our walls, longing and confused, wondering if it is safe to lower our defenses.

Fortress of Love

The weapons of our warfare are powerful to destroy our strongholds. Prayer is powerful. Worship is powerful. Truth is powerful. But of all our weapons, love is the most powerful. When we commit our lives to the first command, we begin to build a greater stronghold on better foundations. Its construction shakes the heart and mind and the strongholds of lies start to fall. The walls of religion crack and crumble. Walls of pride collapse. Greed, lust and selfish ambition all fall as the fortress of God's love is built within us.

Like the strongholds before it, this fortress of love is built through agreement. Every time we agree with God, He strengthens the stronghold of love within us. Every time we cancel an agreement with a lie, the enemy is displaced and his strongholds are cast down. Thought by godly thought, the stronghold of love is built until it takes over and becomes our primary bias. At that time, our brains then start to look for evidence to support our belief in the limitless love of God. And we find the evidence everywhere. Our eyes become open to hear His voice in music, see His hand in creation, sense His presence in His people, and read His heart in His word. Everywhere we look we see signs that God loves us. He deeply, passionately, perfectly loves us.

Pray

Father, I know that you love me. Please conquer my heart! Please tear down every stronghold that stands against you. Let your love flood me and wash away the lies. Please change my whole way of thinking so that I can truly know you and accept your love.

15 | A New Identity

Proverbs 23:7a
For as he thinks in his heart, so is he.

Our identity is primarily expressed in the way we think. All the thoughts that we believe about ourselves flow out through our words and actions. The decisions we make; how we interpret life; how we relate to people; and even how we love—the different aspects of our lives are all deeply affected by our sense of identity.

When our thoughts are shaped by strongholds of lies, our sense of identity is distorted and we lose our ability to fully live in love. To live as God designed, we need to break our agreements with lies and let God begin to overcome our resistances to love. We need to hear the call of John the Baptist and ask God to help us to level the mountains that stand against His love and raise the valleys within us. We need to prepare our hearts for Jesus and get ready to receive a new identity in Christ and a whole new way of thinking.

Out with the Old, in with the New

Ephesians 4:20-24
But that is not the way you learned Christ!— assuming that you have heard about him and were taught in him, as the truth is in Jesus, to put off your old self, which belongs to your former manner of life and is corrupt through deceitful desires, and to be renewed in the spirit of your minds, and to put on the new self, created after the likeness of God in true righteousness and holiness.

When speaking of identity, Scripture uses the terms *old self* and *new self*. The *old self* refers to our old identity apart from Christ. It is the corrupt image of our personality, distorted by our sinful desires and selfishness. The *new self* is our new identity.

To put on the new self means to actively clothe ourselves in our new identity. When we put on the new self, we agree with God's design for our lives. We consciously choose a life of love and unity with Jesus, and we then let this unity change the way we think.

The new self delights in every expression of love. It loves loving and being loved. The new self fits us like a perfectly tailored garment, but it is not an overcoat. We do not put the new self over the top of the old and hope that the world will not see the darkness of our old self. Instead, before we can truly put on our new identity, we must first completely put off the old.

Galatians 2:20 (TDB)
I have been crucified•⁾ with Christ. It is no longer I who live, but Christ who lives in me. And the life I now live in the flesh I live by faith in [from] the Son of God, who loved me and gave himself for me.

I have been crucified with Christ. There is a death that we must experience before we can know the full reality of our new life. Here Paul writes of that death as being crucified with Christ. The word *crucified* is in the Greek perfect tense (•⁾), which describes a completed action with a focus on the ongoing effects. When Paul laid off his old self through the cross of Christ, it set off a cascade of change that affected his entire life. In the same way, when we call on God to crucify us with Christ and circumcise our hearts, it will begin a process of change that will bring about lifelong transformation. The cross will do its work in us and crush our selfishness which will then enable the Holy Spirit to lead us into wholehearted love. As we receive this new life of selfless love, we will no longer think and feel how we used to. Everything will change.

We possess all things in Christ through faith, and faith comes from hearing God's voice. This means that we need to hear God speak to us about our call to be crucified with Christ. Only when He speaks can we receive the faith we need to experience the reality.

Being crucified with Christ is entirely a work of grace, for no one can overcome their selfishness in their own strength. The roots of the selfish nature are simply too deep. Only God can do it. *And He wants to.* He did it for Paul and He will do it for us. Our part is simply to surrender ourselves to the call of the cross: to come and to die.[1]

It is no longer I who live but Christ who lives in me. Because his old self died with Christ, Paul was united with Jesus in a completely new life and identity. This changed his way of thinking forever. Paul now saw himself as a channel for the life of Christ. He recognized that his union with Jesus was still expressed in his earthly body and so the world would still see him as Paul. But within his heart, Paul saw his identity only in terms of the unity he shared with Jesus.

You are in Christ Jesus

2 Corinthians 5:17
Therefore, if anyone is in Christ, he is a new creation. The old has passed away; behold, the new has come.

1 Corinthians 1:30-31 (emphasis added)
And because of him **you are in Christ Jesus**, who became to us wisdom from God, righteousness and sanctification and redemption, so that, as it is written, "Let the one who boasts, boast in the Lord."

You are in Christ Jesus. This is one of the most powerful statements ever about identity. We are in Christ Jesus. He is in us. We share the same spirit.[2] We are one. Through His indwelling presence we are a new creation who thinks entirely differently. It is no longer *I* who lives but *We*—I in Christ and Christ in me: *We*.[3]

We can look at this change of thinking in the context of a marriage. When we are single, we think like single people. When we get married we have to change the way we think to account for our unity. This can be difficult at first. But if we do not change the way we think, our single-mindedness will be a source of tension and distance in our marriage. To have a successful marriage, we need to let go of our old identity and invest ourselves in forging unity with our spouse through love.

The same is true for our relationship with Jesus. When we become one with Christ, we can no longer afford to think in our old ways. We are no longer single. Instead we need to learn to think in terms of our unity with Jesus. It is important to note again that even though we become one with Christ, we do not become Jesus. It is the same in marriage. When a man and woman get married, they do not become each other. They simply stop being single and start a new life of unity together. And this requires a change of thinking. In the same way, when we become one with Christ, we live in a unique unity with Him so that it is no longer *I* who live. It is now *We*: Christ in me and I in Christ. *We.*

Our thinking apart from Jesus usually starts with *I* and can include thoughts like: *I can't do this. I don't have enough money. I'm going to let people down. I'm just not good enough.* Our single-life thoughts are not always negative—we can have positively proud thoughts as well. *I deserve some recognition for what I've done. What will I do with my money? What's in it for me? I'm too good for this, I deserve better.*

There is a simple key to changing our thinking so that we account for our unity with Jesus. When we find ourselves thinking *I*, we simply rephrase the same thought using *We* (adding Jesus). This one small change has the power to force us into the truth. For example, when we think *I can't do this,* we start the thought again using *We. We can do this. Together, we can do anything.* Instead of *I don't want to do this,* we think *We...do we want to do this?* Thinking *We* prompts us to ask Jesus what He thinks and involve Him in our everyday lives. This discipline draws us into the truth and releases us from our natural limitations. It helps us to redefine our identity and accept that we are no longer alone, but we now live forever in unity with Jesus Christ. *What are we doing today?*

Ongoing Renewing

For this kind of thinking to be genuine, the change must come from the Holy Spirit. Naturally thinking *We* is not something we can talk ourselves into and it does not happen in a single moment of revelation. It is a part of an ongoing process of transformation.

> **Romans 12:1-2** (TDB)
> Therefore I urge you, brethren, by the mercies of God, to present your bodies a living and holy sacrifice, acceptable to God, which is your spiritual service of worship. And do not be conformed~ to this world, but be transformed~ by the renewing of your mind, so that you may prove~ what the will of God is, that which is good and acceptable and perfect.

The word *transformed* is written in the Greek present tense (~!), which speaks of an ongoing, continual action. If we are to be living sacrifices, then we need the Spirit of God to continually transform us by renewing our minds and helping us to think *We*. We participate in this transformation by constantly placing all the strongholds of the mind—all our mindsets, worldviews, agendas, assumptions, doctrines, beliefs and theologies—on the altar before God. Every time we offer our minds to God, His fire of love falls and transforms more of our thinking.

> **Matthew 4:17** (TDB)
> From that time Jesus began to preach, saying, "Repent,~ for the kingdom of heaven is at hand."

Echoing the call to ongoing transformation, the Greek present tense (~!) in this verse calls us to repent *all through life*. Our English word *repent* means to be sorry again. However, the Greek word *metanoia* (which is translated as *repent*) literally means to change our mind or to change the way we think.[4] Therefore, when Jesus calls us to repent, He is not calling us to make a one-time decision to follow Him and neither is He calling us to live a sorry life. Instead, Jesus is calling us to let Him continually change the way we think.

84

As our true friend, Jesus is promising to share His mind with us and reshape the way we think. If we let Him, Jesus will affirm our new identity and our unity with Him with one simple word: *We.*

Pray

Jesus, thank you for wanting to change the way I think. I say "yes and amen" to you. I give you full permission to change the way I think about everything. I offer myself as a living sacrifice. Let your fire fall on my whole life and consume me with your love. Let us be forever "We" in heart, thought and action.

16 | Identity in Love

Luke 15:11-24

And he [Jesus] said, "There was a man who had two sons. And the younger of them said to his father, 'Father, give me the share of property that is coming to me.' And he divided his property between them. Not many days later, the younger son gathered all he had and took a journey into a far country, and there he squandered his property in reckless living. And when he had spent everything, a severe famine arose in that country, and he began to be in need. So he went and hired himself out to one of the citizens of that country, who sent him into his fields to feed pigs. And he was longing to be fed with the pods that the pigs ate, and no one gave him anything.

"But when he came to himself, he said, 'How many of my father's hired servants have more than enough bread, but I perish here with hunger! I will arise and go to my father, and I will say to him, "Father, I have sinned against heaven and before you. I am no longer worthy to be called your son. Treat me as one of your hired servants."' And he arose and came to his father. But while he was still a long way off, his father saw him and felt compassion, and ran and embraced him and kissed him. And the son said to him, 'Father, I have sinned against heaven and before you. I am no longer worthy to be called your son.' But the father said to his servants, 'Bring quickly the best robe, and put it on him, and put a ring on his hand, and shoes on his feet. And bring the fattened calf and kill it, and let us eat and celebrate. For this my son was dead, and is alive again; he was lost, and is found.' And they began to celebrate."

This is one of the Bible's most well-known parables. It starts with the younger son asking his father for his share of his inheritance. The son is intent on pursuing pleasure, but in order to truly enjoy the world, he has to travel to a far-off land where no one knows him. There he creates a new identity for himself, out from under the shadow of his father. The son wastes his entire inheritance on selfish living and reduces himself to nothing.

A famine comes to the land and the son begins to starve. As the haze of pleasure lifts, the son starts to see how far he has fallen from his true identity. Rather than endure starvation, he decides to return home.

As the son nears home, his father sees him and runs to him. The father embraces the son and kisses him. He brings him home and clothes him in the best robe, puts a ring on his finger, and gets sandals for his feet. Then he calls for a great celebration. The father gives no rebuke and displays no sense of disappointment or regret over the past. He simply expresses His extravagant, uninhibited love for His child.

A Father's Love

When the prodigal son returned to the father, he carried a profound sense of unworthiness. He knew he had chosen selfishness over love, rejected his father, wasted his life, and dishonored his family. The shame of his actions changed the way he was willing to relate to his father. Though he returned to the father in a spirit of humility and repentance, he did not return in his identity as a son. He believed that he had forfeited his right to be called a son because of his sin. His only hope was that his father would accept him back as a servant and give him the chance to atone for his sin by working in the household. He thought, *I'm not worthy to be a son to my father, but perhaps I can be a servant.* So the son returned to the father.

While he was still a long way off, his father saw him and felt compassion.

The father was waiting and watching for his son and saw him a long way off. The father would have been waiting in a spirit of love, hope, optimism and expectancy.

When the father finally saw his son, he was filled with compassion. The Greek word translated here as *compassion* is the word *splagxnízomai*. This word literally refers to the inner organs like the heart and lungs but when it is used in a figurative sense, *splagxnízomai* is the strongest Greek word for expressing intense compassion.[1] By using this word, Jesus was inspiring the listeners' imagination to see the great affection that flows from the depths of the father's heart.

His father ran

In ancient times, a person of a lower status would quietly approach someone of a higher status as a sign of respect. A non-threatening approach to a superior is a sign of submission and honor and this is still the case today. Dignitaries, royalty and people of status wait while their aides approach. If two people are equal, they will usually approach each other and meet in the middle.

In this passage we would expect the father to wait while the son approaches. We would expect to see the son humble himself at his father's feet and beg for mercy. Yet we see something else entirely. The father sets aside the honor due him and runs to his son. In ancient times it was considered undignified, even shameful, for an older man to run in public. And yet the father *runs*. The father is so moved by the intensity of his love and compassion that he sheds all his dignity and runs to his son.

His father ran to him and embraced him and kissed him

The word *embrace* is from a Greek phrase meaning "to fall upon the neck." In this passage the father falls upon the neck of his son and kisses him. For the father it is a moment of incredible relief. The separation is over. The anguish has ended. The son would have come home dirty, sweaty, and smelling like pigs, but it did not matter in the slightest. The love of the father that has waited so long has finally found its release.

Get the best robe

The son did not return because of love but because of necessity. He was going to die. He started to apologize but the father ignored him. Instead the father called for the best robe, which showed that he was restoring his son into the covering, wealth, and privilege of the family. This was an outward sign that showed everyone that the father had fully accepted his son and set his blessing upon him.

Put shoes on his feet

In ancient times, footwear was important: slaves were forced to go bare foot while free people wore sandals. When the father gave his son new shoes, he was making a statement: *You are no longer a slave.* It was always the son's intention to return as a servant, but the father did not even let him speak the words. He banished any mindset that would tempt his son to accept anything less than his position as a fully loved and fully accepted son.

Put a ring on his hand

Throughout history, a signet ring was used to seal documents and was a sign of authority, belonging and identity. In this single moment of undeserved love, the son received the ring and was restored as a fully empowered member of his family. He now had access to the full authority, protection and provision of his father.

Let us celebrate!

That which was lost was now found and it was the cause for a great celebration.

A Good Father

I once saw a video of a man whose wife had been taken captive and enslaved by radical Islamists. Another man went undercover as someone seeking to purchase a slave and he bought the woman from her captors. He then returned the woman to her husband. The video showed the moment when the couple were reunited. When they saw each other they literally ran and fell upon each other's necks and wept profusely and kissed each other. It was a miraculous and deeply emotional moment. I cried as I watched. That which was lost had been found.

The emotion that the couple experienced at that point in time is only a faint shadow of the emotion that the Father feels towards us. His love is so great that He set aside the glory of heaven and in Christ Jesus, He ran to us. Because of His love, Jesus gave up all His dignity and was humiliated, stripped naked, tortured and crucified. At the cross, the living God ran to us and spread His arms wide, open for our embrace.

Like the prodigal, we come to the cross seeking mercy and forgiveness. We find these and so much more. At the cross, we find our Father running full speed towards us, moved by an unimaginably powerful compassion. The Father's love for us is so intense, His compassion so overwhelming, that when we come to Him, He falls upon our neck and weeps for joy. He embraces us and He does not let go. Through our return, the love that has been welling up for so long in our Father's heart finally finds its release.

Having found our way back into the arms of God, He then lavishes us with His affection. From the depths of His heart, God's love flows to us. His eyes look at us and are so full of love that they do not recognize any trace of failure or guilt. All they see is the child of His love. And so all of heaven celebrates. That which was lost is found at last.

Pray

Father, thank you for your love. I can barely believe that you love me so much. It is beyond anything I could ever hope or dream! I surrender to your love. Thank you for choosing me. Thank you for setting your love upon me. Thank you, thank you, thank you.

17 | Prevailing Grace

Luke 15:25-32

"Now his older son was in the field, and as he came and drew near to the house, he heard music and dancing. And he called one of the servants and asked what these things meant. And he said to him, 'Your brother has come, and your father has killed the fattened calf, because he has received him back safe and sound.' But he was angry and refused to go in. His father came out and entreated him, but he answered his father, 'Look, these many years I have served you, and I never disobeyed your command, yet you never gave me a young goat, that I might celebrate with my friends. But when this son of yours came, who has devoured your property with prostitutes, you killed the fattened calf for him!' And he said to him, 'Son, you are always with me, and all that is mine is yours. It was fitting to celebrate and be glad, for this your brother was dead, and is alive; he was lost, and is found.'"

When the celebrations began, the older son refused to join in. For years he had faithfully served his father and kept his commands. Yet despite his faithfulness, the older son was never given even a young goat in return for his labor. So he was incensed at the display of extravagant love that the father poured out on his younger brother. None of it made any sense. The younger brother deserved to be punished, not celebrated. The prodigal son had done nothing to earn his father's approval and yet the father was showering him with all the love and acceptance that the older brother felt was owed to him. It seemed more than unjust; it seemed like the father was rewarding sin and mocking faithfulness. Why would a loving father not give his son even the smallest of rewards in return for all his years of hard work?

The parable of the prodigal son is not simply a revelation of God's unconditional love and acceptance. It is a powerful story of the grace of God. To understand this parable, we need to learn about grace and what Scripture calls the *law of works*.

Grace and Works

Romans 3:27-28, 4:1-5a

Then what becomes of our boasting? It is excluded. By what kind of law? By a law of works? No, but by the law of faith. For we hold that one is justified by faith apart from works of the law...

What then shall we say was gained by Abraham, our forefather according to the flesh? For if Abraham was justified by works, he has something to boast about, but not before God. For what does the Scripture say? "Abraham believed God, and it was counted to him as righteousness." Now to the one who works, his wages are not counted as a gift but as his due. And to the one who does not work but believes in him who justifies the ungodly, his faith is counted as righteousness...

The word translated as *law* is the Greek word *nomos*. At times *nomos* is used to refer to the first five books of the Bible and at other times it can refer to the whole Old Testament.[1] Often however, *nomos* is used in a broader sense to refer to a system of religious thinking.[2] In this context, the term *law* speaks of the principles that we let govern our spiritual life and frame our relationship with God.[3]

This passage tells us that we can live under the law of faith or the law of works. Each law represents a way of life—a system of belief that shapes our thinking and drives our behavior. The *law of works* is a term that Paul uses to describe legalism.[4] It is called a law of works because it is based on the belief that we gain God's approval by the things we do.[5]

In the parable of the prodigal son, the younger brother thought that he could earn back the acceptance of His father by working as a servant. His hope was that he could atone for his sin through his own works. The older brother thought in a similar way. Like a worker who is entitled to wages for their work, the older brother felt that his years of service made him deserving of his father's blessing.

Both brothers were deceived by legalism. Neither brother understood his place in the heart of the father. Neither truly knew the depth of the father's love and so neither brother had a true sense of identity.

Like the brothers in the parable, legalism deceives us into thinking that we need to try to please God through our works. We think that if we act in a certain way that God will like us more. We think that if we pray in a certain way that God will answer our prayers; if we repent with tears that God will forgive us; if we sing a certain song then the presence of God will come; if we give a certain amount of money then God will bless us but if we do not give then we will be cursed. Legalism reduces our spiritual life to the principle of cause and effect: If we do this then God will bless us, and if we do that then God will punish us. In legalism, we do our best to live a good Christian life and avoid doing anything that would make God angry.

The Nature of Grace

> **Romans 11:6**
> Now if by grace, then it is not by works; otherwise grace ceases to be grace.

> **Romans 11:6** (NLT)
> And since it is through God's kindness, then it is not by their good works. For in that case, God's grace would not be what it really is— free and undeserved.

God never changes; He is the same yesterday, today and forever. Likewise, God's grace never changes. It remains forever free, undeserved, and unconditional.

It is the unchanging grace of God that protects the priceless value of God's love and all the blessings that flow from His love. The grace of God makes it impossible to earn God's love and ensures that God's love always remains free and unconditional. *Free* means that we are completely free to either choose or reject His love. *Unconditional* means that we can receive the love of God without doing anything to earn it. Why is this important? Because forced love is slavery and bought love is prostitution. And the Living God of Love can never be an enslaver nor a prostitute, not even for a moment. The integrity of the loving nature of God depends on the unbending nature of His grace.

Even though we may be full of the best intentions, when we try to earn God's blessing by the things we do, we deny His nature of love and offend His grace. Through our striving, we try to turn His grace from a gift into something that God owes us—wages for our work. This can *never* happen. No matter how hard we try, the priceless love of God can never be bought. Grace can never cease to be grace and love can never cease to be love. It must always be an *entirely* free gift.

Father or Employer?

Romans 4:4 (NLT)
When people work, their wages are not a gift, but something they have earned.

The grace of God can never be earned and yet this is what the older son tries to do. He works hard and so he feels like he deserves the father's blessings.[6] He puts his trust in his own works rather than in his father's love. Like the older son, when we try to earn God's blessing, we demand a fundamental change in our relationship with God. Instead of relating to God as our loving Father, we insist on relating to Him as our Employer. We want Him to tell us what to do and then reward our obedience with His blessing.

When we try to relate to God in this way, we immediately come into conflict with Him. God wants to be our loving Father and we want Him to be our fair Employer. God longs to lavish us with His love, but we insist on earning it. The result is tragic.

The older son was rich beyond his imagination but because of his legalism he lived in poverty, not even receiving a young goat to enjoy with his friends. Yet the father had already given him everything that he was working so hard to attain. All the goats were already his—a gift of his awesome inheritance.

The son had complete access to every blessing of his father, but legalism had blinded him to the riches that were already his. He thought that he had to earn the blessing and so he worked hard, only to find that the exact opposite happened. The more he worked, the more he distanced himself from the love of his father. Even though he was rich, the older son lived in pointless poverty.

A Different Gospel

Galatians 1:6, 3:1, 5:4, 14

I am astonished that you are so quickly deserting him who called you in the grace of Christ and are turning to a different gospel...You are severed from Christ, you who would be justified by the law [of legalism]; you have fallen away from grace...For the whole law [of God] is fulfilled in one word: "You shall love your neighbor as yourself."

When we live like the older son, we too fall into spiritual poverty. In his letters, Paul describes this poverty and the devastating effects that legalism has in our lives. Legalism makes sense and sounds good, but it denies the nature of grace and so removes the need for faith.

From the least to the greatest, every blessing of God is a gift of grace that can only be received through faith. This is why Jesus says that the older son did not receive even a small goat for all his hard work. There is no way we can experience even the smallest blessing of God through our own effort. Each and every blessing must remain a gift of love.

The quickest way to refuse a gift is to insist on paying for it. The enemy therefore uses legalism to compel us to earn God's unearnable blessings, knowing that in every case it will cut us off from the very thing we are trying so hard to attain. This is why Paul writes that legalism is a "different gospel" that "severs us from Christ." By replacing faith with works, legalism locks us out of grace and love, disconnects us from the heart of God, and leads us to reject God as our loving Father.

When we feel distant from God, the voice of legalism then blames us and compels us to try harder to reconnect with God. So we try harder: we pray more and worship more and do everything we are told to do to earn His love. We try to purchase a gift that is not for sale, and the harder we try, the further we fall from God's grace. Rarely do we stop striving long enough to realize that we reject the gift of God's love every time we try to earn it. In effect our actions say: *God, I want your love, but I cannot believe it is a free gift. I cannot bring myself to receive what I do not deserve. I just cannot believe that you want to be so generous with me. So I will not let you be who You are. Instead I will make you my Employer. I will earn your blessings. I will earn your love. I will earn your favor and affection and approval. Watch me try.*

And so our Father watches and waits. He waits for us to receive His love on His terms. Our Father waits for us to give up on our own efforts and simply accept that He loves us. He truly, deeply, passionately loves us.

God's response to our striving is never one of condemnation but of unending compassion: *Come to me and I will give you rest. I am good—better than you can imagine. I have always loved you so don't feel like you need to earn my approval. You can stop striving now; it's yours. I'm yours and everything I have is yours. I long to pour out my love upon you and to see you enjoy all the blessings of heaven. But as long as you keep trying to earn my love, the doors of your heart remain closed. I am knocking. Open the doors. Surrender to my love.*

Pray

Father I thank you that your love cannot be earned and I'm sorry I ever tried to earn it. Please forgive me. I know I need to get free from legalism but I'm not sure if I can overcome the instinct to earn your blessing. I need you to overcome it for me. Please set me free from legalism so that there is no longer any trace of it in my life. Let all legalism die within me so that I might live forever in your amazing grace and unfailing love.

18 | Relationship and Religion

Like the older brother, the Pharisees were people who lived in legalism. They were zealous for all the rules and commands of Scripture and spent their lives trying to please God by doing what was right and avoiding what was sinful.

> **Matthew 23:13**
>
> "But woe to you, scribes and Pharisees, hypocrites! For you shut the kingdom of heaven in people's faces. For you neither enter yourselves nor allow those who would enter to go in."

The Pharisees were victims of a grave deception that compelled them to deceive others. For generations, a spirit of religion had been speaking to the Pharisees, saying, *Look at all the commands of the law—you need to keep every single one perfectly to please God. If you disobey any, God will judge you without mercy. You must obey every command to the highest degree and teach others to obey as well.*

By the time of Jesus, the faith of Abraham and the love of Moses were long lost in the haze of legalism. The word *Law,* which once inspired a holy awe, had now become just another name for legalism. Something had to change. At the perfect time, Jesus came to bring grace and truth. He came to fulfil the true Law and to break the bondage of legalism. He came to set His people free.

Often the Pharisees are painted as the enemy of Christ, but Jesus loved them. He understood their deception and with firm love He told the Pharisees how legalism was locking them out of the kingdom of heaven. He forcefully pointed them to the love of God and called them to keep the first command. As a result, there were some Pharisees who turned from their dead works and embraced a life of faith and love.

John 5:36-42

[Talking to the Pharisees Jesus says:] "But the testimony that I have is greater than that of John. For the works that the Father has given me to accomplish, the very works that I am doing, bear witness about me that the Father has sent me. And the Father who sent me has himself borne witness about me. His voice you have never heard, his form you have never seen, and you do not have his word abiding in you, for you do not believe the one whom he has sent. You search the Scriptures because you think that in them you have eternal life; and it is they that bear witness about me, yet you refuse to come to me that you may have life. I do not receive glory from people. But I know that you do not have the love of God within you."

Jesus loved the Pharisees enough to tell them the truth. He also loves us enough to tell us the truth. Through the Pharisees, Jesus shows us what legalism does to a believer. In this passage we find that the Pharisees:

1. Knew the Scriptures but did not have the word of God abiding in them
2. Did not hear the voice of God
3. Did not believe Jesus
4. Did not come to Jesus and find life (so were spiritually dead)
5. Did not have the love of God within them

The Pharisees dedicated their lives to obeying the word of God, yet they did not have the word of God in the hearts. Their focus was set on outward obedience rather than inward love and unity. They had an unsurpassed knowledge of Scripture, but without the Holy Spirit, they could not see Jesus revealed in the word of God. They failed to understand that Scripture was given to us as a tutor to lead us *into* Jesus through faith.[1]

Faith comes by hearing God's voice and Jesus says that the Pharisees had never heard His voice. They did not listen to the voice of the Spirit because they believed that they had everything they needed in the Scriptures. The result was that the Pharisees rejected Jesus. This is how the spirit of religion used the Scripture against those who loved it most. Through legalism, the religious spirit stripped the Pharisees of their humanity and robbed them of a life of wholehearted love. It worked to ensure that the Pharisees remained spiritually dead, imprisoned in the futility of a religion that insisted on earning the unearnable.

Legalism works in the same way today. By replacing the voice of God with the principles of Scripture, legalism removes the need for relationship. This sets in motion a devastating cascade of spiritual loss. By silencing God's voice, legalism strips us of a living faith.[2] This loss of faith then disconnects us from God's grace. Without grace, we cannot receive the gift of love.[3] And it is love alone that gives our actions eternal value. No matter how hard we try, when we strive without love, Scripture says that our works achieve nothing.[4]

Through all this, legalism replaces our relationship with God with something altogether different and absolutely inferior: religion. This is why Paul was so vehemently against legalism. It takes the children of God, separates them from His presence, robs them of His love, strips them of their value, and reduces them to nothing.

A Perfect Law?

How could the Pharisees accept religion over relationship? How could they know the Scriptures so well and yet miss the obvious call of faith and grace? How could they recite the Shema twice every day and not experience the reality of love and union with God?

We can explore these questions by looking at the New Testament's almost contradictory perspective on the Law. In some places it speaks harshly about the Law, calling it a law of sin and death. It says that the Law imparts the knowledge of sin and arouses the selfish nature and brings condemnation, guilt and slavery.[5] Yet in other places the New Testament speaks of the Law as being perfect, holy, righteous and good, calling it the law of Spirit and life and the perfect law of liberty.[6] So which is it?

In the beginning, humanity was given a choice between two trees. Today we have this choice in every sphere of life and even in Scripture itself. When we open the Bible, it is like a garden with two trees and how we read the Scripture determines which tree we eat from. When we read the Bible through the lens of love, we see every passage in the context of the first two commands (on which they depend), and we eat from the tree of life. The word of God comes to life and becomes a law of love that restores, inspires and transforms us. Through the lens of love, we hear all the commands of Scripture calling us out of selfishness and *into* Jesus to experience life as God intended: a life of wholehearted love, of hearing His voice, and living in union with Him.

When we read Scripture through the lens of legalism, it becomes like the tree of the knowledge of good and evil. When we eat from this tree, the Bible becomes the standard by which we judge between right and wrong. It makes sense and appears empowering: *Do this and be blessed; do that and die.* Its fruit appears good to eat, and like a serpent, the religious spirit would try to seduce us into reaching out for the fruit of this tree. It tempts us to doubt the voice of God and then to doubt God's nature of love. *You shall surely not die if you try to do it on your own—God is lying to you. The tree of knowledge is a blessing that will make you like Him. He wants to keep the blessing from you because He doesn't fully love you. He is not as good as He says He is. You can take the blessing, just reach out, stretch farther, try harder...*Like Eve, we so easily doubt the love of God and believe the lie. We believe that there is a blessing we can get apart from grace—one that we can possess through our own strength. So we deny our unity with Christ, thinking *I* not *we*. We reach out, take the fruit, and we eat. However, it is only after we taste of the fruit that we find that legalism is a tree without life. Its only fruit is condemnation, isolation, guilt and spiritual despair.

We can think of this in terms of the way our brains filter life through our own beliefs. We do this with Scripture as well, subconsciously interpreting the Bible in a way that reinforces what we already believe. This is why the Pharisees remained bound in legalism. They constantly read verses about faith and love and recited the Shema twice every day. Yet through the lens of legalism, they redefined love as obedience. When they read of the call to hear God's voice, they understood it as a call to obey the Scriptures in every detail. Union with God became a matter of doctrine rather than heart and spirit. Everything made sense to them through the lens of legalism.

Psalm 119:97

Oh how I love your law!
It is my meditation all the day.

Matthew 22:37-40

And he said to him, "You shall love the LORD your God with all your heart and with all your soul and with all your mind. This is the great and first commandment. And a second is like it: You shall love your neighbor as yourself. On these two commandments depend all the Law and the Prophets."

Like the Pharisees, if we believe that we can earn God's blessing then the Scriptures will confirm our bias towards legalism. However, Jesus makes it clear: All the Scripture are written in the context of love and so we must learn to read Scripture with a bias of love. Only then will we be able to correctly filter the word of God. Only then we will experience Scripture as the perfect law of liberty—the law that enlightens the eyes and revives our soul with the awesome love of God.

The Early Church

Galatians 3:2-3

Let me ask you only this: Did you receive the Spirit by works of the law or by hearing with faith? Are you so foolish? Having begun by the Spirit, are you now being perfected by the flesh?

The early church burst forth into history in the glorious grace of God. The Galatian church started their journey with God like the prodigal son. They were brought out of darkness into the love of the Father by grace and through faith. They began in the Spirit but were then seduced into legalism. They followed the path of the older son and started striving in their own strength to please God.

> **Galatians 5:4, 16-18**
> You are severed from Christ, you who would be justified by the law; you have fallen away from grace...But I say, walk by the Spirit, and you will not gratify the desires of the flesh. For the desires of the flesh are against the Spirit, and the desires of the Spirit are against the flesh, for these are opposed to each other, to keep you from doing the things you want to do. But if you are led by the Spirit, you are not under the law.

If we are led by the Spirit, we are not under the law of legalism. *If.*

Like the believers in the early church found, it is all too easy to fall into legalism. The letter to the Galatians was written to Christians who through legalism were busy severing themselves from Christ. We cannot afford to think that because we talk about grace that we are immune to legalism. Like the Galatian believers, no matter how mature we are in Christ, we can fall into the trap of legalism and begin seeking God's approval through our works.

Legalism is the arch enemy of love and the body of Christ is yet to truly overcome it. Knowing the devastating power of legalism, it is critical that we learn how to identify and conquer legalism in our lives. We simply have to know: how can we overcome legalism?

Pray

Father, I give you glory. I know your heart towards the Pharisees was one of total love. Please speak the truth to me too. If I am dishonoring you in any area of my life or trying to be righteous on my own, then I pray that you would expose it and deal with it. I ask you to set me free so that I may be free indeed.

19 | Life in Love

Though they had originally come to Christ through faith and grace, the Galatian believers were being led astray by false teachers. These teachers taught that in order to be righteous, people had to perform certain outward works such as physical circumcision.[1] Like the Pharisees before them, these teachers called people to strict obedience rather than selfless love. By doing so, they denied the first command and prevented people from knowing their design of love.

Paul often wrote about the threat of false teachers and legalism. In his letter to the Galatians, Paul especially warned people against trying to mix legalism and grace.

Galatians 5:3

I testify again to every man who accepts circumcision that he is obligated to keep the whole law.

In terms of mixture, the typical experience of a believer is not one of perfect grace nor is it a life of total legalism. There are threads of grace in every believer's life which is why we can still have a relationship with God even when we live under legalism. However, because of this, most people accept mixture as a normal part of our spiritual life. Yet here Paul says that if we consciously submit to legalism in any area of our lives then we are committed to living fully and perfectly in legalism. There can be no room for mixture because we cannot serve two masters. Grace cannot be mostly grace and a little bit wages. The unconditional love of God cannot be mostly priceless and a little bit earnable with a few conditions. God's blessing cannot be a gift that is both freely given and partly bought. God cannot be mostly good and a little bit cruel. In every area, it is all or nothing.

Mixing legalism and grace only brings confusion—confusion in our relationship with God and with others. We therefore need to allow God to remove every shred of legalism in our lives. This involves testing the teaching we hear, discerning our thoughts, and exposing the lies that create space for legalism in our lives.

Testing the Teaching

Jesus warned His disciples to beware of the leaven of the Pharisees: legalism and hypocrisy. He has warned us. The teaching of legalism is one of the single greatest threats to the life of a believer. If we want to live with Jesus in His design of love, then we must learn to test every teaching.

> **2 Corinthians 11:3-4** (NASB)
> But I am afraid that, as the serpent deceived Eve by his craftiness, your minds will be led astray from the simplicity and purity of devotion to Christ. For if one comes and preaches another Jesus whom we have not preached, or you receive a different spirit which you have not received, or a different gospel which you have not accepted, you bear this beautifully.

> **Deuteronomy 13:1-4** (emphasis added)
> "If a prophet or a dreamer of dreams arises among you and gives you a sign or a wonder, and the sign or wonder that he tells you comes to pass, and if he says, 'Let us go after other gods,' which you have not known, 'and let us serve them,' you shall not listen to the words of that prophet or that dreamer of dreams. **For the LORD your God is testing you, to know whether you love the LORD your God with all your heart and with all your soul.** You shall walk after the LORD your God and fear him [revere and not be casual with him] and keep his commandments and obey his voice, and you shall serve him and hold fast to him [be one with Him]."[2]

When someone preaches legalism, they proclaim another Jesus—a Jesus who demands strict moral obedience and is ready to punish any failure. They also share a different gospel, one that claims that we can earn God's approval by our own works. **And God allows this to happen.** He permits false teachers and prophets to speak to us and even to perform signs and wonders that come true. Why? Because He wants to see if we truly love Him with all our heart and soul.

Our best protection against deception is therefore not found in our knowledge of the Scriptures but in our unwavering commitment to the first command. This devotion to a life of wholehearted love is a powerful form of discernment—it is the key to testing what we hear and overcoming legalism. When a person shares a prophecy or teaching, we simply ask:

- Does the teaching put the first command into first place as our top priority in life?
- Is the teacher or prophet devoted to their first love?
- Is love the goal of the teaching?
- Does their word compel us to hear God's voice for ourselves?
- Does it lead us into a greater unity with Jesus?
- Are they calling us to depend more on the Spirit of Jesus?
- Or does it put our works before our love?

The Early Church believers became vulnerable to deception because they lost sight of their call to love God and to love each other.[3] In their infancy, they drifted from their first love and lost the ability to discern the spirit behind a teaching. Through the fear of judgment, criticism and condemnation, many of these believers were swept away into legalism. They exchanged love for works and started to strive on their own to act the right way and do the right thing. It was a deadly mistake that cost them faith, love and intimacy with God.

Let us not make the same mistake.

Discerning the Thoughts
Because legalism uses the principles of the Bible, legalistic thoughts sound good and are often true. For example, Scripture calls us to preach the gospel, and so we think *I should share my faith more*.[4] And it is true: we probably

should share the gospel more with people. However, legalism removes the call to preach the gospel from its context of love and disconnects it from the voice of God. While we may keep our good intentions, if our preaching does not flow from our love and unity with God, it is all a worthless waste of time.

1 John 5:3
For this is the love of God, that we keep his commandments. And his commandments are not burdensome.

All the commands of Scripture are intended to be life-giving, inspiring and easy. Not even one is burdensome. Christ's yoke is easy and His burden is light because Jesus does all the heavy lifting. We simply live in union with Him and let Jesus share His desire and energy with us.

Like a branch that is snapped off the vine, legalism severs our union with Jesus. In our thinking, it replaces *we* with *I* and puts the weight of obedience upon our shoulders. It focuses us on working *for* God rather than *with* Him. Legalism often controls us by using words like *I should, I ought to* and *I must. I should worship more. I must pray more often. I should tithe more faithfully— that's why I have no money. I ought to go to the prayer meeting. I should do this because the Bible says so. I ought to drive more slowly. I should fast more regularly. If I don't give more, God won't bless me. I should forgive my parents. I shouldn't hold this grudge. I'm a failure. I'm just not enough.* Thoughts like these are all designed to bring us under a yoke of obligation and set us up for judgment and failure.[5]

There are a few simple keys to taking legalistic thoughts captive. Firstly, replace *I* with *we* (and *me* with *us*) so we can start thinking again in terms of our unity with Jesus. Then turn the statements into questions. Instead of *I should pray more*, turn it into: *Holy Spirit, are you giving me your grace to pray more?* Or instead of, *I should share my faith more*, turn it into: *Jesus, can you please give me an opportunity to share our faith and love today?* As soon as we involve the Spirit of God, He removes the burden of obedience and we instantly feel lighter.

Legalism manifests in both thought and feeling. When we live under legalism, we experience feelings of fear, control, guilt and obligation. These feelings compel us to act out of a sense of duty, not because the Spirit is leading us to act but because we feel that we need to act a certain way to please God. We cannot blindly accept such feelings. Rather, just like our thoughts, we need to take our feelings captive. This often requires more than just a prayer. It requires that we put the axe to the root.

The thoughts and feelings of legalism are usually the fruit of lies that we have let take root in our hearts. One of the key lies of legalism is that God is not entirely good. Another is that we can earn His love. Another is that God wants to use us more than love us. Another lie is that God only likes us when we are obedient and that He is quick to punish us when we sin.

It is essential that we overcome all these lies. Why? Because when we believe a lie we make an agreement. Remember back to the café where the owner had agreed with a spirit of lust. His agreement allowed that spirit to fill his life with lust and then sow lust into the people who came into his café. In the same way, when we believe the lies of legalism, we give permission to a religious spirit to fill our lives with thoughts and feelings of legalism. The spirit of religion comes to enslave us, but the Spirit of Christ comes to set us free. With His help, we can cancel every agreement we have made with legalism and replace its lies with the truth of God.

Life over Legalism

Galatians 2:19

For through the law I died to the law [of legalism], so that I might live to God.

Like Paul, we need to die to legalism so that we might live a life of love, intimacy, and unity with God. For many people, legalism is not so much a sin or deception; it is a stronghold of the heart. For such people, the call to repent of legalism can seem like a call to change their religion. And in many ways, it is. Legalism is a false gospel that looks like Christianity. It uses all the same terms found in Scripture. It speaks about Jesus and salvation, righteousness and eternal life. But because legalism is based on works and not faith, it denies us the experience of God's love, prevents us from hearing His voice, and keeps us from becoming one with Him.

If you are confused or struggling with the call to be free from legalism, turn to God first. Call on God to reveal His truth and then search the Scriptures. Read what the Scriptures have to say about the law of works (legalism), and how it requires striving, arouses sin within us and brings condemnation. Read in Romans about what life is like under legalism. Read Philippians and see the value of our religious works when compared to the value of knowing Christ through faith. Read about the devastating spiritual impact of legalism in Galatians. Read about the call to repent from dead works and turn to faith in Hebrews. Read Colossians and see the futility of legalism in overcoming the selfish nature. Read about the Pharisees in any of the gospels and see how legalism robs people of their life, love and value in God. Read in John about how God's love offers mercy and life whereas legalism demands justice and death. Read in Matthew about how legalism leads us to control, manipulate, judge, and condemn each other. Read the prophets like Isaiah, Hosea, or Micah and see that apart from love, all our so-called righteous acts of legalism are utterly worthless in the eyes of God.

There is a reason why the Bible devotes so much space to our call to live in grace and overcome legalism. God has created us for love but legalism prevents us from ever entering our design of love. If we are to keep the first command and love God with our entire being, it is essential that we die to the law.[6] All legalism must go so that our hearts can be wholly consumed by the love of God.

Reflect

The following questions can be helpful in discovering the extent that legalism is currently shaping our relationship with God:

- Am I thankful to God or do I feel like I deserve some of God's blessings?
- Am I consumed by guilt, shame and condemnation when I sin?
- Do I expect God to punish me for my sin?
- Do I feel like I need to earn God's forgiveness?
- Is the focus of my faith on sinning less or loving more?
- Do I judge, criticize or accuse others?
- Do I feel like I get spiritually manipulated by others?
- Am I quick to speak and slow to listen?
- Am I relying on people to tell me what God is saying?
- Do I fear being judged or criticized by others?
- Do I worry about what other people think of me?
- Do I focus on doctrine or love as the basis of unity?
- Do I act out of a sense of obligation (because I should)?
- Do I feel controlled?
- Do I feel safest when I am in control?
- Do I give money and time freely or out of compulsion?
- Do I give money expecting a return from God?
- Do I worry about the consequences of saying "No" to people?
- Does the Holy Spirit lead me to give or is my giving based on principles?
- Am I generous?
- In uncertain situations, do I expect the Holy Spirit to speak to me, or do I try to work things out myself?
- Am I weighed down or inspired by the commands of Scripture?
- Am I known for my devotion to love or for something else?
- Do I feel truly dependent on God in my life?
- Do I get stressed over spiritual things?

Pray

If we discern the presence of legalism in our lives, then we need to deal with it as a sin and a deception. We need to repent of all legalism and then turn to God who alone can deliver us from its burden and bondage. Because of the deep roots that legalism often has, this may take some time. But God is good and Jesus has promised us: If we come to Him, He will give us rest from our legalism and make our obedience easy and our burden light.[7] Faithful is He who calls us, He is able to do it.

Oh Father, I call on you now to keep your word: give me rest from all my striving. I repent for ever trying to earn your favor and love. I repent for dishonoring your grace. I did not know what I was doing. Now I ask you to set me free from every chain of legalism. I give you permission to enter every place within my heart and soul and purge legalism entirely from my life. Please replace the lies with your truth. Replace the striving with your rest. Please teach me what it is to live by faith, to continually hear your voice and to receive your love. I love you Lord and I want to love you more. Take my life and prepare me for a greater love. I am yours.

20 | Breaking the Cycle

In terms of my own relationship with God, I struggled for years under the yoke of legalism. Every so often I would switch between living as the prodigal son and living as the older son. I found myself caught in a cycle of legalism that was never-ending and soul-destroying. For me it looked something like this:

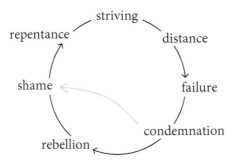

I would do my best to please God, but my striving only led to a sense of spiritual exhaustion. There was the constant thought that nothing I did was ever good enough for our perfect God. This left me with a profound sense of disappointment and failure which distanced me from God. Failure led to condemnation and because I felt like a failure, I thought that I may as well live as one—I may as well fail properly. So I would escape to the mire to look for something to fill the emptiness I felt in my heart. I would seek out some sort of worldly pleasure to escape the reality that deep down I did not feel loved—not by God nor by anyone else.

The world would give me a fleeting high but then leave me emptier than before. When the emptiness became too much to bear, I would return to God in shame, determined to atone for my sin by becoming like the older son and working as a slave for God. I followed the same logic as the prodigal son: *My worth is based on what I do. I have sinned therefore I am unworthy. I must try to become worthy again. Therefore, I will try to do what is righteous so I can restore my value to God.*

On my return, instead of receiving the Father's love and blessing, I would run past His open arms and go straight out to the fields to get to work. I simply could not bring myself to receive what I did not deserve. So I would strive even harder for God's approval and begin the cycle all over again.

I found that I was not alone in my experience of the destructive cycle of legalism. For some people the cycle repeats itself over days or weeks, for others it plays out over years. So many leaders over the ages have given their best for God only to buckle under the pressure to perform for God and for His people. From the outside people would say that these leaders fell from grace. But the reality was that so many of these people were not living in grace to start with. They were struggling under the yoke of legalism, trying to perform their best for God but ultimately failing. And we need to share some of the responsibility for their failure. We supported the culture of legalism. We valued form over substance and excellence over authenticity. We praised their performances and celebrated every achievement without stopping to think of love, which alone gives value to our actions. We forgot the greatest command and we let our leaders forget their first love. We lifted them up to a place where grace is hard to find and then shook our heads as they fell down.

One prominent worship leader wrote of his experience:

"I just always thought I was failing. There was this longstanding frustration that I could never be the person that I felt that people needed me to be... I struggled throughout the week trying to lead the worship, but feeling very much that I was failing. I really fell apart emotionally within a month of the conference ending. My face was on all the posters, I was writing songs which everyone was singing, but inside I was asking myself 'Why am I always struggling? Why can't I just rise up in faith and be the man of God that everybody else says I should be, that this movement says I should be?'

"[My marriage was suffering] but we just thought OK, we'll just have to work harder - serve God harder - we'll do more for God and he will bless us...

"The greatest tragedy was the consequences that years of poor stewardship and a woeful lack of priorities had visited on all of us. After about ten months I fell in love with somebody I'd known a long time. I was so despondent, and disappointed with the way everything had gone, that basically, when I hit a rock in the middle of a raging stream I held on to it. And it just...it happened. There are no excuses. We broke many lives, we disappointed many friends, we hurt many people. As the dust cleared, we realized that we couldn't go back and 'fix' what was broken. All we could do was slowly work through all the consequences. We still do. We always will.

"I had got to the point where even my integrity had deserted me. At that point I had no desire to continue in ministry because I had disqualified myself, and I didn't need anyone else to tell me that."[1]

This is a common story in Christian circles because it is the reality of legalism. Striving disconnects us from grace and prevents us from receiving God's love, which leads to isolation, failure, condemnation and rebellion. God's heart was never for any of His children to have to strive *at all* to please Him. He knows what striving does to the soul and the desolation it brings. He knows how legalism devastates our love and intimacy with Him. God does not want us to labor in legalism only to exhaust ourselves with dead works. Our great Father has something far better in mind for us.

Ending the Cycle

2 Timothy 2:20-21

Now in a great house there are not only vessels of gold and silver but also of wood and clay, some for honorable use, some for dishonorable. Therefore, if anyone cleanses himself from what is dishonorable, he will be a vessel for honorable use, set apart as holy, useful to the master of the house, ready for every good work.

After a brief period of rebellion, I returned once again to God, not sure of how much more He could take. I feared being lost, so I cried out to God.

"Lord, I do not care what kind of vessel I am in your house, I just want to be in your house!"

Condemnation covered me and I felt that my sin had disqualified me, not just from a place of honor, but from any place in the house altogether. Like the prodigal son, I was returning once again from the mire back to the Father, hoping to become like a servant or slave in the house. And it felt right. I had sinned, so I no longer deserved a place of honor. In fact, I did not deserve to be in the house at all. Like the younger son I thought that perhaps God would be merciful to me and let me have a place of a dishcloth or rag in the kitchen. Even if it was the lowest place in the house, at least I would have a place.

Legalism had blinded me to God's mercy and His heart for intimacy. I was convinced that I had to atone for my own sin and work for God to somehow balance the divine scales. This cycle continued for years. One day, He spoke to bring the cycle to an end.

"I will not be who you want Me to be. I will be who I AM." The voice of God was clear and emphatic, but I was slow to understand. He continued.

"A part of you wants me to be angry with you and to punish you for your sin. But Jesus has already fully dealt with your sin. There is no punishment left for you. If you want to know my heart towards a person who sins it is this: Think of a loving father whose only daughter self-harms. I am not angry or offended or frustrated. I grieve over the pain and I only want to bring freedom from the addiction of sin. I only want to heal all your wounds and erase your scars. I do not want to punish you."

I thought of a close friend who had been through a period of self-harming. She said it felt good to watch the life-blood flow out from her arms. I thought of my own sin. It felt good to sin; it comforted some of the brokenness within me. I never realized that when I sinned, I was wounding myself. I was hardening my heart with the scars of sin and destroying the beauty that God had created in me.

I realized then that by trying to earn God's forgiveness for my sin I was missing what I truly needed: healing. I needed the healing of being embraced by my Father. I needed the healing of His acceptance. I needed to let my Father minister to the root of my sin and heal my orphan heart. I needed the healing that could only come by being loved.

I had tried for so long to get it right on my own. And now I was tired. I was finally ready to be healed. I was ready to accept God's love and to receive His robe and put on His ring. I was ready to give up trying and simply fall into the arms and onto the neck of the One who always loved me. And so I fell.

Pray

Father, thank you for your love. Thank you that you have given me a place in your house. Please cleanse me from every impurity that I might be a vessel of honor. Please heal my heart and make me whole.

21 | Crime and Punishment

The idea that God did not want to punish me for my sin was a struggle to accept. I wanted to be punished so that I could feel like I had earned a fresh start with God. Therefore, if God would not punish me for my sin, I would tend to emotionally punish myself. I simply felt that I had to atone for what I had done.

I was blind to the impact that my desire for punishment was having on my relationship with God. Legalism allowed me to relate to God as my good Father when I was doing well. But if I sinned then legalism forced me to relate to God as my Judge and Jury. Judges are not given to embracing those on trial and so I never expected any intimacy in times of sin and restoration. Instead I would expect only punishment. When I read the Old Testament through the lens of legalism, it seemed to confirm this perspective on sin and punishment.

Exodus 32:34 (NASB)
"But go now, lead the people where I told you. Behold, My angel shall go before you; nevertheless in the day when I punish, I will punish them for their sin."

Here it seems clear that God punishes His people for their sin. However, if we look at the Hebrew word translated here as *punish*, we find the word *paqad* which means "to make a personal visit...to attend to the real need of the person or situation."[1] Another word that is translated as *punish* in the Old Testament is the word *yasar*. This word means "to correct by necessary discipline; to educate, train with positive discipline to equip people to succeed in life."[2] Yet another word is *shub* meaning to "change direction, return, restore, or turn back to."[3]

None of these Hebrew words above is adequately translated by the English word *punish*. Because of this, some translations prefer to use the words *discipline* or *chastise* (make pure) for *yasar*, the word *repay* for *shub*, and the word *visit* for *paqad*.

So what does our word *punish* really mean and why does God refuse to punish us for our sin?

Punishment and Justice

> **Punish**: To inflict a penalty or sanction on someone as retribution for an offence, especially a transgression of a legal or moral code.[4] To cause someone who has done something wrong or committed a crime to suffer, by hurting them, forcing them to pay money, sending them to prison etc.[5]

Punishment is a penalty that the law imposes to balance the scales of justice. Modern society is built on civil law, which uses the threat of punishment to govern people's behavior. As a society, we feel safe knowing every crime has its just punishment. Yet while it may bring stability to society, punishment does nothing to change a person's heart. Later in *First Love,* we will read of a woman who was almost beaten to death by two men. Both men were caught and sentenced to prison. In the eyes of the law, punishment was given and justice was done. But did the punishment that these men bore change their hearts? Did their sentences bring healing to the woman? No. It simply meant that society's need for justice was satisfied and the threat of punishment was maintained.

> **1 John 4:18**
> There is no fear in love, but perfect love casts out fear. For fear has to do with punishment, and whoever fears has not been perfected in love.

Legalism is the spiritual equivalent of the civil laws that govern us. This is why legalism seems to make sense and feels so familiar. Legalism controls our behavior through the fear of punishment and in doing so it appeals to our natural sense of justice. Yet grace is so different. The grace of God focuses on authentic love rather than moral control. God does not use the threat of punishment because it does nothing to inspire or change our hearts. It does not lead us into an authentic love for God nor help us to keep the first command. It also does nothing for justice. Through Jesus' death, every need for justice concerning sin was forever satisfied. God does not need us to punish us to atone for our sin because the cross was the full and final atonement. At the cross, Jesus died to heal us and restore us into His love, forever free from the threat of punishment.

Because we have believed into Jesus, we will *never* be subject to any punishment from God. Therefore, now is the time to accept the power of the cross and to let go of the idea that we can atone for our sin. Now is the time to give up seeking the punishment we believe we deserve. There is no punishment to be found at the cross; instead there is only the love and forgiveness of God.

"Hold on. Are you saying God doesn't punish our sin? Because I have found that when I sin, everything goes wrong but when I obey God, everything goes right. If God isn't punishing me for my sin, then why does everything go wrong when I sin?"

A friend asked me this during a Bible study and I understood exactly where she was coming from. The way she interpreted life was being shaped by the belief that God blesses us when we do what is right and punishes us when we sin. *This went wrong so God must be punishing me. This went right—God is blessing me!* She was viewing life through the lens of legalism and getting a distorted view of God. Instead of knowing God as a loving Father, she was relating to Him as an employer who rewards faithfulness but punishes failure.

Still the question was a valid one. If God does not punish our sin, then why do things go wrong when we sin? Is it simply a case of reaping and sowing? Or is there another dynamic at work?

Hedge of Thorns

As we learned earlier, we can only understand the Scriptures in their context of love. Therefore, it is important that we look at God's response to sin through the lens of love. When we read the Old Testament and combine the meanings of the Hebrew words *paqad, yasar* and *shub,* we find that God's response to sin is to address the real need of the person sinning. With our permission, God goes to the heart of the issue and heals the brokenness behind the sin. If we refuse to give up our sin, God does whatever it takes to inspire us to turn around and return to His love. It has always been this way.

But if this is true, how do we understand verses like "I will punish you again sevenfold for your sins" as in the passage below?

> Leviticus 26:14-19 (ESV)
> "But if you will not listen to me and will not do all these commandments, if you spurn my statutes, and if your soul abhors my rules, so that you will not do all my commandments, but break my covenant, then I will do this to you: I will visit you [*paqad*] with panic, with wasting disease and fever that consume the eyes and make the heart ache. And you shall sow your seed in vain, for your enemies shall eat it. I will set my face against you, and you shall be struck down before your enemies. Those who hate you shall rule over you, and you shall flee when none pursues you.
>
> "And if in spite of this you will not listen to me, then I will discipline [NASB: *punish*] you again sevenfold for your sins, and I will break the pride of your power, and I will make your heavens like iron and your earth like bronze."

Where some versions use the word *punish* in this passage, the ESV and others use the word *discipline.* The shift in the tone of the passage is profound. The word *punish* portrays God as a judge who coldly serves justice upon His people. The word *discipline* presents God as a Father who corrects His children and restores them into His love.

This passage is written for people who intentionally turn away from God's call to love. If our soul abhors the first command and we pursue a life of selfishness, we can expect God to discipline us. If we do not respond to His discipline, then God will increase the intensity of His discipline, even sevenfold. God does not enjoy this process but because His love for us is so great, He lets us experience a level of temporary pain or loss to inspire us to return to His love.

We can see this principle at work in the book of Hosea. Here God beautifully reveals His heart towards us when we sin and why things often go wrong when we abandon His way of love.

Hosea 2:5-7

"For their mother has played the harlot;
>She who conceived them has behaved shamefully.
>For she said, 'I will go after my lovers,
>Who give me my bread and my water,
>My wool and my linen,
>My oil and my drink.'
"Therefore, behold,
>I will hedge up your way with thorns,
>And wall her in,
>So that she cannot find her paths.
>She will chase her lovers,
>But not overtake them;
>Yes, she will seek them, but not find them.
>Then she will say,
>'I will go and return to my first husband,
>For then it was better for me than now.'"

God is love and can only ever act in love. Even His judgment is His love. When we fall into sin or run after temptations, God loves us by hedging up our way with thorns. In the natural realm, thorns are painful and so we generally think of them as negative. But the reality is that we need pain. Pain tells us that something is wrong, and the sting of pain motivates us to restore our bodies back to their healthy design. The same is true spiritually. When we stray from God's design, the emotional or spiritual pain that we feel because of sin motivates us to return to our design of love.

The legalistic mind interprets these thorns and frustrations as God's punishment on our sin. *I've sinned; God has cursed me!* Yet when we view these thorns in the light of grace, we see that they are all expressions of God's relentless love. When we sin and things go wrong, it is not because God has abandoned us or is angry with us and is punishing us for our selfishness. He is simply blessing us with a bit of pain and frustration to inspire us to return to Him and once again enjoy His intimate love.

This is exactly what happens in the parable of the prodigal son. In the parable, God sent a famine on the land. He hedged the son in with hunger to lead him back to love. The famine that people considered to be a curse turned out to be the amazing grace of God in action. Through this grace, the son returned home and was restored into his place in the family as a beloved son. The prodigal was received back with joy and celebration, without the slightest hint of any need for punishment.

Like the prodigal son, we will keep on going through the cycle of rebellion and restoration until we accept our identity as children of God. This can take some time, but God is patient. Every time we turn our back on God to pursue our selfish desires, He hedges up our way with thorns to help us find our way back to love. He then waits and watches for us. He waits not only for our return, but for the day that we finally accept His love and enter His embrace. He waits for the day that we take our place as His children and know Him as our Abba Father.

Pray

Father, thank you that you love me so much that you won't let me be satisfied outside your love. Thank you for the hedges of thorns and walls that separate me from the world. May I never even come close to those boundaries again. Please take away all my affections for the world and all my agreements with it, and let me live in union with you, in wholehearted, extravagant love.

22 | Sin and Deception

1 John 4:18

There is no fear in love, but perfect love casts out fear. For fear has to do with punishment, and whoever fears has not been perfected in love.

Legalism leads us to replace grace with works; love with striving; freedom with bondage; discipline with punishment; and faith with fear. When Scripture speaks positively about fear, it is in the sense of having a deep respect and awe of God. It is a holy fear that draws us to God in childlike wonder. The fear that John is speaking of in this verse is entirely different. Like a child who runs away from an angry parent to avoid being punished, this is a fear that makes us want to run from God.

When we believe that God punishes us for our sin, we create space for this kind of fear. By believing the lie about punishment, we then forfeit a measure of intimacy with our Father, which robs Him of our affection. The only way to find deliverance from this kind of fear is to open our hearts to the perfect love of God.

Effects of Sin

If God sets us free from our fear of punishment, does that mean that we can sin or be selfish and not suffer any consequences in our lives? Does the cross mean that our sin no longer has any effect on our relationship with God?

Before we look at the effects of sin, we need to look at the extremes of teaching about sin in the church. At one extreme, legalism makes us believe that sin is a failure that needs to be punished before it can be forgiven. In many Christian circles the pendulum is now swinging away from legalism. However, instead of stopping at the center of balance in a place called *grace*, the pendulum is swinging towards the opposite extreme: license.

Forgiveness: A License to Sin

Jude 1:3-5 (BSB)

Beloved, although I made every effort to write you about the salvation we share, I felt it necessary to write and urge you to contend earnestly for the faith entrusted once for all to the saints. For certain men have crept in among you unnoticed—ungodly ones who were designated long ago for condemnation. They turn the grace of our God into a license for immorality, and they deny our only Master and Lord, Jesus Christ.

Legalism enslaves people through the commands and principles of Scripture. License (or licentiousness) does the opposite. It removes all the commands and rules. It turns the grace of God into a license to sin by teaching that forgiveness has already removed the consequences of sin. The teachings of license sound something like this: *Jesus forgave all your sin over 2000 years ago—before you committed a single sin! Because of the cross, as soon as you sin, it is already forgiven and forgotten. Your place in heaven is forever secure. Even if you continue to sin, God will still love you. He sees you as perfect so draw close to God without feeling guilty about your sin. You are the righteousness of God in Christ and no amount of sin will change that fact. Remember: God gave you everything to enjoy and He wants you to love yourself. So do not worry about enjoying some sin now and again. God's grace is greater.*

Like legalism, the teaching of license distorts the love and grace of God. It proclaims a Jesus who accepts our selfishness rather than cuts it out of our hearts. This is a Jesus who loves us so much that He lets us follow Him in a life of lukewarmness and compromise. Like the boyfriend of a prostitute, this Jesus does not mind sharing us with the world. This is a Jesus who saves us for heaven but does little to bring us into a wholehearted love for God in this present life. This is not the real Jesus.

Free from Sin or Free to Sin?

2 Corinthians 12:20-21

For I fear that perhaps when I come I may find you not as I wish, and that you may find me not as you wish—that perhaps there may be quarrelling, jealousy, anger, hostility, slander, gossip, conceit, and disorder. I fear that when I come again my God may humble me before you, and I may have to mourn over many of those who sinned earlier and have not repented of the impurity, sexual immorality, and sensuality that they have practiced.

Galatians 5:13

For you were called to freedom, brothers. Only do not use your freedom as an opportunity for the flesh, but through love serve one another.

1 Peter 2:16

Live as people who are free, not using your freedom as a cover-up for evil, but living as servants of God.

Most of the early church fellowships struggled with the dual threats of legalism and license. People who were excited to be free from the bondage of legalism were often easily tempted to indulge their selfish nature. Instead of turning from their sin, they practiced it in their lives and accommodated it in their theologies. Those who fell into license threw off the yoke of the law and embraced lawlessness, most likely believing that God had forgiven all their sin and they would still go to heaven. And they have a point. If our future in heaven is already secure because we once said a prayer, then why not enjoy the pleasures of sin in this life?

Deceptive Power of Sin

Hebrews 3:13 (NLT)

You must warn each other every day, while it is still "today," so that none of you will be deceived by sin and hardened against God.

Romans 7:11

> ...for sin, taking an opportunity through the commandment, deceived
> me and through it killed me.

All sin brings a deception. Why? Because in order to sin, we must first deny the truth.[1] We must deny our unity with Jesus and turn our back on our true identity. We must move our thinking from *we* to *I* and embrace a lie. In order to sin, we need to take off our breastplate and let our enemy tear the truth from our hearts. The unavoidable reality is that every time we sin we fall deeper into deception and further out of love.

Warn each other every day...so that none of you will be deceived by sin and hardened against God. All sin brings a hardening of the heart. Like a person who self-harms, every sin is a cut into our heart that creates a hardness against love and numbs us to the pain of sin. This hardening of the heart makes it easier for us to sin again and to become even harder. Because of the numbness of our hearts, we fail to feel death entering us every time we sin—not necessarily physical death, but the self-gratifying, love-destroying death of selfishness.

Like our words or thoughts, our sinful acts create a legal agreement between us and our enemy. Every time we sin, we give the enemy permission to speak into our lives and change the way we think and how we feel. We need to know that habit creates habitat. If we continue to sin, we effectively surrender to our enemy and allow him to turn our lives into his habitation. Instead of being a glorious dwelling place for the Spirit of Love, we make ourselves a dwelling place for enslaving spirits. Rather than bringing us into the glory and beauty of being the Bride of Christ, sin disfigures our hearts, corrupts our souls and betroths us to another.

Worse still is the fact that we have to stop loving in order to sin. God designed our hearts to flow His love back to Him. But every time we sin, we suspend the flow of love through our hearts. This means that every sin has spiritual consequences that are ultimately felt by God Himself. Why? Because every sin robs God of a measure of the love He died for. This is worth repeating: Every time we sin, we rob God of a measure of the love He died for. So does sin have consequences? Yes, far more than we will ever truly know.

Sin and Identity

Matthew 18:9

"And if your eye causes you to sin, tear it out and throw it away. It is better for you to enter life with one eye than with two eyes to be thrown into the hell of fire."

Jesus knows the true impact of sin because He feels the loss that our sin incurs. In this passage, Jesus is not calling us to literally cut out our eyes, but rather He is using a word-picture to call us to take extreme action against sin. Sin is everything we are not. We need to join with Him to eliminate sin from our lives, both in the present and in our past.

If God has already forgiven our past sin, why do we need to deal with the past? It is because our past affects our present. Our brains constantly use our past experiences to predict our future behavior. Because I had been through the cycle of striving and failure so many times, I had come to expect failure in the future. A pattern of past sin had distorted my identity. I believed I was broken and that it was only ever a matter of time before I would fall again. Then one day God spoke into my brokenness.

"You cannot let your past define you. Not even five minutes ago. I alone have the right to define you."

I realized that even though I knew I was forgiven, the memory of sin was still there, distorting my sense of identity. *I sinned before in this area—it's just a matter of time before I sin again. It's inevitable. Deep down, I am a sinner.* The enemy uses such thoughts of our past to steer us towards defeat. When we accept these thoughts, we quietly redefine our identity as sinful and corrupt.

Hebrews 10:15-17

And the Holy Spirit also bears witness to us; for after saying,

"This is the covenant that I will make with them

after those days, declares the LORD:

I will put my laws on their hearts,

and write them on their minds," then he adds,

"I will remember their sins and their lawless deeds no more."

I will remember their sins no more. When God forgives our sin, He erases it from His own memory. And if God can share His mind with us, He can also share His forgetfulness.

As long as we hold on to our memory of sin, it will continue to distort our identity and affect our future. To end our past sins' power over us, we need to make what we can right with the people we have hurt, accept the forgiveness of God, and then ask God to help us to forget. This does not mean that we deny our past or hide our failings. Rather it simply means that we agree with God. We agree that the blood of Jesus has taken away all our sin and forever wiped our guilt from the memory of God.[2] Through our union with Jesus, we are a new creation, one made pure and holy in Him.

Healing the Heart

It is so easy to think of sin as the barrier to heaven. Yet Jesus did not take our sin just so we could go to heaven when we die. He died to restore us into our design of love. The question of sin for the believer is therefore not about jeopardizing our place in heaven. It is a question of love both now and into eternity. God designed us for love and when we sin, we close our hearts to love and move in the exact opposite: selfishness.

If we do sin, we need to remember that no sin will ever change the Father's heart of love toward us. God never puts His love for us on hold, not even in times of sin and discipline. He loves us with an unbreakable, uninterruptible, everlasting love. *He loves us.* God's response to sin is to always give us what we need. And because love is the goal, our hearts need to be healed rather than punished. It is only God's healing that will remove the hardness of our hearts and restore our capacity for love. It is only His healing that will take away the deception of sin and restore us into His truth. It is only His healing that will bring us back into our identity of love.

This healing of God is found at the cross. Like a master surgeon with the cross as His scalpel, Jesus circumcises the sin and selfishness from our hearts so that we might live and love God with all our heart and soul. There is no place for striving in this. Like a patient on the operating table, all we need to do is lie still and abandon ourselves to God. He will do the rest.

Pray

Father, I can see the way of grace is really narrow. On either side are deep ditches of license and legalism. Please help me not to fall. Let us walk together. Better yet, take me on your shoulders. Let us live as one today.

23 | Teaching Grace

Deuteronomy 6:4-8
"Hear, O Israel: The LORD our God, the LORD is one! You shall love the LORD your God with all your heart, with all your soul, and with all your strength.

"And these words which I command you today shall be in your heart. You shall teach them diligently to your children, and shall talk of them when you sit in your house, when you walk by the way, when you lie down, and when you rise up. You shall bind them as a sign on your hand, and they shall be as frontlets between your eyes."

Bind them as a sign on your hands

God did not intend us to take this command literally and bind physical copies of the first command to our hands. Instead, He is using the hands as a symbol of our works. This connection between our hands and our works is common in Scripture.[1] Those who have clean hands and a pure heart are those who have done no evil outwardly (with their hands) and harbor no evil in their hearts. By calling us to bind the command of love on our hands, this passage is calling us to let the love of God infuse *all* our works.

1 Corinthians 16:14
Let all that you do be done in love.

We can only love in unity with Jesus, and this unity is not reserved for spiritual acts like praying for people. The Spirit of Jesus is one with us all the time. Jesus is one with us as we cook and clean, as we read and write, as we learn and teach, as we build and work. This means that Jesus can release His love through us in the everyday tasks of life. The more we think *we*, the more we find that all our work, no matter how small or great, how menial or honorable, how secular or spiritual; all our work can express the love of God.

They shall be as frontlets between your eyes

The first command is to be our vision and goal. Through the grace of God, we are to constantly focus and refocus on our call to love.

Earlier we saw how we need to read the Bible through the lens of love. This verse challenges us to take this principle beyond the pages of Scriptures and learn to view all of life through the lens of love. In every situation, we need to ask God how we can give, receive or grow in our love. When we filter life through the first command, we begin to see the potential in every circumstance for love to prevail. As we respond to this potential and act in love, we invest eternal value into each situation.

Teach them diligently to your children

It is in our childhood that we develop our sense of identity and discover our place in creation. As we have seen, the world will teach our children nothing of their true design. Instead it offers them a different model to imprint on— one of a selfishness and self-defined identity.

If our children are to learn what it means to be human, then we need to show them the mirror of the word. We need to use the word to teach our children about our God of love and His design of love for all people. As we do this, it is important to remember that children imprint on what they see more than what they hear. Therefore, the best way to show our children their design of love is for us to love God with all our heart and soul, and parent our children in union with Him.

As parents, it is so easy to put all our energy into loving our children, and they will gladly soak up all the love we can give. However, we need to realize that like anyone, children can receive amazing amounts of love and affection and yet remain deeply selfish. We do not want our children to become like the Dead Sea, with love flowing in but never out. To lead our children into their design of love, we need to teach them to love others.

Remember Jesus' call to hear *and* obey. Theory is perfected in practice and so we need to ask the Holy Spirit how we can practically teach our children to love. A good place to start is by involving our children as we love others. Are we giving to meet a financial need? Involve the children. Tell them of the need and invite them to help. Are we cooking a meal for someone in need? Involve the children. Have them cook and then deliver the meal. Are we giving firewood to someone in need? Involve the children. Let them see the face of the person they are helping as they unload and stack the wood.

Children are as capable of love as adults. Recently a five-year-old girl called Madison heard of the Freeslaves.org project and was so moved by the story of Christian families struggling in slavery that she did small jobs around her neighborhood for almost five months. She raised over $3000USD and set two families free. She then got to meet the families on a video-call and see the faces of those she set free. And she felt the reward of her love.

All children can love and can feel the joy of love. Even if they are resistant at first, their biology of love will start to take effect as they act. Oxytocin will flow, and their bodies will be telling them what we have been teaching: that God has created them for a life of love.

Love and Discipline

Teaching our children to love God and love others takes time. When we model love to our children, we are not just teaching them about their design—we are teaching them about God Himself. Whether we like it or not, the way we raise our children will shape the way they relate to God—for good or for bad. We need to remember this, especially in times of discipline. When we discipline in love, we edify our children (though they may not agree at the time) and we strengthen our relationship with them. Punishment does neither. Punishing children damages our relationship, destroys intimacy, and creates a platform for legalism in their lives. If we plant the seeds of legalism in our children, then those seeds will have a lifetime to grow roots that penetrate the very depths of their hearts. This will then shut the doors of their hearts to the love of God. It is essential that we stop the cycle of legalism repeating in the next generation. To do this, we need to start by asking God to share His love for our children with us. As the love of God flows through us, we need to make sure that this love remains *unearnable* and *unconditional*. With the Spirit, we can then learn how to discipline our children in a way that expresses the love of God.

Hebrews 12:5-6

And have you forgotten the exhortation that addresses you as sons?
"My son, do not regard lightly the discipline of the Lord,
    nor be weary when reproved by him.
For the Lord disciplines the one he loves,
    and chastises every son whom he receives."

When we turn away from God, He hedges us in with thorns to draw us back into His love. He lets us feel the pain of sin, but that pain is not punishment. It is a sign of His grace that tells us we are leaving the way of love. When we return to God, He then addresses our real need and offers us healing for our brokenness and truth in place of our deception. Our Father continues to discipline us when needed as He empowers us to live as His children.

As parents, when we withhold discipline from our children, we remove the boundaries that are designed to keep them safe and directed to love. A lack of boundaries creates an environment for license, which enslaves a child to their selfish nature. We want to see our children free from the bondage of selfishness and so it is essential that we learn how to raise and fully discipline our children without punishing them. The easiest way to do this is to create hedges of thorns—clear boundaries with clear consequences that will motivate our children back to love. When these boundaries are in place, we can be like the father of the prodigal son. We can be free to let our children cross the boundaries and feel the thorns. We can trust that when our children experience the consequences of their actions they will be inspired to return to love.

Punishment and Anger

If discipline involves creating firm boundaries with consequences, then what is the real difference between discipline and punishment?

It is the presence of anger that turns discipline into punishment and creates ungodly fear in our children. When we discipline our children with a negative emotion such as anger, frustration, resentment or offence, we arouse fear in our children and communicate a false image of God. Though we may try to reassure them of our love, whenever our discipline is infused with a dark emotion, it makes the child feel like we have suspended our love and unleashed our fury. True discipline affirms their place in our love, but emotionally charged punishment damages our children and makes them feel like they have become our enemies. Through punishment they learn that our love is conditional. They see that good behavior is rewarded and bad behavior is punished and so they learn to perform in such a way as to earn our love. If this is what we teach our children, this is how they will relate to God.

As parents, we can be a living gospel to our children, revealing the good news that God is not angry with us. He loves us and He is always good to us. We never need to fear His wrath or punishment ever again.

Isaiah 54:9-10
"This is like the days of Noah to me:
  as I swore that the waters of Noah
  should no more go over the earth,
  so I have sworn that I will not be angry with you,
  and will not rebuke you.
"For the mountains may depart
  and the hills be removed,
  but my steadfast love shall not depart from you,
  and my covenant of peace shall not be removed,"
  says the LORD, who has compassion on you.

Punishment and anger may be normal in the world, but it is not the way of God. Quite simply, there is no wrath or punishment for those within the kingdom of God. Why? Because the cross was like the flood of Noah. At the cross, God poured out His judgment and spent all His anger as He flooded the sin of humanity. At the cross, the blood of Jesus became the flood that overwhelmed sin and selfishness, and He became the ark that carried His people safely into a new life. And like He did with Noah, at the cross God made an everlasting covenant with us: He will not be angry with us, nor will His unfailing love ever depart from us. *His unfailing love will never, ever depart from us.* Even if we sin, we can know that our God is not a god who punishes in anger, but a God of compassion who keeps His promise. When confronted with our sin and selfishness, our God runs to us and embraces us. He acts to meet our true need by healing our hearts and restoring us back into a life of love.

This discipline of God gives us a sense of security in life that far excels the false security of punishment and legalism. When we live in the kingdom of God, the first two commandments are our only law. They are our life. If we happen to stray from the law of love, we can expect to encounter hedges of thorns and walls of frustration. These are the firm boundaries of our loving Father and His discipline is proof of His love. Yet while we can expect His loving discipline, as children of God, we never need to fear any punishment. For us there is only love in its many glorious forms.

Pray

Father, I thank you that you discipline me and keep me in the way of love. Thank you for the grace to love. Lord, please let the greatest command become my vision and let it would infuse everything I do. Help me to teach your command in word and in action. Let us love together.

24 | Love in Eternity

"You must see your call to love me with all your heart and soul in the light of eternity…" God spoke with compassion and conviction. "…You only take into eternity the capacity for love that you have cultivated in this life."

It was one of those pivotal moments. Though my heart was set on love, I had not thought of the first command in the light of eternity. But it made sense. God has defined life as the state of wholehearted love and union with Him which means that eternal life must be a state of love and union *that lasts forever.* When we die, everything of the natural realm will pass away. All we will take into eternity is the love and unity with Christ that we have forged in this life.

This invitation to see our call to love in the light of eternity raises some questions. How do we get an eternal perspective on love? Does every believer receive the same inheritance of love in heaven? Or are we going to be unique in our love for God?

The Infinite Greatness

In many ways love is like light. Love defeats selfishness in the same way that light overcomes darkness. A defining quality of light is its speed—by nature, light cannot stop moving. Like light, love never stops flowing. Instead, love exists as a life-giving flow of affection and action.

> Isaiah 57:15
> For thus says the One who is high and lifted up, who inhabits eternity, whose name is Holy: "I dwell in the high and holy place, and also with him who is of a contrite and lowly spirit, to revive the spirit of the lowly, and to revive the heart of the contrite."

God is the uncreated One who inhabits eternity. Because God is love and He has always existed, love itself has always been in existence. But if love must always flow in order to be love, where did God's love flow to before creation?

> **John 17:24** (emphasis added)
> Father, I desire that they also, whom you have given me, may be with me where I am, to see my glory that you have given me because **you loved me before the foundation of the world.**

Before and beyond all time and creation, God exists in an infinite and eternal flow of love: Father to Son and Son to Father through one shared and holy Spirit. God is love and He is not dependent on any created thing to sustain His nature of love. Rather, the eternal flow of love has always existed within God Himself, outside creation.

By calling us to be one with Jesus and to share His love for the Father, God Himself is inviting us to be a part of the divine flow of love that exists at the center of eternity. He is inviting us to share in the glory of His love forever.

Unique in Glory

> **1 Corinthians 15:40-44**
> There are heavenly bodies and earthly bodies, but the glory of the heavenly is of one kind, and the glory of the earthly is of another. There is one glory of the sun, and another glory of the moon, and another glory of the stars; for star differs from star in glory.
>
> So is it with the resurrection of the dead. What is sown is perishable; what is raised is imperishable. It is sown in dishonor; it is raised in glory. It is sown in weakness; it is raised in power. It is sown a natural body; it is raised a spiritual body. If there is a natural body, there is also a spiritual body.

God is infinitely creative and He has created every person who ever lived as an entirely unique expression of His love and goodness. No two people are exactly alike in the physical realm nor in the spirit. We are all unique in this life and at the end of time, when the dead are raised and all humanity passes into eternity, we will still all be absolutely unique. Paul describes this using the sun, moon and stars. Just as each star has its own glory that is different from every other star, each person in heaven will radiate their own unique glory in Christ. The more we grow in our unity with Jesus and increase our capacity for His love, the more radiant our glory in eternity will be.

All the Same?

It has been taught that everyone receives the same salvation on earth and so everyone will receive the same glorification in heaven. Yet this teaching is not based in Scripture. In Luke 12, Jesus tells us to give to the poor and so build up our treasure in heaven.[1] Different people will respond in varying degrees to Christ's call and so everyone will have varying degrees of treasure in heaven. In Matthew 13, Jesus shares the parable of the sower and shows how people will yield a different harvest from the same seed. In the parable of the talents, people are given unique amounts of gold and are responsible for multiplying their love. In the book of Revelation, Jesus calls the churches to overcome and describes the glory for those who overcome and the consequences for those who do not overcome. God does not create us all as unique individuals now only to make us all the same later. We will never be the same—not now, not ever. Like the stars of heaven, the glory of each person will be unique for eternity and that glory will be largely determined by each person's life of love.

Eternally One

I once had an insight into life in heaven. It was sparked by a lingering question I had concerning my heart towards my father. My earthly father and I were never close so when he died, I felt no loss or even the slightest sense of grief. I knew he was secure in heaven, but the void of emotion made me wonder if I was carrying some sort of emotional wounding that had hardened my heart. I asked God about it but did not hear anything specific, so I left it with Him.

Then in answer to my question, one night I had an incredibly real dream. I was sitting next to Melanie at some kind of service. I was trying to talk to her, but she could not hear me. I looked around and saw that I was at a funeral—my funeral! I could see the coffin and my children. I turned to my left and I saw my earthly father in the heavenly realms. I figured that because no one could hear me, there was no point in staying at the funeral service. So I started moving towards my father. As I did, the earthly world dissolved away and I found myself in heaven, standing before my father.

I looked in his eyes and I instantly knew everything about him. With a single look, I could see his entire soul, right down to the atomic level. Except at that level, I did not see physical atoms. Instead I saw the love of God, giving substance and life to my father. My father was still uniquely himself with his own personality, but he was, at the same time, an entirely unique expression of the Father's love. He was also so completely one with Christ that it was impossible to separate him from Christ, any more than we can separate our own bodies from the atoms that compose us.

I then looked at myself and I could see down to the same level. Again, all I could see was the light of God's love giving me substance and life. I looked back at my father again, and he said nothing, but opened his arms. We embraced. As we connected, the two loves touched and the pure power of love radiated out of us like a shockwave. I was literally alive with love. I then had two thoughts. The first was a realization that this realm of unlimited love and unity with God is why people cannot explain what heaven is like; there are simply no words to describe how awesome and glorious it truly is. The second thought was that there was no way I was going back. Melanie and the kids would be with me in heaven before they knew it. I was staying.

And then I woke up, disappointed to still be alive. I felt the Lord speak to me saying, "I want you to see yourself for who you are. You are nothing but a being of pure light and love."

We all have an eternal identity in heaven, free from all the limitations and distorted perspectives that we accept in this life. If we are to come to a true sense of identity, we need to start with our eternal identity and bring it into our present experience. Only then can we know what it is to be a creation of love, a person who bears the image of Christ in absolute unity with Him.

Heavenly Reality

I cannot say if the dream was spiritually real or not, but as well as giving me a new sense of identity, it also gave me a vision for heaven. As a child, I had thought that heaven was all about worshipping Jesus around His throne. And this will certainly happen throughout eternity and will be exhilarating in joy. But we will also have eternity to love Jesus *through one another.* We will be able to fully appreciate the unique expression of God's heart that each one of us carries, and as we love God through each other, it will be glorious beyond words.

All through history there have been testimonies of people who have been caught up to heaven, including some from people who have died and come back to life. Some of these can be found online.

Many of these testimonies carry a common thread. People describe heaven as a "hyper-reality" or "ultra-real."[2] There is life and music in the words of heaven. The colors of heaven are living and real, far more vibrant than any of the colors of earth. People say how the reality of heaven makes their lives on earth seem like a rapidly fading dream. I can understand what they mean. When I look back on my life, my entire history already seems like a fleeting dream. And I know that this is exactly how I will feel when I am soon on my deathbed. This life is like a dream; eternity is the reality.

Whenever we dream, we have a liberty to break the rules of our natural lives. In the same way, as we start to view our physical life like a dream and see our heavenly life as the reality, we discover the freedom to break the rules of our natural thinking. We can give extravagantly and take risks of love with Jesus that seem insane to the natural mind. We can take these risks because we know that the dream will shortly be over and we will soon wake up to our eternal reality.

Numbered Days

James 4:14b

What is your life? For you are a mist that appears for a little time and then vanishes.

Psalm 39:4-5 (NLT)

"LORD, remind me how brief my time on earth will be.
Remind me that my days are numbered—how fleeting my life is.
You have made my life no longer than the width of my hand.
My entire lifetime is just a moment to you; at best, each of us is but a breath."

Our time in this life is short. I tried to communicate this to a small group of young people who were amused at the idea that life is fleeting.

"When you look back over the last fifteen years of your life, does it seem like fifteen years has gone by? How does it feel?" The group all agreed—the first fifteen years of their lives had vanished all too quickly.

"I'm 41 now and I can assure you: When you turn 41, you will feel exactly the same way. And when you turn 81, you will still feel the same way. Your entire history—your entire life—it all passes by in a moment."

That statement gave the young people cause for reflection and it is something that we all need to accept. Our life is a series of moments, each one valuable, yet each one passing away into history as soon as it has arrived. Because we only live in the present moment, there is no great difference between a minute, an hour, day or year. Whether we live to 18 or 80, our life will vanish into history like a passing morning mist.

One day soon, the dream will end and this life will be over before we know it. It is therefore essential that we see our call to love in the light of eternity. We only take into eternity the capacity for love that we have cultivated here on earth. So let us love! As we let the love of Christ flow through us, His love redeems our time by investing it with eternal value that makes every moment significant. Time itself is a gift from God that we can use to change eternity.[3]

So let us make the best use of our time. Let us take every opportunity to love God and love others, and so change our eternal glory.

Pray

Father, please remind me how brief my time on earth is. Please help me to view my call to love you with all my heart and soul and mind and strength in the light of eternity. Please help me to constantly grow my capacity for love.

25 | Multiplying Love

Matthew 25:14-30

"For it will be like a man going on a journey, who called his servants and entrusted to them his property. To one he gave five talents, to another two, to another one, to each according to his ability. Then he went away. He who had received the five talents went at once and traded with them, and he made five talents more. So also he who had the two talents made two talents more. But he who had received the one talent went and dug in the ground and hid his master's money.

"Now after a long time the master of those servants came and settled accounts with them. And he who had received the five talents came forward, bringing five talents more, saying, 'Master, you delivered to me five talents; here, I have made five talents more.' His master said to him, 'Well done, good and faithful servant. You have been faithful over a little; I will set you over much. Enter into the joy of your master.' And he also who had the two talents came forward, saying, 'Master, you delivered to me two talents; here, I have made two talents more.' His master said to him, 'Well done, good and faithful servant. You have been faithful over a little; I will set you over much. Enter into the joy of your master.'

"He also who had received the one talent came forward, saying, 'Master, I knew you to be a hard man, reaping where you did not sow, and gathering where you scattered no seed, so I was afraid, and I went and hid your talent in the ground. Here, you have what is yours.' But his master answered him, 'You wicked and slothful servant! You knew that I reap where I have not sown and gather where I scattered no seed? Then you ought to have invested my money with the bankers, and at my coming I should have received what was my own with interest. So take the talent from him and give it to him who has the ten talents. For to everyone who has will more be given, and he will have an abundance. But from the one who has not, even what he has will be taken away. And cast the worthless servant into the outer darkness. In that place there will be weeping and gnashing of teeth.'"

In this parable, Jesus describes God like a man who entrusts His servants with varying levels of wealth. A talent is a weight of gold, approximately 35 kgs or 75 lbs. In Scripture gold is the unit of highest value and as such, it represents the love of God—the element of ultimate value.

Often when people read this parable, they read the word *talent* literally and think it refers to their own talents, giftings or abilities. The message they take away is that they need to use their talents and gifts to be found faithful before God. And in many ways, this is true. Yet, Scripture is clear about the value of our own abilities when compared to love.

The Value of Love

Matthew 7:21-23

"Not everyone who says to me, 'Lord, Lord,' will enter the kingdom of heaven, but the one who does the will of my Father who is in heaven. On that day many will say to me, 'Lord, Lord, did we not prophesy in your name, and cast out demons in your name, and do many mighty works in your name?' And then will I declare to them, 'I never knew you; depart from me, you workers of lawlessness.'

1 Corinthians 13:1-3

If I speak in the tongues of men and of angels, but have not love, I am a noisy gong or a clanging cymbal. And if I have prophetic powers, and understand all mysteries and all knowledge, and if I have all faith, so as to remove mountains, but have not love, I am nothing. If I give away all I have, and if I deliver up my body to be burned, but have not love, I gain nothing.

We may move in the gifts, have faith for miracles, preach to millions and prophesy to nations. We may think that we are something in our own eyes or in the eyes of other believers. But without love we are nothing, we have nothing, and we can do nothing. Love is the only currency in eternity. Without love we are both broke and broken.

A couple of years ago, I led a group in a nearby town in which we focused on loving God with all our heart and loving one another. A woman called

Desi was a part of that group. She carried the deep scars of 13 years of unspeakable abuse and tragedy. Over the course of the group, she fell hopelessly in love with Jesus. She devoted her life to loving Him with all her heart, and He responded by making it possible. He healed her broken heart, taking away all the nightmares and ending the flashbacks that caused her to relive the emotional trauma. His love washed over her and filled her and gave her a whole new identity in Him. She became more than His follower; she became His bride. And then she became terminally ill.

Desi heard that I had been invited to do a meeting close to her and so she asked her husband to bring her. Another friend called Drew came with me to the meeting to help minister. Drew moves beautifully in the prophetic, healing, and deliverance. He shared some words of knowledge for different people and prayed for them. We then invited him over to pray for Desi. He looked in her eyes and immediately burst into tears.

"I have nothing to offer you. Can you please pray for me?" was all he could say.

"Sure thing," she quietly replied. Desi took his hands and simply said, "Jesus, you know what he needs. Just give him more Lord."

On the way home, I asked Drew what happened.

He said, "I looked into her eyes, and I saw the love of God burning in her. And I realized that I don't have that love in me...It has never been more real to me, that I can prophesy all things but without love it's all worth nothing. I feel like this is a conversion moment." The love of Christ in Desi was so real and powerful that it changed Drew with just a look.

It is this flow of Christ's love through us that gives value to our actions. In our zeal for God, it is easy to become so busy in ministry that we lose sight of the essential need for love in everything we do. We need to be constantly reminded: If we lack love, all our activities are worthless. Without love, we are destined to accomplish nothing for God and to make ourselves nothing in the process. But with love, we become channels of the divine nature of God. And as His love flows through us, we take on the highest value in all creation!

Many people often wonder how someone can move so powerfully in the spiritual gifts and yet lack love or even live in willful sin. Why would God allow such people to move in spiritual power without love?

It can be helpful to think of spiritual gifts like natural gifts. A person may be a gifted pianist. One day they may play with great passion and emotion. On another day, they may play with no passion at all. Their ability remains the same, but a discerning listener will hear the difference. It is the same for our spiritual gifts. We may heal the sick and prophesy accurately, we may cast out demons, we may teach mysteries of the word of God, we may have the faith to move mountains, and we may even sacrifice our very lives. Yet none of these abilities requires love to operate, and without love, it all counts as nothing. In order to avoid wasting our lives, we need to see past our ministry or gifting and be converted to God's design of love.

Multiplying the Wealth

Each of the servants in the parable was given a different amount of wealth. After a time, the servants were called to account for the wealth they had been given. Those who had multiplied their wealth received the blessing of great joy and glory.

Our spiritual wealth is our capacity for love. Each one of us is born into an entirely unique family situation with a unique bloodline that shapes our capacity for love. Some people are born into incredibly difficult circumstances and are raised in environments almost entirely void of any love. Like Desi, they may endure years of horrific abuse and neglect. Yet despite their circumstances, when they come to Christ they are still entrusted with a measure of love. Even if that measure is small, in the spiritual realm the value of that love is incredibly valuable and worth multiplying.

Other people may be born into the best environments and they may be lavished with love their entire lives. When they come to Christ, they naturally have a greater capacity for love. Yet to whom much is given, much is expected. In the end, what matters is not the amount of love that we have been entrusted to begin with, but how much we have increased that love.

This means that no one is at a disadvantage before God. We all have access to the same grace of God and so we are all able to multiply our love.

Giving Love

In the natural realm, we increase our wealth through working, trading and hoarding. In the spiritual realm, it is the opposite: we increase our love by giving it away. Therefore, if we want to multiply our wealth, Jesus simply calls us to love and keep loving.

> **Proverbs 27:5**
> Better is open rebuke than hidden love.

The foolish servant buried his gold in the ground because he was fearful of losing what he had been given. If we insist on hiding our love, like the foolish servant we will one day lose that love altogether. This is not a threat that God uses to control us; it is simply a fact about love. The nature of love demands expression. Just as a river that stops flowing ceases to be a river, so love that is hidden ceases to be love. The only way to keep love is to give it away.

> **Revelation 3:15-19**
> "I know your works: you are neither cold nor hot. Would that you were either cold or hot! So, because you are lukewarm, and neither hot nor cold, I will spit you out of my mouth. For you say, I am rich, I have prospered, and I need nothing, not realizing that you are wretched, pitiable, poor, blind, and naked. I counsel you to buy from me gold refined by fire, so that you may be rich, and white garments so that you may clothe yourself and the shame of your nakedness may not be seen, and salve to anoint your eyes, so that you may see. Those whom I love, I reprove and discipline, so be zealous and repent."

The church at Laodicea was a living example of people who had buried their gold. Their material wealth and comfort had led them into a life of complacency and lukewarmness. Like Sodom, they had "pride, excess of food, and prosperous ease," but they were spiritually blind, living in the outer darkness of their own spiritual poverty.[1] And they were enjoying it.

The Laodicean believers had wasted their inheritance of love and yet instead of judgment, Jesus offered them grace and love in the face of their poverty. *Buy from me gold refined by fire.* Jesus gave them a chance to start over in the love of God. However, this gold is bought at a price: Everything they had in life would need to be taken out of the domain of selfishness and brought into the domain of love. All their material wealth would no longer be their own, but it would be consecrated to expressing the love of God for others. By using their wealth as a channel of love, their earthly riches would turn to spiritual gold and take on true eternal value.

God's grace is always amazing, and this was an amazing second chance, given while there was still time to change. We can take heart in this triumph of mercy over judgment, knowing that if we have failed to multiply our love, it is not yet too late. Now is the time to devote our lives to love and ask Jesus to share His love with us and make us truly rich. If we call on Him, He will heal our sight so we can see through the lens of love and clothe us in His garments of selfless love and righteousness.

Having been healed, restored, and enriched by Jesus, we can then ask Him to help us to multiply our love. With Jesus, we can invest our gold in others and make them wealthy in the love of God while multiplying our own love. Even though it may seem costly at times, when we love with Jesus, our brains will reward us with oxytocin and give us a sense of fulfilment, satisfaction and wholeness. It will feel awesome. And best of all, it will all be to God's great pleasure and eternal glory.

Pray

Father, I love you. I thank you that you have made me rich. I never want to lose your love by keeping it to myself. So please give me opportunities to multiply this wealth today. Let your love, in all its joy, passion and glory, flow through me today. I love you!

26 | Love Like This

In order to multiply the love we have, we need to learn how love is shared, both in word and action.

> **Matthew 22:34-40** (BSB)
> And when the Pharisees heard that Jesus had silenced the Sadducees, they themselves gathered together. One of them, an expert in the law, tested Him with a question: "Teacher, which commandment is the greatest in the Law?"
>
> Jesus declared, "'Love the Lord your God with all your heart and with all your soul and with all your mind.' This is the first and greatest commandment. And the second is like it: 'Love your neighbor as yourself.' All the Law and the Prophets depend on these two commandments.'"

In the command to love others, Jesus calls us to appreciate the unity we share with one another and love our neighbor as ourselves—as if they were us. This is essentially the golden rule. It is a call to put ourselves in another person's position and act as we would like others to act towards us.

In many Christian circles, people reword this verse so that it reads, "love your neighbor as [much as you love] yourself." They reason that we cannot possibly love others if we do not first love ourselves, and so they focus on teaching people to love themselves. There can be real fruit in helping people to accept their true identity in Christ and overcome self-rejection. However, the danger of this teaching is that people can be tempted to use their brokenness to justify disobedience. *I cannot love others because I am not loving myself. I have to focus on me.* For many people, rather than leading to a life of selfless love, their efforts to "love themselves" only lead them to become more selfish—the exact opposite of love.

God has promised to make it possible for us to love Him with our whole heart. So if our heart is not whole—if we are broken and need healing—then God has guaranteed to heal us, but we need to commit our lives to keeping the greatest command *first*. If we demand that God heal us before we are willing to embrace our design of love, then we make our pain and brokenness idols that bind us in a life of disobedience. If we are in this place, then we need to repent and quickly shift our focus from ourselves onto Jesus. Instead of thinking, "I can't love until He heals me," we need to think, "I will love Him despite my brokenness. I choose to become a channel of His love." If we would only dare to follow Jesus into our design of selfless love, we would find that He quickly heals us along the way.

John 15:12-14
"This is my commandment, that you love one another as [*kathos*] I have loved you. Greater love has no one than this, that someone lay down his life for his friends. You are my friends if you do what I command you.

Kathos (kath-oce): *As much as*
An adverb derived from katá, meaning "according to" and hōs, meaning "as compared to, to the extent of." Properly, in proportion; to the degree that; just as (in direct proportion); corresponding to fully (exactly).[1]

Jesus never calls us to love others as much as we love ourselves. On the contrary, Jesus deliberately uses the word *kathos* to call us to "love one another [in exactly the same way] as I have loved you." His love is the only standard. Jesus loves us with a selfless, pure, extravagant, unconditional, and unfailing love. He loves us with a relentless devotion to our very best. He loves us in a way that we could not possibly hope to imitate. And yet this is the very love that Jesus calls us to share with one another.

Romans 5:5 (BSB)

And hope does not disappoint us, because God has poured out His love into our hearts through the Holy Spirit, whom He has given us.

Only Jesus can love like Jesus. For this reason, God gives us the same Spirit that lived within Jesus and He pours into our hearts the same love that dwelt in Jesus. *We have the same love!* Therefore, rather than strive to love like Him, our role is simply to offer ourselves as living channels of His love and let Jesus love through us.

The New Commandment

John 13:34-35

A new commandment I give to you, that you love one another, just as I have loved you, you also are to love one another. By this all people will know that you are my disciples, if you have love for one another.

Here Jesus gives us a new command to govern our entire life with Him. The term *new* here is translated from the Greek word *kainos*, which means "new in quality or fresh in development."[2] By giving us a new command to love one another, Jesus is not replacing the greatest command—to love God with our entire being—nor is He elevating the second command to first place.[3] The first command will be in first place forever. Instead Jesus is bringing a fresh development to the commands of love. He is combining the first and second command together in one new command and showing us that the primary way we love God is by loving one another.

1 John 4:15

Whoever confesses that Jesus is the Son of God, God abides in him, and he in God.

Whoever follows Jesus has the Spirit of God living within them. Because God is present in His people, we can love Him through one another. In fact, this is the very design of God. He created us to live in unity with Jesus and to be channels of His love rather than generators of our own love. To this end, the

Holy Spirit pours out His presence and love into our hearts, which then flows back to God as we love one another.[4] It is a stunning design.

Love in Word

Luke 6:45 (NLT)

A good person produces good things from the treasury of a good heart, and an evil person produces evil things from the treasury of an evil heart. What you say flows from what is in your heart.

We can only love through words and actions. In terms of speech, the words we speak flow from our heart. So instead of striving to speak words of love, we simply need to let God's love fill our hearts. When we have an abundance of love within us, it will flow effortlessly through our words.

In our relationship with God, we tend to think of expressing our love and affection for God through our prayers and songs. Praying and singing can be powerful ways of connecting with God when they honestly express our heart towards Him. But if our words are insincere; if we are only praying what we think God wants to hear, then our words are worthless and our time is wasted. Loving God through our words begins with being truly honest.

But why be honest with God when He knows everything anyway? God does not call us to be honest so He can learn something He does not already know. Rather, He calls us to honesty because He loves intimacy. When we share our hopes and desires with God as well as our disappointments and struggles, we give Him access to the intimate depths of our heart. This increases our unity with Jesus and delights the heart of God. It also makes us more honest with ourselves, which brings the blessing of humility and makes our lives more real. This gives us a powerful starting place to truly grow in God.

Ephesians 4:15

Rather, speaking the truth in love, we are to grow up in every way into him who is the head, into Christ, from whom the whole body, joined and held together by every joint with which it is equipped, when each part is working properly, makes the body grow so that it builds itself up in love.

1 John 1:7
But if we walk in the light, as he is in the light, we have fellowship with one another, and the blood of Jesus his Son cleanses us from all sin.

Speaking the truth in love is about heart-to-heart communication. This kind of honesty is essential if we are to grow in our relationship with God and it is key to loving Him through one another. Without honesty, we cannot have trust or true fellowship with other believers. Honesty alone brings a sense of authenticity to our relationships, which provides the soil for intimacy, unity and love to flourish.

When we trust in each other's love, we can be free to confess our sins and failings to one another without any fear of judgment. This brings freedom, especially in terms of our identity. When we hide our sin, we take ownership of it and it becomes a part of who we are. But when we bring it into the light and confess it to another person, we actively reject it from our identity and set ourselves free to live more in love and holiness.

Love in the Light

When we live in the light with one another, we open channels for the love of God to flow between us. This flow of love brings indescribable strength and healing to the body of Christ. Because of this, the enemy seeks to prevent love from flowing by undermining our fellowship. One of the main ways he does this is through offense.

In simple terms, an offense is a resentment brought about by a perceived insult. Most often offence comes through the expectations that we place upon people. *I expected them to be on time, but they were late. They have no respect for me.* Without love and grace, our expectations are merely standards that define failure. If people meet our expectations, all is well. If they fail to meet our expectations, we are disappointed or offended.

Expectations are closely followed by assumptions. When someone fails to meet our expectations, we often assume the reason why. *My friend didn't call me when my grandmother died. If he truly loved me, he would have contacted me. He didn't call because he doesn't care about me. If that's the way it's going to be, then I don't care about him either.*

When we allow expectations and assumptions into our relationships, we create the perfect conditions for offence to enter our hearts. This offence then leads to resentment, with all its bitterness and pain. We naturally want to avoid feeling the pain, but rather than dealing with the offence, we avoid the person. We stop communicating. We avoid eye contact. We live in the dark. Where possible, we cut off the relationship, and in doing so, we deny our design of love and grieve the heart of God.

The restoration of relationships is going to require some courage. If we are carrying an offence, then we need to go to that person and confess it. We need to ask God for the humility to give and request forgiveness. It is not important how the other person responds. Even if they reject us, we can feel at peace in knowing that when we let go of our offence, we allow God to heal our own hearts and restore our ability to love. The key is to take the first step and initiate. It may not be as scary as we think.

"Hey, can we talk?"

"Sure, what's up?"

"Well, the other day, I really needed you to be on time. And when you weren't, I was a bit upset and kind of took it personally. I'm sorry. I don't want to be offended, it just happened."

"Yeah, I'm sorry too. I had a feeling that I should have left earlier but didn't and then I got stuck in traffic. That was dumb. Can I buy you a coffee?"

Eliminating Assumption

The battle against offence is often fought throughout life. The easiest way to overcome is to deal with our assumptions before they can lead to offence. We all know the feeling that grows within us when we start to assume things about other people. It is often like a twisting in the heart or a heavy weight that dissolves our joy. As soon as we start feeling this heaviness, we need to see the danger and enter the battle. If we cannot take our assumptions captive in our own mind, then we need to talk to the other person and test our assumptions. We need to look them in the eye and speak honestly. This takes vulnerability and humility and it can be immensely difficult at first. But for the love of Christ, we need to do it. We need to pick up the phone or make a visit and have a conversation. Breathe. Dial.

"Hey, I'm glad you called. How's it going?"

"Actually, I'm not so good. Didn't you hear? My grandmother died last week."

"No way. I didn't know. I'm so sorry to hear that, I know how close you were to her. Do you feel like visitors? Can I come around?"

"Yeah, it would be good to see you."

Assumption tested. Relationship saved. Love wins again.

As long as we keep our assumptions in the dark, the enemy has power to undermine our relationships and steal love from Jesus. But when we check our assumptions with each other, we bring our thoughts into the light and we can have fellowship with one another. It may take courage to come into the light, but the reward of the temporary discomfort is the joy found in loving others and being loved. This is a joy worth fighting for.

Pray

Lord Jesus, I thank you for calling me to love others with you. Please help me to see your presence in people and to honor you and love you through them. I give you my voice. Please let us speak words of spirit and life together. May all our speech be uplifting, inspiring, positive and encouraging. Please forgive me for allowing disappointment and offence to keep me from loving you through others. Please wash away my sin. Help me to live in the light with others and to share your love through heart-to-heart conversation. Where there are broken relationships, please help me to have some brave conversations and give me the grace to forgive. Let us be one in love!

27 | Loving and Giving

In the last chapter, we looked at expressing love through our words. But what does the love of Christ look like in action?

When we look at Scripture, we find that Jesus loved people primarily by meeting their needs. When the people needed teaching, Jesus taught them. When they needed feeding, He fed them. When they needed healing, He healed them. And when people needed saving, Jesus saved them.

> **1 John 3:16-18**
>
> By this we know love, that he laid down his life for us, and we ought to lay down our lives for the brothers. But if anyone has the world's goods and sees his brother in need, yet closes his heart against him, how does God's love abide in him? Little children, let us not love in word or talk but in deed and in truth.

Jesus laid down His life, not only at the cross, but every day as He met the needs of those around Him. He made Himself the least of all by constantly putting other people's needs ahead of His own. Just as it did for Jesus, when the self-sacrificial love of God is poured into our hearts, it compels us to lay down our lives for others by meeting their needs. It compels us to give and keep giving.

There are many different expressions of love, yet every expression shares this foundation of giving. We give affection. We give respect. We give encouragement. We give attention. We give help. We give money. We give time. We give care, advice, honor, gifts, wisdom and effort. Because of the foundation of giving, our love for others is not measured by the way we feel but by our level of our generosity. Loving is giving.

Loving Jesus Through Others

Matthew 25:34-40

"Then the King will say to those on his right, 'Come, you who are blessed by my Father, inherit the kingdom prepared for you from the foundation of the world. For I was hungry and you gave me food, I was thirsty and you gave me drink, I was a stranger and you welcomed me, I was naked and you clothed me, I was sick and you visited me, I was in prison and you came to me.' Then the righteous will answer him, saying, 'Lord, when did we see you hungry and feed you, or thirsty and give you drink? And when did we see you a stranger and welcome you, or naked and clothe you? And when did we see you sick or in prison and visit you?' And the King will answer them, 'Truly, I say to you, as you did it to one of the least of these my brothers, you did it to me.'"

It is one thing to think about how we are personally changed when the Spirit of Jesus lives within us, but it is something else to think about how Jesus is impacted by living within us. When His Spirit fills us, Jesus shares all our experiences. So when we are in need, Jesus suffers our need with us.

I saw this when I was recently asked to pray with a woman for her friend, Michelle.[1] As the friend arrived, the Holy Spirit whispered, "Just look her in the eyes and listen."

I sat as Michelle shared her experience of being raised in a foster home "so evil and dark you could taste it." She spoke of a life of heartbreaking trauma and abuse, and then looked at me and said, "Jesus was never a woman! He doesn't know what it's like."

Michelle had every right to be broken and hurt and angry. There was nothing I could say, so I asked if we could pray. As we waited on God, a question came to mind, so I asked her, "Where was Jesus during your time of darkness?" I waited, expecting her to express a sense of abandonment, believing Jesus was gone when she needed Him most. Instead she gasped as the Holy Spirit opened her eyes.

"He was with me," she replied to our mutual surprise.

156

"How did He feel during the time of darkness?" I asked. Again, Michelle waited. Her reply came as a whisper: "He suffered. Oh, He suffered."[2]

Jesus shares our suffering. We know that the same God who created us all with the freedom to choose love also made us free to choose selfishness and violence. When we suffer because other people use their freedom to hurt us, we can be quick to blame God for the injustice and pain, but slow to realize that He is there with us the whole time, suffering with us. He shares our pain and He wants to set us free through His healing love.

It is therefore a literal reality that whatever we do for God's people, even the very "least of these," we do for Jesus. He is present in His people and that is where we truly love Him.

In the Body of Christ, we are all at different stages of maturity. Some of us may be a bit broken and may have little to give back. Yet every one of us possesses a unique unity with Jesus which means that every relationship we have with another believer is a channel through which we can love Jesus.

The presence of the Spirit of Jesus within each believer is why we are called to honor one another and fervently love one another from our heart.[3] In the same way that Jesus experiences our need with us, He also experiences our love! All the honor and love we share with one another flows through each one of us and is then received by Jesus Christ Himself! This is especially true for the least among us—those who cannot repay us for our love. What we do for every follower of Christ, we do for Him. And He loves it.

Loving Later

Mark 12:41-44

And he [Jesus] sat down opposite the treasury and watched the people putting money into the offering box. Many rich people put in large sums. And a poor widow came and put in two small copper coins, which make a penny. And he called his disciples to him and said to them, "Truly, I say to you, this poor widow has put in more than all those who are contributing to the offering box. For they all contributed out of their abundance, but she out of her poverty has put in everything she had, all she had to live on."

157

In this passage, Jesus shows us that the amount we give is not relevant *at all* to God. It is the sacrifice and risk behind our giving that reveals the depth of our love for Him. In the eyes of God, this widow offered more than all the wealthy givers put together because she gave out of her poverty.

Often people who have little to give use their poverty to justify their lack of giving. This is not only true for those who are financially poor. A lot of people are time-poor and use it as an excuse for not giving their time to people in need. Some are resource-poor, some have a poverty of energy, many have poor attention spans, and others suffer a poverty of empathy. Yet like the widow, we can use our poverty to bring us deeper into love by giving despite our poverty. Even when we have no time, we make time for those in need. When we have no money, we give what we do have to those in need and trust God for our provision. Whenever we give out of our poverty, our giving forces us to depend on God to make up the difference.

In our first year of marriage, God told me and Melanie not to ask anyone for money for ourselves. He wanted us to trust entirely in Him to provide what we need, when we need it. He gives this promise to every believer. He will provide our every need for the rest of our lives if we simply seek first His kingdom. This promise of provision sets us free to extravagantly love one another, knowing that we will always have everything we need.

Melanie and I have been faithful to trust in God and He has never let us down. However, there have been times when He has stretched us beyond what we expected. At one such time, Melanie was feeling the discomfort that comes with being stretched and so she took it to God in prayer.

"Lord, I'm tired of living by faith."[4] Melanie poured out her feelings to God. The Father instantly replied, not with a rebuke, but with a tender insight into dependency.

"You do not know how privileged you are. So few people depend on Me for their provision. And you need to know: dependency builds intimacy." When we stepped back, we could see this was true. Every time God provided for one of our needs, it increased the sense of intimacy and joy in our relationship with Him. If only people knew what they were missing. If only people knew how trustworthy God is to keep His promise; if only they knew how it feels to see God come through over and over again. If people knew what they were missing, they would look for ways they could become more dependent on God. Instead, the opposite is more often true. It is common for people to focus on building a life in which they do not need to depend on God. Some people even call it wisdom. Yet what we fail to see is that when we strive to become self-sufficient, we sacrifice a great measure of intimacy with God.

This quest for independence is often justified as a spiritual pursuit. In their zeal to help God, many people invest years in building businesses, ministries, or careers with the intention of one day channeling great profits into the kingdom of God. Their focus is on creating a surplus that can then be used to bless people. This is good when it is led by the Holy Spirit. However, in practice it is often based on the mindset of *I'll do this now so I can love later.* The tragedy is that by attempting to increase their financial wealth for God, people lose their true wealth by burying their love while they work on their projects. It is an illusion to love later. When later comes, people will search in vain for the love they buried. Love lives in the moment and responds to the need it sees now.

People who focus on building wealth now in order to love later often miss the spiritual dimension to giving in love. Giving out of a great surplus may have a significant impact on the world, but if it does not require great sacrifice then it is not an expression of great love. All the wealthy givers at the temple combined did not offer as much as the widow. The true spiritual value is found in the risk involved in the giving. *God this is all I have. By giving this to you, I am giving my life to you. I trust you.*

It is one thing to know the theory behind sacrificially giving to those in need, and something else entirely to put it into practice. It seems so risky. The essential key is to be led by the voice of the Holy Spirit. If we let the Spirit lead us in our giving, we would find that the risks we take with Him are rewarded with greater dependence, intimacy, love and unity with God.

One day I was preparing dinner in the kitchen. We had heard of some flooding in Pakistan that had devastated villages and created a desperate level of need for many people there. I took the situation before God, feeling frustrated that we had so little to give.

"God, I wish I had more money to send to Pakistan." God replied by putting a picture of a jar of oil into my mind. There was only a thin layer of oil at the bottom of the jar. I recognized it as the jar of oil belonging to the widow of Zarephath.[5]

"Pour out what you've got, and I'll fill it back up." God spoke and I remembered how He always refilled the widow's jar so that she never ran out of oil. I immediately sent money over to Pakistan. I trusted that God would keep His promise and figured that the people in Pakistan needed the money now whereas we only needed it later, and their need outweighed our own. The feedback was inspiring. People who had not eaten for days received food, supplies were given to those in need and we helped people to rebuild their homes. Then our own bills came in: $3800. *God's bills now.*

We did not share our need with anyone, and no one asked. With one week before the bills were due, I received a phone call.

"I've just sold a house. The money came through today so I'm going to put $4000 into your account tonight."

Someone once said that you can never out-give God. If only we truly believed that. We measure our capacity to give based on our surplus. We want to give more so we keep filling up our own jar of oil until it starts overflowing and then we give out of our overflow. But if God has promised to meet all our needs and to always replace our supply, what difference does it make if our jar is overflowing or almost empty? Regardless of whether we are rich or poor, when we give in love, we all have equal access to the infinite reserves of God.

"Love is not a choice… It's not an option. It's not a recommendation. It's not a suggestion. It is a commandment…So if we don't do it, what are we? In one simple word, we are *disobedient*. So we have two options. We can either love one another the way Jesus loved us and be obedient, or we can fail to love one other and be disobedient. But remember, this is not a suggestion. It is not a recommendation. It is a commandment."

- Derek Prince[6]

Pray

Lord Jesus, I acknowledge your heart and your desire. I hear your call to love others with your love. There is no way I could ever do this on my own. If I am to love like you, I need you to live within me and your love to flow through me. I hear your command to love and I embrace it. I give you permission to fulfil that command through me and to keep fulfilling it. Please keep pouring out more of your love into me and it flow through every area of my life.

Father, I need to need you more. The whole world is telling me I need to be secure. I want my security to be found only in you. Please give me the faith, love and courage to embrace a greater dependency on you.

28 | Giving in Unity

Psalm 23:1
The LORD is my shepherd; I shall not want.

The Lord Jesus is our shepherd and He will supply our every need. But if this is true then why is there need in the body of Christ? Why are there believers who go without? Is God failing to keep His promise to us? Or are we failing each other?

Needing Need

One day, Melanie arrived home after a meeting with a friend who is a single mother. Melanie told me of how this woman's car had broken down and how she and her son were having to walk or bus everywhere in winter.

"I really feel that we should help pay for the repairs. She needs $1200," Melanie said. Unfortunately at that time, we had no money to give.

"Sure thing," I replied. "We will just need God to give us $1200 first and then we can give it to her." Within three days, a friend unexpectedly repaid a loan that we had forgotten about and $1250 was put into our bank account. We gave the $1200 to our friend which encouraged her in her own journey of faith. However, it made me think: Why did God not directly give her the money she needed or miraculously fix her car? Why would He give us the money to give it to her? We find the answer in John 17.

John 17:22-23
And the glory which You gave Me I have given them, that they may be one just as We are one: I in them, and You in Me; that they may be made perfect in one, and that the world may know that You have sent Me, and have loved them as You have loved Me.

Jesus prayed to the Father that we might become one in Him. But how does the Father answer this prayer? What creates unity within the body of Christ?

Colossians 3:14
And over all these virtues put on love, which is the bond of perfect unity.

Love is the only bond that produces real unity. The Father allowed our friend to endure a need so that His love could flow through us to her and unite us together. This is how the body of Christ is designed to connect together and become one. Love is like the blood in the body: it flows from the heart and brings life to the whole body. When we look at need through the lens of love we realize that having a need does not mean that God has let us down or that we lack faith for His provision or that we have failed in some way. On the contrary, every need is a blessing that God gives us so that others can share His love by meeting our need, which then increases our unity. And it may not be a financial need. In one group I asked if there were any needs and one woman burst into tears and cried, "I'm so lonely!" We can experience need in the spiritual, emotional, relational, educational, economic, material realms and more. The key is to realize that **God blesses us with need** so that our love for one another can flow and make us more one in Christ. As a living body, we need.

Acts 4:32-35
Now the full number of those who believed were of one heart and soul, and no one said that any of the things that belonged to him was his own, but they had everything in common. And with great power the apostles were giving their testimony to the resurrection of the Lord Jesus, and great grace was upon them all. There was not a needy person among them, for as many as were owners of lands or houses sold them and brought the proceeds of what was sold and laid it at the apostles' feet, and it was distributed to each as any had need.

The early church had no need because the love of God was constantly flowing between the believers and meeting every need. The result was that everyone, the full number of believers, were of one heart and soul. This love that flowed between believers created an unbreakable unity. Through the meeting of need, the Father answered Jesus' prayer that His children would be one.

Sharing Our Need

The heart of God is still to make us one. However, for this to happen, we need to be willing to share our needs and to help meet the needs of others. And this is not always easy. We live in a world that prizes material success and views having need as a kind of failure. We do not want people to think that we are failing at life, so we naturally hide our need. Yet while we may keep our pride and reputation intact, when we conceal our need from other believers, we close the arteries of love within the body of Christ. By hiding our need, we waste the opportunity for life, unity and strength to grow within the Body of Christ.

It is no small thing to share our need with other people. It takes humility and vulnerability. It feels like failure. But that feeling fades when we come to see need as a blessing that God gives us to create unity in His body.

"So, what do you need?" A man asked me as we met over lunch for the first time. For some reason the question jolted me. I realized that what he was really asking me was, *How can I love you?* The impact of the question was instant. *Wow. This guy cares. He's in my corner.* I shared some needs with him and we left lunch as friends.

After that lunch I wondered why the question came as such as surprise. I had never been asked that question before but neither had I asked others what they needed. I just assumed that if a person was in need then it would be obvious. The only problem is that most of us hide our need. It is not obvious. It makes no sense to believe that love is primarily expressed in meeting needs but then not to ask anyone about their need. How did we miss such an obvious connection? Why are we not asking others to share their needs with us?

I then realized why. If the love of Christ is yet to overcome our selfishness, this question brings us into a place of conflict. If we have the resources to meet a need and we give, we suffer loss. But if we refuse to give, we make ourselves appear like loveless hypocrites. So we decide to avoid the conflict by staying silent. And by not asking, we close our hearts to love.

Giving in Unity

If we love in unity with Jesus, we give in unity with Jesus. The reason we are reluctant to meet the needs of others is because we do not truly believe in our unity with God. If we were fully convinced that Jesus lives within us and that He shares His wealth with us, we would be generous beyond measure. We would know that everything we have is a gift from God and so we would give it freely with Him. We would know that we never need to fear for our own provision because Jesus has promised to always look after us.

To be transformed in our giving, we need to be renewed in our mind concerning our unity with Jesus. Jesus wants to be involved in all our giving, and we involve Him by asking. Hearing His voice sets us free from relying on principles or percentages that may limit our love. Instead, when we see a need, we can simply ask the Spirit of Jesus to direct our giving. We did this one night with the family over dinner.

"OK everyone, we're going to pray. Close your eyes and ask Jesus: 'What have you given me to give away?' Then let the Holy Spirit put a thought in your mind." Everyone prayed and then listened. Afterwards we shared the thoughts that had come to mind. My eldest son Jacob shared the thought that first came to his mind: his iPhone. He had been given the phone as a gift only two months earlier. Around that time, we heard that my sister-in-law, who works with the poor in India, needed a new phone. This was Jacob's moment. He wrapped up the iPhone and sent it over. It was beautiful to watch love in action, led by the Spirit, meeting need.

Balancing it Out

Acts 20:35

In all things I have shown you that by working hard in this way we must help the weak and remember the words of the Lord Jesus, how he himself said, "It is more blessed to give than to receive."

When the body connects by meeting need, it is better to be the giver than the receiver. When we receive, we feel loved. But when we give, we grow in our unity with Jesus and affirm our identity as channels of His love.

A story is often told of Alexander the Great. As his procession passed a beggar, Alexander called his servant who kept his purse.

"Give the beggar two gold coins," Alexander instructed.

"But my lord, one copper coin is becoming of the beggar," the servant objected.

"But two gold coins is becoming of me," replied Alexander the Great.

Our giving is an expression of who we are. When we give in unity with Jesus, we define ourselves as one with Christ. And it feels amazing. By giving to meet the needs of others, we feel the oxytocin warm our hearts as God's love flows through us, which creates a real sense of identity. In so many ways, it is better to give than receive.

Even though we may prefer to give than receive, we need to create space for others to give and this can take humility. Many people struggle to accept love, even when it meets a genuine need. The solution to this struggle is simple. If someone offers to meet your need, just smile and say, "Thank you." Maybe give them a hug. Do not argue or refuse the gift, and do not or mistake insecurity for humility and pretend that you are not worthy. Rejecting a gift denies the giver a blessing and prevents the love of Christ from flowing in His Body. Instead of resisting love, just humble yourself and let the love flow.

I have met several people over the years who believe that God has told them not to ask people for money for themselves. Like us, this is a matter of dependence on God rather than doctrine. But if God says this to us, does it mean that we need to hide our need from others?

When we advertise our need, it can easily turn into manipulation. *If you loved me, you would help me with this need.* Every believer is called to trust in God to provide. If we look to people to provide our needs instead of God, we fall into idolatry. It is therefore important that we neither advertise nor hide our need. Instead, we can just be honest when asked. This is the key that brings balance to giving and receiving. In our relationships we seek to give rather than receive and to love rather than to be loved. But we do not conceal our need when asked nor do we refuse the love of others. We are simply honest and trust that people are being led by God. If He meets our need through a person, we smile and give thanks to God and to His channel.

All for One

For the body to function well, the call to love cannot be carried just by the few. On one occasion I was asked to speak in a church. I asked God what He wanted to say.

"Talk about the great commandment and the great commission and how you cannot outsource them to your pastor." He revealed that people in this fellowship did not feel the need to create disciples because their pastor was running a Bible study. They did not connect with each other outside their Sunday meetings because they believed it was the pastor's job to make sure other people were ok. This was never God's design. No one else can obey God for us by loving on our behalf. God's design requires all of us to work together to build an environment of love. This means that everyone needs to keep asking one another if there are any needs. When everyone is actively seeking out need, no one will have to ask for help on their own behalf.[1]

If we discover a need that we cannot meet by ourselves then we can join with others to meet the need together. If the whole fellowship combined does not have the resources to meet the need then people can come together and pray. As we all give what we have to meet each other's needs, we will find that like the Early Church, God will make us of one heart and soul. Together we will experience the joy and unity that comes from keeping Christ's one simple command: love one another.

167

Pray

Lord Jesus, I thank you that you live within me. Please help me to live in the awareness of our unity. I pray that you would make it more and more real to me and that our unity would transform my giving. Let your love flow through me to meet the needs of those around me. Let us be extravagant in love and generous in giving together. Please bless others through me. Love others and meet their needs through me. I am yours and we are one. I love you.

29 | Love Discerns

Romans 12:1-2

I appeal to you therefore, brothers, by the mercies of God, to present your bodies as a living sacrifice, holy and acceptable to God, which is your spiritual worship. Do not be conformed to this world, but be [continually] transformed by the renewal of your mind, that by testing you may discern what is the will of God, what is good and acceptable and perfect.

As we learned earlier, Jesus wants to share His thoughts with us so that we no longer think like the world. A key aspect of this is changing the way we think about love. Because we have been raised in the world, we often have distorted ideas about love and what it means to love. If we are to be free to love, we need to understand how the world sees love.

The world thinks of love mainly as an emotion. In terms of loving others, the pattern of the world is: *feel and do*. If we feel compassion or affection towards a person, then we let those feelings move us to act. Likewise, if we do not feel compassion towards someone then we can justify our inaction based on our lack of emotion. Even though we may perceive a need, in our unrenewed state we follow the pattern of the world and only act when we feel like it.

The love of God is entirely different. In the world, people love others by doing what they think is best. However, only God truly knows what is in a person's best interest. He knows His design and He sees the real need that only love can meet.

Because true love is only found in the will of God, it can only be out-worked in relationship with God. Therefore, instead of the worldly pattern of love, which is *feel and do,* the spiritual pattern of love is *discern then act.*[1]

This is why the Holy Spirit renews our mind, so that by testing our thoughts we might "discern the will of God—what is good, acceptable and perfect." Only after we discern God's will can we know what it means to truly love.

The How of Love

Discernment focuses us on *how* to love. With love reigning over us, the *what* and *why* of our lives never change. The *what* is the goal: to love God with all our heart, soul, mind and strength, in union with Him. The *why* is the reason: because He created us for love and union; it is encoded into the core of our being and we will only find fulfilment within our design of love.

Unlike the *what* and *why*, the *how* of our lives is a moving target. The *how* of doing the will of God is outworked in the many small circumstances of life. When Israel was taking the Promised Land, God never let His people put their trust in a formula or principle. They had to rely on His voice and constantly seek God for His strategy. The same is true for love. To know how to love in specific situations, we need to know the specific will of God. A similar situation at a different time may call for an entirely different act of love or it may call for no action at all.[2] God calls us to constantly discern His voice so that we always remain dependent on Him.

Learning to Listen

Before we discern the will of God, we need to first discern a person's need. The easiest way to do this is to listen and ask open questions. Often people are not sure what they need and it can take some time to get to the heart of the issue. At other times, we can ask, "What do you need?" and a person can answer straight away. The key is to listen and sense the heart.

> **James 1:19** (NLT)
> Understand this, my dear brothers and sisters: You must all be quick
> to listen, slow to speak, and slow to get angry.

As Christians it is so tempting to think that we love others by talking to them. However, the reality is that most people do not feel loved when we talk. They feel loved when we listen. For this reason, Scripture calls us to be slow to speak and quick to listen. Few people take the time to learn how to truly listen. It takes humility. It takes focus. It takes practice. It takes patience and kindness to draw a person out and get to the heart behind the words. It takes sensitivity to the Holy Spirit to know where He is directing the conversation. Yet if we invest our time in people, not only will they feel loved as they talk with us, we will also be able to discover their need. We can then take this need to God and see how He wants to meet their need.

Hearing, Obeying and Loving

Prayer is a key part of discerning the will of God. Yet so often people have shared their need with others only to hear the words, "I'll pray for you." People who live in legalism have often used this as a way of avoiding meeting the needs of others. *You're in need? I'll pray for you.* Like the priests and teachers in the parable of the Good Samaritan, we have used prayer to cross to the other side of the road and distance ourselves from a person's need. But God's love always meets need, every time. Therefore, we seek discernment, not to determine *if* we should respond to a need or not, but to discover *how* we should respond. Instead of using prayer as an escape, we use prayer to learn how we can love someone with Jesus. *Lord, I see a need. How shall we respond to this need?*

> **Deuteronomy 30:19-20a**
> I call heaven and earth to witness against you today, that I have set before you life and death, the blessing and the curse. So choose life in order that you may live, you and your descendants, by loving the LORD your God, by obeying [*shema*] His voice, and by living in union with Him; for this is your life...

The need for discernment is found in the call to choose life. As we learned earlier, the word *shema* literally means *to hear*, but it has such a strong sense of obedience that it is often simply translated as *obey*. If we are to live a life of love, we need to discern the voice of the Spirit and then act on what He says. This is what it means to truly hear and obey. This is what it means to truly live. It all happens in active relationship with God.

I learned the importance of discerning the voice of God after a close friend phoned me one night, utterly distraught. She was clearly in emotional need, so I went around to her place and talked her through the situation, trying to comfort and counsel her. When I returned home, I heard the voice of God.

"That wasn't Me." God showed me that I had not paused to discern His will and so had not acted in love. The reality of the situation was that she was in pain because she did not want to embrace the will of God. She was falling on the rock of Christ to be broken by His grace, and I was trying to soften her fall.[3] While my intentions were good, I had not taken the time to discern God's will and I ended up interfering with the work of His Spirit and acting against the will of God. I eased the pain that God was using for her good and completely failed to love her.

What this shows is that there can be times when our principles can lead us to act against the will of God. In the situation above, I thought I was acting according to the principle in Scripture which calls us to comfort those in affliction and mourn with those who mourn.[4] I was being led by principles rather than by the Holy Spirit. But does this mean that we need to abandon our principles in order to follow the voice of God? No. The voice of God is always consistent with the principles of Scripture. We simply need to let the Holy Spirit determine which principles we act on, when and how. In the case above, God was not calling me to comfort my friend. Instead He was wanting me to act according to different principles by spurring her onto love and compelling her to take up her cross with Christ.[5] He had the best plan.

This experience reinforced the truth that only God knows the true need of a person. If we would only stop to listen to His voice, we would find it so much easier to love others. I once had a friend who needed money to buy a car. I wanted to help and so for days I tried to source some money for a car. Nothing worked out, and the more I thought about the money and the car, the more I lost my peace. I finally took the situation before God.

"He doesn't need a car. He needs a job." The Spirit saw the real need behind the obvious need. Within a few days, another friend asked, "Do you know anyone who needs a job?" The need was met and love was shared, but it was not in the way I first expected. Love discerns.

Love and Emotion

Just because we act according to a Christian principle does not mean that we are doing the will of God. Likewise, just because we feel a sense of compassion does not necessarily mean that God is moving us with His compassion. It can often simply be a response of our natural mind. When we feel a strong emotion, we simply need to remember: love discerns then acts.

There is simply no replacement in life for the voice of God. Like our principles, our emotions are not a replacement for discernment and nor are they an essential component of love. If we act according to God's will, the emotions of love may precede or follow our action, or we may not feel any emotional reward at all. The result of acting in love may even at times be an emotionally crushing rejection.[6] Yet in Christ, we cannot love for reward and act only when it suits us or makes us feel good. That may be the way of the world, but it is not the way of God. He created us to live in selfless love and in this place, love becomes its own reward.

So does this mean that there is no emotion in love? Scripture speaks of love as a fine wine, which has the power to intoxicate us both spiritually and emotionally.[7] Oftentimes, flowing in the love of God can be a deeply emotional experience, but God's love is not limited to, defined by, or bound by emotion. The love of God both encompasses and surpasses emotion. It takes us beyond our feelings to a place where the world and our selfish nature cannot come. That place is simply called *the will of God*.

Pray

Holy Spirit, please take my heart, my principles, and all my emotions. Please rule over them. I only want to feel how you feel. I want to share your heart and experience your emotions. I ask you to lead me throughout my day. I know I cannot love without you. I need you. Please help me to live in a constant conversation with you. Let us walk in step together and love together.

30 | Will of God

Luke 18:19
And Jesus said to him, "Why do you call me good? No one is good except God alone."

True love always acts in another person's best interest, leading to their ultimate good. But who can say what is actually good? Here we find that God alone is good; He is infinitely, eternally, inexpressibly good! As the source of all goodness, God alone has the right to define what is truly good for us. God knows what He is capable of and His desires for us far surpass anything we could possibly desire for ourselves. The only best is God's best, and it never changes. No matter how we feel or how far we have wandered from His arms, God's best will for us is as constant as His love.

John 14:15
"If you love me, you will keep my commandments."

1 John 5:3
For this is the love of God, that we keep his commandments. And his commandments are not burdensome.

All the commands of Scripture express His awesome will for us: the heights of His love, the depths of His presence, and the blessings of a life lived in union with Him. But this is all only possible with our participation. God cannot force us to receive His goodness and so He humbles Himself to bless us as much as our faith allows. If we are to increase our faith and remove the limits we place on God, we need to seek the revelation that God is *infinitely* good—far better than we could ever imagine. The more confident we become in God's goodness, the more inspired we will be to genuinely seek His will for our lives.

Seeking His Will

"Would you pray for me?" a woman asked one night after a Bible study.

"Sure, I'd love to. What's up?"

"We have saved all this money to buy a farm, but we're not sure on how to invest it. We have three options and we've been praying about it, but we're not sure what God's will is."

"OK. Are you willing to give it all away?" I asked.

"What?!" She was genuinely surprised. "God wouldn't ask us to do that."

"Well, He has in the past with other people," I said. I went on to explain that we are deceiving ourselves if we think we are seeking the will of God when we decide the options He can choose from. We need to surrender every option to Him. If we cannot sincerely put all the options before Him, then we need to ask: *Why?* What is it in our hearts that is preventing us from surrendering every option to God? Is it insecurity or selfishness? Is it fear? Once God reveals the root cause of our resistance, we can then take it to the cross and ask God to help us to come to a place of full surrender. When we are equally at peace with every option, we can then seek God's will in the confidence that we will obey His will, no matter what it costs us.

If we sense this kind of conflict in our heart, it is important to remember that God's will is always for love. Is God asking you to sell something? It is because He is inviting you to grow in love by selling. Is He asking you not to sell something? It is because He wants to use it with you as a channel of His love. Is He asking you to go? Go and love. Is He asking you to stay? Stay and love. Simply trust that God's will is His love and that no matter what, His Spirit will always give you the grace to obey.

Like the woman who had her heart set on a farm, too often we decide what we think is best and then pray that God would do our will. When we do this, we misunderstand the will of God, the design of love, and the nature of prayer.

Exchanging Desires

1 Thessalonians 5:17
Pray without ceasing...

Matthew 6:9-10
"[Continually] Pray then like this:
'Our Father in heaven,
hallowed be your name.
Your kingdom come,
Your will [*thelema*: desire] be done,
on earth as it is in heaven.'"

The Greek word *thelema* is often translated as *will* but it is based on the root word *thelo,* which means *desire.* The Greek word *proseúxomai,* which is translated as *pray,* means *to exchange desires.*[1]

It is natural for friends to share their desires with each other. We share our desires both through conversation and action. If we love sport, we talk about sport with our friends and we invite them to play with us. If we love reading, we share good books with our friends. Sharing what we love is a natural part of friendship and the same is true for God. When we pray, we share our desires with God and He shares His desires with us.

Prayer is a conversation with God where we pour out our heart before God and lay all our desires at His feet. We then enter into an exchange. We ask the Spirit of Jesus to take our desires and establish His desires in their place. In this way, prayer is not about getting God to act for us. It is about coming into agreement with the will of God and receiving His desires in exchange for our own.

Let Your will be done is therefore a powerful prayer of exchange that calls forth unity: *Let our will be one.* Jesus is teaching us to pray by asking God to impart His desires to us so that we can obey His will.

While the will of God is expressed in His many small desires, God's highest will is revealed in the greatest, most important command: that we would love Him with all our heart and soul in unity with Him. This desire for a life of consuming love and unity is one of the greatest expressions of His goodness to us, and if we embrace this will, it will bring both temporal transformation and eternal glory.

Because the greatest command is God's greatest desire, every time we pray, *Let Your will be done*, we are really praying, *Let us love You with all our heart, soul, mind and strength.* If we are not really devoted to loving God, then it is a delusion to think that we are truly seeking the will of God. God's will is not a buffet. We cannot pick and choose which parts of God's will we want done in our lives. If we do not want to obey the first command, then we need to be honest with God and stop praying for His will to be done. He can handle it. If this is how we feel, we can exchange our lack of desire with Him. We can pray, *Lord I do not have the desire to love you with all my heart and soul. But I want it. Please put your desire for the first command in my heart so that I can pray from my heart, "Let your will be done."*

Prayer and Action

James 2:26
For as the body without the spirit is dead, so faith without works is dead also.

Too often people recite the Lord's Prayer without understanding, conviction or faith. Prayer without faith is dead and so as a ritual this prayer achieves nothing. Likewise, faith without works is also dead and so every prayer of faith should ultimately lead to some form of action. This means that we cannot simply pray for God's will to be done and then do whatever we want with our lives. True prayer calls us to lay down our own desires and to yield to the will of the King of kings, the Lord Jesus Christ. It demands that we wait on God for the revelation of His will and then receive His desires as our own. Having exchanged desires with Him, we then need to offer our time, energy and wealth in acting on the will of God.[2]

Philippians 2:13 (NLT)

For God is working in you, giving you the desire and the power to do
what pleases him.

Through prayer, God gives us His desires as a gift of grace. However, His
grace does not end there. In His goodness, God also offers the motivation
and energy we need to act in love. This power comes from His Spirit within
us and like all gifts of grace, we access this power through faith. *Thank you
for the grace and energy to act right now—I receive it!* Trusting God to act
with us sets us free from having to obey God in our own strength. We can
pour out what we have in unity with His Spirit, knowing that His love, grace,
provision, and joy are inexhaustible.

I experienced this during a trip to Fiji. I was at a meeting in a home-
church when I noticed a woman sitting on the floor. She looked overwhelmed with discouragement.

"She is weighed down by financial needs and is doubting My provision,"
the Spirit said through a quiet thought as He moved me to pray for her. With
her permission, I then prayed for faith in God's provision, for love, blessing,
grace, joy, and favor. When I had finished praying, the Holy Spirit reminded
me that real prayer in real faith leads to real action. I could not sincerely pray
for this woman without doing something to minister to her need. As she
turned away, I took $50 and slipped it into the pages of her Bible. It was a
small gift that I hoped would be an encouragement.

That Sunday I was asked to speak at a different gathering. I was surprised
to find that the woman's husband was leading the fellowship. The meeting
opened with testimonies and everyone was free to share. This woman stood
up, beaming with the most beautiful smile. The joy of Christ radiated out
from her as she began to speak.

"Church! Our God is a God of miracles!" she began. "On Wednesday
morning I was praying to God and He asked me, 'Do you believe I can put
$50 in your Bible?' I said, 'Yes Lord, I believe,' and I opened my Bible and

look—$50!" She began waving the money. "Look church! It has never been used. It's fresh from heaven!"

Even though I gave the money to the woman, God took the credit. Why? Because we acted in unity. We loved that woman together and it all started with hearing God's voice, receiving His desire, and then acting with Him. This is life as God designed.

This experience of God's love will now stay with that woman for her life. The joy that she received and then imparted to others was worth so much more than $50. It truly is so much better to give than receive and I count myself blessed to have been able to act with God as He loved His daughter.

God's will for people is awesome and it is exciting to act with Him. It all starts with exchanging our will with God's and then letting Him lead us from prayer to action. As we act with Him, there will be times when we get to see some of the fruit of our love. At these times we will simply smile and celebrate the wonderful nature of God. The Lord is good and His love endures forever!

Pray

Father, you know my heart. I want it to be one with your heart. So let your will be done. Let your kingdom come. Let your love reign within me and flow through me, and let the world be changed. I am yours.

31 | Founded in Love

I remember hearing a person tell the story of an engineer who was asked to investigate cracks that were appearing on the 16th floor of a building. When he arrived at the building, he asked to go down to the basement. The building manager was confused. The cracks were on the 16th floor. However, the engineer knew that the cracks above were only symptoms of a problem below. He went down to inspect the foundations and fix the problem.

Most of the time we give little thought to the foundations of our lives until the cracks start appearing. Even then, it can be tempting to plaster over the cracks rather than inspect the foundations. However, unless we fix our foundations, the cracks will keep on reappearing. If we are wise and courageous, we can ask God to expose the foundations of our lives.

Matthew 7:24-27

"Everyone then who hears these words of mine and does them will be like a wise man who built his house on the rock. And the rain fell, and the floods came, and the winds blew and beat on that house, but it did not fall, because it had been founded on the rock. And everyone who hears these words of mine and does not do them will be like a foolish man who built his house on the sand. And the rain fell, and the floods came, and the winds blew and beat against that house, and it fell, and great was the fall of it."

In this passage, Jesus likens our lives to a home built on a foundation. The one who hears the words of Christ and does them is like a wise man who builds upon the rock. Here Jesus teaches us that the only way to build our lives on solid foundations is through faith *and* action. It is not enough just to believe in the truth. Too many people believe in Jesus but live for themselves and waste their time building upon shifting sands. To have solid foundations we need to believe the truth and let it change the way we live.

God promises that the storms of life will come. These storms will expose our life-foundations and they will come with or without our permission. So why wait for the storms to arrive? Let us prepare ourselves now by inspecting our foundations. What are we basing our life on? What gives substance and stability to our lives?

Laying Foundations

Themélios (them-el-ee-os): *Foundation*
From the root *tithemi* meaning to place, lay or set.

Katabolē (kat-ab-ol-ay'): *Foundation*
Properly, a foundation cast according to a blueprint (original design), i.e. the *substructure* which determines the entire direction (destination) of all that follows; the foundation-plan upon which the entire super-structure is built; (figuratively) the *beginning* (*founding*) which also purposefully designs all that follows.

Every foundation is built according to a plan. The plan determines the design and direction of everything that is built upon it. In other words, everything in our lives gets its value and sense of purpose from our foundation. This is true for good or for bad. For example, if we are building on a foundation of worldly security, we will value our possessions because they add to our sense of security. However, if we are building our lives on a foundation of love, we will value our possessions because of their potential as channels of love. In this way, our foundation shapes the way we view life.

1 Corinthians 3:10-15

According to the grace of God given to me, like a skilled master builder I laid a foundation, and someone else is building upon it. Let each one take care how he builds upon it. For no one can lay a foundation other than that which is laid, which is Jesus Christ. Now if anyone builds on the foundation with gold, silver, precious stones, wood, hay, straw— each one's work will become manifest, for the Day will disclose it, because it will be revealed by fire, and the fire will test what sort of work each one has done. If the work that anyone has built on the foundation survives, he will receive a reward. If anyone's work is burned up, he will suffer loss, though he himself will be saved, but only as through fire.

There is only one sure foundation for our lives: the solid rock of Jesus Christ. Each person can build differently upon the foundation, but eventually it will all be tested. The storms will come and the fire will fall. With this in mind, Paul calls us to build carefully.

The foundation of Christ is far more than just a doctrine of Jesus' life, death, and resurrection. If we build our lives upon doctrine alone, we will face the storms with merely a philosophy of Christ. Remember that truth means *reality*. Jesus is real. His Spirit is real. To build upon Christ is not to build upon a doctrine but a reality. It is to build a life of unity with Jesus, by loving Him, hearing His voice, and acting with Him.

Rooted and Grounded

Ephesians 3:14-19

For this reason I bow my knees to the Father of our Lord Jesus Christ, from whom the whole family in heaven and earth is named, that He would grant you, according to the riches of His glory, to be strengthened with might through His Spirit in the inner man, that Christ may dwell in your hearts through faith; that you, being rooted and grounded in love, may be able to comprehend with all the saints what is the width and length and depth and height— to know the love of Christ which passes knowledge; that you may be filled with all the fullness of God.

Here Paul prays that we might be rooted and grounded (or founded) in love so that we might come to experience the love of Christ that surpasses knowledge.[1] Paul is extreme in His language here. He is calling us to embrace an intense, experiential knowledge of the love of Christ, which will bring us into an ever-increasing fullness of His Spirit.

The only way to build upon this foundation of love is to do the will of God. And Scripture has made God's will crystal clear and put it within reach of every person. The ultimate will of God is revealed in the first and second commands. We cannot pretend to build on the foundation of Christ and neglect His top two priorities. They must become our vision, our passion, our mission, and our message. If we are to build on solid rock, we must give ourselves to loving God with all our heart, soul, mind and strength, and loving others as ourselves. This is what it means to build with gold and precious stones. It is all about living a life of love.

The Gift that Works

Colossians 2:6-7

Therefore, as you received Christ Jesus the Lord, so walk in him, rooted and built up [*epoikodomeo*] in him and established in the faith, just as you were taught, abounding in thanksgiving.

Epoikodomeo (ep-oy-kod-om-eh'-o): "built up"

To build on a foundation; properly, appropriately build on, as when following a plan and its pre-designed (pre-defined) specifications.

Here again Paul speaks of being rooted and grounded in Christ. Being "rooted in Christ" uses the metaphor of a living plant or tree. We are like a tree that grows its roots into God and draws life and love from His presence. Being "built up" in Christ uses the metaphor of building our lives upon a foundation. While a tree might effortlessly draw nourishment through its roots, building requires effort. Our foundation is laid only by God's grace, but His grace requires our active participation. We must be prepared to build.

Romans 11:6

But if it is by grace, it is no longer on the basis of works; otherwise grace would no longer be grace.

By its very nature, grace is a gift that reflects the heart of the giver. This is why people speak of grace as the unmerited favor of God. The Father gives His countless blessings to us because He loves us and cannot hold back His goodness towards us. Grace has nothing to do with our worth because grace can never be earned in any way. God cannot put Himself, His love, or His blessings on sale. For grace to remain a true reflection of God's nature and character, it must always be entirely unearned.

> **1 Corinthians 15:10**
> But by the grace of God I am what I am, and his grace toward me was not in vain. On the contrary, I worked harder than any of them, though it was not I, but the grace of God that is with me.

"By the grace of God, I am what I am."

Grace is the free gift of God that brings us into our true identity in Christ. But while grace can never be earned, the reality is that grace is anything but passive. As Paul writes, the grace of God works hard—really hard. Grace is the gift of God that energizes us to love God with all our strength. Grace connects our heart with our hands, enabling us to outwork our wholehearted love for God with wholehearted effort. And unlike the striving of legalism, the work of grace is not a heavy burden. It does not exhaust us or leave us feeling spiritually empty. Instead the grace of God motivates us through joy to build with Christ. It sets the first command as its goal and brings us into the thrilling pursuit of love.

Contending for Love

> **1 Timothy 6:12**
> Fight the good fight of the faith. Take hold of the eternal life to which you were called and about which you made the good confession in the presence of many witnesses.

Like Timothy, God is calling us to fight the good fight and take hold of eternal life. As we know, eternal life is the unending, wholehearted love for

God. This is not something that we can receive passively. Rather, we are called to keep fighting for wholehearted love.

The intensity of this fight is revealed in the Greek word *epilambanomai* (translated as "take hold"). This word conveys the sense of a focused, aggressive pursuit. While eternal life is a gift that is only given by God's grace, Scripture calls us to receive the gift with resolve and determination. In this fight, complacency, compromise, and apathy are our enemies. We simply cannot afford to be casual or half-hearted in our response to the greatest command. As it is written, the way to life is difficult.[2] If we want to build our lives upon the first and second commands, we must be prepared to pursue and attain, to fight and overcome.

We learned from the word *katabole* that a foundation sets the design and direction of all that is built upon it. As we build upon the Rock of Christ, His love begins to determine the entire direction of our lives. Every decision, every action, every relationship, every word, everything we are and have; everything in our lives is given meaning by this foundation of love. Knowing how short our lives are compared to eternity, we need to begin to build our lives upon a foundation of love *right now*. We start building by making a covenant with God, to love Him with all our heart and soul, and to love others. We then begin to restructure our lives for love.

Pray

Father, I cannot think of a better foundation for my life than Jesus Christ. I choose to build my entire life on Him. Let the first two commands shape my entire life—everything I am and everything I do. Please energize my heart and soul to desire as you desire. Please energize my mind and body to act with you in wholehearted devotion. I love you and I call on you to make this all a reality in my life. Empower me for wholehearted love and life in union with your Son. Love Him through me and let it be real, now and forever.

32 | All of You

1 Peter 2:4-5

As you come to him, a living stone rejected by men but in the sight of God chosen and precious, you yourselves like living stones are being built up as a spiritual house, to be a holy priesthood, to offer spiritual sacrifices acceptable to God through Jesus Christ.

In the original Greek, the word *you* here is plural, meaning *all of you*. Together we are being built up into a holy house and every house needs a good foundation. Our call is therefore not just to build strong foundations as individuals but to come together to build strong foundations in fellowship with one another.

Our spiritual foundations are laid according to God's precise design. Earlier we learned how we instinctively form our sense of design and identity from what we see around us. For this reason, church gatherings all around the world generally follow a similar pattern. Because everyone follows the same format, we assume that we are all living according to God's design. However, the book of James makes it clear: it is only the word of God that reveals God's design for us. Instead of looking at what everyone else is doing, we need to let God determine His design for our lives both as individuals and as corporate groups of believers.

John 15:12

This is my commandment, that you love one another as I have loved you.

God's corporate design for us is not defined by structure but by character, and it is revealed in one command: that we love one another. This is a design that can never be changed or improved on. If we are to walk in the will of God, then we must establish love as the foundation of our relationships.

Laying a foundation of love together requires a conscious agreement with others. Once we all commit to laying a foundation of love, the Spirit of God can then build us together into a living stronghold of love. As a stronghold, love will be the primary bias within our relationships. It will become the filter of our mind through which we interpret the words and actions of one another. And as a shared foundation, love will give meaning to everything we do in a corporate setting.

We learned earlier how God blesses us with need so that love can flow as we meet each other's needs. All these needs are in some way connected to our design. Our physical bodies are designed to get energy from food and so everyone needs to eat. Therefore, when people are hungry, we love them by feeding them. People are designed to need shelter. Without it, people die and so we love others by providing shelter. People are designed to live in freedom and so we love others by freeing those who are in slavery. Love meets need and our needs are determined by our design.

Hebrews 10:24-25
And let us consider how to stir up one another to love and good works, not neglecting to meet together, as is the habit of some, but encouraging one another, and all the more as you see the Day drawing near.

While a person's physical needs are both urgent and important, we cannot lose focus of a person's spiritual needs, which all stem from their spiritual design. In the spiritual realm, we are designed to love God with all our heart and soul, to hear His voice, and to live in union with Jesus. All our spiritual needs flow out from this perfect design. So while people may not realize it, we all *need* to love God with all our heart. We all *need* to hear His voice and live in union with Him. For this reason, Scripture calls us to continue to meet together to spur each other onto love. When we meet, we love one another by encouraging each other to keep the first and second commands. We love one another by helping each other to hear the voice of God. We love one another by inspiring each other to go deeper into union with Jesus. We love by opposing selfishness in ourselves and others. We love by calling one another to let God circumcise our hearts and make us channels of His love.

Moving Foundations

Mark 7:8

"Neglecting the commandment of God, you hold to the tradition of men."

As individuals, it can require a process of real change to rebuild our lives on a foundation of love. The same is true corporately.

We can test the foundations of our corporate meetings by asking, "Why do we do what we do? Is love the motivation and the goal?" If we test our meetings by the standard of love, we may find that some of the things we do are motivated out of tradition rather than love. Our traditions feel familiar, safe, and even righteous, but so often they can lead us to focus on activities rather than love. When we meet together, our traditions can lead us to follow a predictable pattern rather than the voice of the Holy Spirit. When this happens, our traditions become idols that lead us to neglect God's design of love.[1] These idols must fall.

Because people are so comfortable with engrained traditions, it can be a difficult process to move a corporate group to a foundation of love. People tend to resist change, but we simply must do it. What other choice do we have? We either build on a firm foundation of love or build upon the shifting sands of our own good ideas, traditions, and legalism. And God promises that one day the storms will come. We know that love is the only foundation that will stand in times of shaking. Therefore, we must contend for love both individually and corporately. We must rid our lives of everything that hinders love so that the love of Christ might reign over us.

Less is More

As individuals, the more we restructure our lives for love, the more joy we find in the restructuring. What begins as something scary quickly becomes both exciting and empowering. When we convert our lives to love, we realize that there is no real sacrifice in moving to a foundation of love. God only calls us to give up the chains that we were once so fond of, and in return He gives us the blessing and privilege of being founded on His love.

This is also true corporately. Restructuring our corporate lives for love will seem terrifying at first. It will require us to connect with each other and participate rather than spectate. It will require us to become vulnerable with one another and trust each other. We will need to humble ourselves to connect heart-to-heart and share our struggles and our joys with each other. It will cost us more of our time, money and energy. We may even miss some of our old traditions. But the reward is worth far more than the cost. God has designed us spiritually and physically in such a way that the more we give ourselves to loving others, the more joy and fulfilment we will experience in life. And that will feel amazing.

Not Neglecting to Meet Together

Love always flows from someone to someone. We cannot love in isolation, which means we can only obey Christ's command of love together. Our very obedience to God can only come as we connect with one other and open the channels of love in our relationships. For this reason, Scripture calls us to keep gathering together and not to give up. If we are to live in our design of love, we need to keep on meeting in a way that allows us to truly love one another.

For centuries, the Church has made the weekly service its primary gathering. In our zeal for God, we focused on building a style of service that could attract large numbers of people. However, we failed to think about how the flow of love is affected by large numbers. The problem with investing primarily in a weekly service is that our experience of love decreases as the number of people in a group increases. This is not anyone's fault; it is simply the nature of love. Love flows through intimacy, and intimacy gets lost in the crowd. In this respect, love is like a conversation. It is something that happens in small numbers. So while large gatherings have their place in the Body of Christ, we need to focus on creating space for obedience by meeting together in small numbers with a single goal: to love one another.

Matthew 18:19-20

"Again I say to you, if two of you agree on earth about anything they ask, it will be done for them by my Father in heaven. For where two or three are gathered in my name, there am I among them."

Just as we cannot love alone, neither can we love a crowd. Life itself teaches us that we find love in relationships rather than at events. We find love in family and in friendships. We feel far more comfortable being vulnerable in twos and threes than in 12s and 20s. And where someone will hide their need in front of ten people, they will often share it with one or two.

Love only needs a few people to flow. In fact, love flows strongest in the smallest numbers. Therefore, if we are going to build upon a foundation of love then we need to start with twos and threes as the building blocks of the Church. These twos and threes do not have to be fixed or structured. They can be dynamic—changing, mixing and evolving as the Spirit leads. These twos and threes can then come together as small families of faith. Then, when we bring all these families together, we will find that the love we have poured into one another through our small groups will gloriously transform our larger corporate meetings.

It can be daunting to think about moving a large fellowship to a foundation of love. However, the great news is that we do not need to move from being an organization to a family overnight. We can start small and begin with just two or three people who are devoted to loving God through one another. We can then share that love with others and watch Jesus as He builds His church, living stone by living stone, fitted and bound together by love.

Love Attracts

John 13:34-35

"A new commandment I give to you, that you love one another, just as I have loved you, you also are to love one another. By this all people will know that you are my disciples, if you have love for one another."

God is love and so He naturally wants us to become known in the world by our love. However, for Jesus' desire to be fulfilled, two conditions must first be met:

1. We must love one another,
2. The world must be able to see our love.

When we meet these conditions, something amazing happens.

Earlier we learned about God's biological design for our bodies. We react to love by releasing oxytocin, which gives us a sense of wholeness, wellbeing, and deep fulfilment. Oxytocin is the peace that we feel when we are around people we like. It is the inner warmth we feel when we are embraced by someone we love. Oxytocin is the shiver that comes from singing with other people.[2] It is the warm fuzzy feeling that we feel when we watch someone do something selfless to help another person. God has designed the brain to be so affected by love that we do not even need to participate in love to feel its effects. We simply need to see love in action and the flow of oxytocin through our bloodstream will tell us: *I was designed for love.*

God's desire is to draw people to Himself through love. When we invite non-believers to our small group meetings, their hearts will resonate as they see our love for one another. Even if they have strongholds against God in their minds, they will not be able to stop their hearts from responding to genuine love. Just imagine a meeting of believers who truly love one another. Imagine a non-believer coming to a meeting and seeing people—men and women—embracing each other with a pure love and showing a genuine interest in each other. Imagine a non-believer watching people give to each other with joy. Imagine their response as they experience the presence of the

Holy Spirit and the love of His people. Imagine their thoughts as they hear the truth of God's love and see it manifest in His people. Though their minds may not be able to articulate it, their hearts will be telling them: *I want this! I was made for this! How can I have this in my life?*

Pray

Father, I see your design for fellowship and hear your call to meet together and to spur each other on to love and good works. I know you want us to love one another and to let our love be seen. Please help us to do this. On behalf of your Body, I ask for the humility and courage to embrace this call of love. Please let your love flow through us and make us one together with you. May you be lifted up in our love and may you draw all people to yourself.

33 | Infinite Love

Matthew 28:16-20

Now the eleven disciples went to Galilee, to the mountain to which Jesus had directed them. And when they saw him they worshiped him, but some doubted. And Jesus came and said to them, "All authority in heaven and on earth has been given to me. Go therefore and make disciples of all nations, baptizing them in [Greek: *eis*] the name of the Father and of the Son and of the Holy Spirit, teaching them to observe all that I have commanded you. And behold, I am with you always, to the end of the age."

The great commission is not just a call to share the gospel with the world. It is something far, far greater. As He did for His disciples, Jesus gives us His authority so we can make disciples by baptizing people in the name of the Father, Son and Spirit, and by teaching them to obey the commands of love.

But what does it mean to baptize people in the name of God? Does it refer only to the words we speak at water baptism or something more?

In order to see the spiritual reality of being baptized in the name of God, we need to break the sentence down. In Scripture, a person's name is often used to speak of their character and nature.[1] The name of God is therefore much more than just a word or identifier; it is His nature of pure, divine love.

In Chapter Five we discovered that the Greek word *eis* means *into*—an action that produces union. In Chapter Ten we learned that baptism in the Spirit is an ongoing immersion in God, which makes us one spirit with Jesus. Put together, we find that our call is not simply to baptize people in water, but to immerse them into God's nature of extravagant love, taking them on a journey into love and unity with Him. This immersion can begin even before we share the gospel with people and it is the key to making disciples.

Often people hesitate to share the gospel with others for fear of rejection. However, one of the hardest things in the world to reject is real love. So if we focus first on sharing God's self-sacrificial love with people, our fears will dissolve and it will not be long before people ask us to share the gospel. Remember: everyone is biologically designed to respond to love. If our love is real, we have no reason to fear rejection. Few people can resist God's love forever.

"I am so sick of that guy hassling me about God. He always tells me that I shouldn't be drinking and having sex and he keeps asking me to go to church. I'm sick of it." I listened as a friend complained about her Christian work-mate.

"You know, I think he says those things because he cares about you," I replied. She looked at me and narrowed her eyes.

"*I've been to church.* I know what it is like. All they want is your money."

"You know, it wasn't always that way," I said. "When Jesus was around, He said that life was all about loving God and loving each other. Love was the only thing that mattered."

"What?" She seemed genuinely surprised. We talked for a while about God's love and then picked up the conversation again some days later. She then shared a remarkable story with me.

"I don't usually tell anyone this, but when I was twenty, I was attacked. Two men had to kill someone as part of a gang initiation. They grabbed me off the street and they took me down an alley and started hitting me. They kept going until they thought I was dead. The doctors thought I had been hit over 70 times. The men left me in agony, drowning in my own blood. I was dying and then a man appeared next to me. He touched me and all my pain went away and I could breathe. He then carried me out of the alley to the street, laid me down and disappeared. A young couple found me and called for help and I was taken to the hospital. My uncle says that it was an angel or

God that saved my life, but I don't know. After everything I've done, I just can't believe how God could ever love me."

After everything I've done, I just can't believe how God could ever love me. That is the real heart of the issue. We can be so focused on sharing the gospel that we fail to see that often what people need is simply to know that God loves them. That is their good news. God sees them, He knows them, and He passionately loves them.

Come to Know and Believe

Non-believers often see through the script and are quick to raise their defenses if they sense agendas when we talk with them. But more often than not, people open up to love. This is because beyond the walls of the mind is a heart that carries a profound need for love. Deep down, people desperately want to feel loved. If we are going to minister to that need, our primary focus needs to be on revealing the love of God. Before we can do this, we first need to learn how much God actually loves people. Is the love of God dependent on how people act? Does it ever change?

> 1 John 4:16 (AMP)
> We have come to know [by personal observation and experience], and have believed [with deep, consistent faith] the love which God has for us. God is love, and the one who abides in love abides in God, and God abides continually in him.

We can learn about the love of God in Scripture. However, love is not a theory. To truly know the love of God, we need to combine observation with personal experience. This can only come through the Holy Spirit. He is the source of revelation that makes the theory of love a reality. When He leads us into a personal experience of God's love, we can then share His love with others in a deeply authentic way.

196

Love of the Father

John 3:35

The Father loves the Son and has given all things into his hand.

As we learned earlier, we can position our hearts for revelation by meditating on the word of God. From the Scriptures, we know that God is love and that He is the Source of all love. We know He designed us for love. But when we look more closely at the Father, we find a profoundly simple statement: *The Father loves the Son.*

Before we can begin to understand how much God loves people, we need to explore the love that the Father has for Jesus. This is not a love that can be comprehended by the human mind. It is a love that exists so far beyond the realms of thought that we can barely begin to imagine such love. We can only hope that as we ask the Spirit of God, He will give us a glimpse of the love that the Father has for Jesus.

Imagine

At this point, we need to stop reading and spend some time meditating on the Father's love for Jesus. Ask the Spirit of God to give you insight and revelation in the knowledge of God's love. Then ask: what does it mean for the Father to love the Son? What is the Father's love for Jesus like?

Take some time to engage your imagination. Imagine being in eternity and seeing the love of God flowing from the Father to the Son and back again. Take your time. Let the Spirit of God open the eyes of your heart to see the Father's love for Jesus like a consuming fire. Take a few minutes to let it all settle in your heart and then come back and continue reading.

How would we describe the Father's love for Jesus? Perfect, infinite, eternal, overwhelming, unbreakable, passionate, intense, unwavering, consuming, intimate, uniting, extravagant, consummate, indescribable, perfectly pure, and beyond all comprehension…All of these words fall short of describing the glory of the Father's love for Jesus. No language could ever convey the depth and quality of the Father's love for Jesus. It is something that far exceeds the greatest love that we could ever dream of. It is absolute, unreserved, awesome, infinite, and wonderfully divine.

Now, how would we describe the Father's love for us?

That the World May Know

John 17:20-23 (NLT)

"I am praying not only for these disciples but also for all who will ever believe in me through their message. I pray that they will all be one, just as you and I are one—as you are in me, Father, and I am in you. And may they be in us so that the world will believe you sent me.

I have given them the glory you gave me, so they may be one as we are one. I am in them and you are in me. May they experience such perfect unity that the world will know that you sent me and that you love them as much as [Greek: *kathos*] you love me."

Here Jesus prays that God would make us one with Him. He wants us to be one with Him so that the world would know that Jesus was sent by God and that the Father loves us *just as much as He loves Jesus*. This truth deserves repeating: The Father loves us just as much as He loves Jesus.

In other words, the passionate, eternal, incomprehensible love that the Father has for Jesus is the same love that the Father feels for us. *It is the same love.* It can take a lot of Spirit-inspired imagination to believe, but it remains true: our Father is as intensely consumed with love for us as He is for Jesus.

John 15:9-11 (NASB)

"Just as [*kathos*] the Father has loved Me, I have also loved you; abide in My love. If you keep My commandments, you will abide in My love; just as I have kept My Father's commandments and abide in His love. These things I have spoken to you so that My joy may be in you, and that your joy may be made full."

Earlier we looked at the Greek word *kathos,* which is used to describe two things that are directly comparable or exactly the same. Here again, Jesus uses the word *kathos* to show us that He loves us in exactly the same way that the Father loves Him!

What this shows is that both the Father and Son only have one setting for their love: FULL ON! There is no turning off or turning down the love of God. His love for the greatest of saints is the same as it is for the greatest of sinners, which is the same as it is for Jesus. This is evident by the fact that it was while we were still sinners that the Father gave His Son for us.[2] Christ's sacrifice was the greatest expression of love that the world has ever seen and will ever see. And it was made *while we were still sinners.* We did not earn God's affection or Jesus' sacrifice. The greatest expression of love in all eternity was shown to us solely because God is love and He cannot deny His own nature. He loves us like we were Jesus Christ appearing before Him. He runs to us and embraces us like He was embracing Jesus Christ. As incredible as it may seem, the Father loves us to the same degree that He loves Jesus.

This is the gospel that the world needs to hear, that the Father loves us all with an unreserved, unending passion. He seeks and saves the lost, taking away our pain and carrying us out of dark alleys because He loves us just as much as He loves Jesus. In all His dealings with us, the Father treats us in exactly the same way that He would treat Jesus—with extravagant, infinite, relentless love. This is the love that God wants to share with the world through us. Are we ready?

Pray

Father, I really want to know and believe the love that you have for me. Holy Spirit, please give me a revelation of the Father's love. I want to experience His love. I want to possess His love. Please make the love of God real in me!

34 | The Simple Gospel

1 John 3:21-23

Beloved, if our heart does not condemn us, we have confidence before God; and whatever we ask we receive from him, because we keep his commandments and do what pleases him. And this is his commandment: that we believe in the name of his Son Jesus Christ and love one another, just as he has commanded us.

This is God's commandment: that we believe in the name (and nature) of his Son Jesus Christ *and* love one another. One commandment, two parts. God commands us not just to believe, but to believe *and* love.

All through Scripture, the Spirit of God interweaves faith and love. In the parable of the wise and foolish builders, Jesus calls us to hear (have faith) and to obey (act in love).[1] In the teaching of the sheep and the goats, Jesus reveals that we are not judged on the quality of our theology but on how we loved Him through one another. Paul writes of faith and love as joining to form one spiritual breastplate and explains that the only thing that matters is faith working through love.[2] Faith and love are so united that both James and John challenge us to measure our faith not by what we believe, but by how much we love others.[3] It is love that gives value and substance to our faith and so we can never separate faith from love.[4] The call to faith is a call to love.

1 Peter 1:22-23

Since you have in obedience to the truth purified your souls for a sincere love of the brethren, fervently love one another from the heart, for you have been born again not of seed which is perishable but imperishable, that is, through the living and enduring word of God.

We can see the connection between faith and love again in this passage. Our souls are purified through faith in the blood of Christ *for* a sincere love of the brethren. Love is the goal.

Gospel of Love

This unity between faith and love needs to be remembered when we share the gospel with people. We are not calling people only to believe in Jesus. We are calling the lost to surrender their entire lives to the love of God.

> **Romans 1:16**
> For I am not ashamed of the gospel, for it is the power of God for salvation to everyone who believes, to the Jew first and also to the Greek.

The gospel is the power of salvation for all those who would believe. Paul calls this good news the "glorious gospel of our blessed God."[5] This good news of God and our design of love is glorious beyond words!

We often think of the gospel in terms of a summary of the message of salvation and new life in Christ. However, the word *gospel* not only refers to the summary version of the message, but it extends to the whole body of Scripture.[6] As we learned earlier, all of Scripture hangs on the first two commands. Therefore, regardless of whether it is in summary or in whole, our gospel must be framed entirely by love. When the love of God infuses our message, there is simply no way we could ever feel ashamed of the gospel.

So, if we were to bring faith and love together when we share the gospel with non-believers, what would we say?

Get Ready

> **Ephesians 6:14-15**
> Stand therefore, having fastened on the belt of truth, and having put on the breastplate of righteousness, and, as shoes for your feet, having put on the readiness [*hetoimos*] given by the gospel of peace.

We are in a battle and we need to make ourselves ready. The Greek word translated as *readiness* is the word *hetoimos*, which means "ready because prepared."[7] God is calling us to prepare ourselves in advance so that we can make the most of our future opportunities to share the gospel of peace. This requires more than building our knowledge of the gospel; to get truly ready, we need to live in the reality of God's design of love. This ensures that not only do we have a personal testimony of love, but we have love itself to share.

> **John 3:16**
> For God so loved the world, that he gave his only Son, that whoever believes in him should not perish but have eternal life.

For centuries we have preached a gospel that has sought to make converts rather than disciples. Why? Because we believed that the goal of Jesus' death was to get us into heaven. We read John 3:16 and we missed the call to union. We thought that eternal life was all about heaven after we die so we made this the focus of our gospel. We wanted to save as many people as we could, so we made entry to heaven as easy as our theology would allow. *Say this prayer and you're in.* But the true goal of the gospel is to lead people into union with Jesus so they can live in their design of love. And this takes time. It takes love. It is so much easier to get someone to say a prayer than it is to truly disciple them into the love of God. But the reward of making disciples is that we can open new channels for the love of God to flow. That makes all the investment more than worthwhile. It also makes sharing our faith with others more than a duty. When we realize how blessed God is to receive the love of His people, our call to make disciples becomes an incredible honor.

The Glorious Gospel

> **John 3:16** (expanded)
> For God loved the world in this way: He gave His one and only Son so that whoever believes into union with Him should not perish, but rather experience eternal life here and now through the ongoing, wholehearted love of God.

John 3:16 has always been used as a one-verse summary of the gospel. But when we read it with a better understanding, we see a better gospel. John 3:16 reveals the reason why Jesus came. He lived, died, and was raised again so that we might be brought back into union with Him. When we become one with the Spirit of Jesus through faith, we begin to experience the reality of eternal life right now. We grow in this life as we share the wholehearted love that Jesus has for the Father. The is the glorious gospel of redemption, love, intimacy, unity, and joy.

If we were to expand on this summary, we could start at the beginning. God is love and has always been love. He never changes. Before creation, God existed (and still exists) in an unimaginably awesome flow of love between the Father and the Son, Jesus Christ. The Father made all of creation as an expression of His love and goodness. Unlike the rest of creation, God specifically created us to live in union with Jesus and have lives that radiate with His love.

Rather than live in love, humanity chose to be selfish--the exact opposite of love. That choice shut down the unique flow of love through our hearts. Because the love of God is so precious, our selfishness created a debt with God that we could never possibly pay back. No amount of works could replace the value of God's love that was lost when we chose to serve ourselves.

To bring us out of our selfishness and back into our design of love, Jesus became human. He revealed the nature of the Father to us and showed us what the love of God is like. He taught us that the first and second commands reveal God's design for our lives and define our identity in Him. Jesus called us to love God by loving one another in humility, sincerity and with resolve. He then died to repay our debt of love and give us a fresh start.

Having been raised from the dead, Jesus has made it possible for anyone to be restored to their design of love. If a person is willing to turn from their old life of selfishness and sin to a life of love, Jesus will forgive them, put His Spirit in them and bring them into unity with Him. If they are willing, Jesus will circumcise their heart, immerse them in His love, energize them with His life, and empower them to love God with all their heart and soul.

Jesus will speak to anyone with a heart to listen. He offers all people eternal life; not just a life in heaven, but life on earth as He designed. This is a life found in loving God, hearing His voice, and living in union with Him. It will cost us our lives—all of our selfishness, all our possessions, everything we are and have—but it will all be worth it. If we come to the cross and offer ourselves to God, He will make an exchange with us. In return for our sin and selfishness, God will give us a life of love that lasts forever. This is the good news. This is the great and glorious gospel. This is why God created us.

I was sharing this with a man on an orchard one afternoon. We had only just met but when he learned of my faith, he wanted to find out more. I shared about my own experience of the love of God and then brought his own experience into the conversation.

"How long does it feel good when you do something selfish?" I asked.

"Not long." He was quick to admit what we all know is true.

"What about when someone shows you love or you do something loving for someone else. How long does that feel good for?"

"Yeah…a long time."

"Did you ever wonder why? It's because God designed you for love. And I think you know it. God is love and He has created you to share His love. That's why love feels so good. That's what life is really all about."

"But are you saying that a billion Muslims and a billion Hindus aren't going to go to heaven?"[8]

"Is getting into heaven the goal?" I asked. "Because according to the Bible it's not. The goal of believing is about having your whole life changed by love. It is not just about getting into heaven after we die. It's about finding life in God's love right now."

The conversation continued and we agreed to meet again over dinner. It can take time for people to process the idea of being designed for love and we do not have to share the whole gospel all at once. We are making disciples rather than converts and so we need to be prepared to go on a journey with people. God is good and no matter how much people lie to themselves, there is a part of their heart that knows they are created for love. No one can deny the truth forever.

In the meantime, God is patient. He keeps waiting and watching for His children to return to His arms. Let us join with the Spirit and call His children back home. Let us take His love into the world and find people who will accept the limitless goodness of the Father. Then let us watch as the Father once again runs to His child and wraps them in His arms. Let us celebrate that His love has once again found its release. And let us not grow weary in our call to love others and to make disciples. For as long as we stay upon our foundations of love, we will always overcome. As Scripture says: the love of God never fails. Love always wins.

Pray

Father, I love you. Thank you for the glorious gospel. Your design for creation is amazing. Lord, I long to see people restored into your love. Please help me to know my identity and to live in the reality of your love so that I'm not just sharing a theory with people. Let it be real. Father, please lead me to people who are ready to respond to the call of love. Help me to meet their need and to reveal your love to them.

35 | Revival Fire

It is an awesome privilege to see people come to faith in Jesus. As wonderful as this is, we need to have a vision that sees beyond conversion and instead focuses on discipleship. How do we disciple someone who wants to follow Jesus? What do we do if whole crowds of people want to follow Jesus? Is it possible to disciple masses of people?

In recent years, God has been giving different people a vision for revival that involves great numbers of people turning to follow Jesus. History has so many stories of how the Spirit of God has brought revival to different places that it is easy to see it happening again. It would be amazing to witness multitudes coming to know God and falling in love with Him.

"Lord, what's the story with revival?" I asked.

"There can be no revival for the holes in the net are too big." God used the imagery of people fishing for souls. I pictured a net with holes so big that the fish swam quietly in and out of the net. Not long after this, our family went on holiday and we took one of Jacob's friends with us. After three days the friend came to us.

"Will you pray for me?" he asked.

"Sure, we'd love to. Do you know God? Have you experienced Him before or heard His voice?" I figured that if he was asking for prayer that he may have a background relationship with God.

"No. Mum took me to church for a couple of years when I was younger, but I've never experienced God or heard His voice."

"Never? You went to a church for two years and you never encountered God?"

"No. After that my sister's boyfriend convinced me that God wasn't real. But after being with you guys, I realize that He is real. Can you pray for me?"

This young man had sat in a church for two years as an unbeliever. Like a fish, he swam through the net every Sunday but was never caught and brought to the shore. *The holes in the net are too big.*

Another friend shared with me his vision for a community event he runs every year.

"I can see 5,000 people coming to faith at this event. If the Spirit of God shows up, I can see thousands getting saved." He spoke with an inspiring passion.

"That would be awesome. But then what? What will you do with them after they are saved?" I was not trying to dampen his vision, but to extend it beyond conversion.

"I hadn't thought of that," he replied. If a massive revival is coming, then we need to start asking these questions. If 5,000 people or more gave their lives to Christ in our town, how could we effectively disciple them all? Right now, the holes in the net are simply too big for the net to hold the harvest. If revival is to come, we need a strong net, tightly bound.

Revival Defined

While the modern church is like a net with large holes, the reality is that God is fixing the net. A great harvest is coming and now is the time to prepare. First we need to ask: what is revival? What does it look like?

Many people have defined revival as an outpouring of the Holy Spirit with lots of signs and wonders, coupled with multitudes of people coming to faith in Jesus. But is this really revival?

> **Psalm 85:6**
> Will you not revive [*chayah*] us again, that your people may rejoice in you?

> **Psalm 19:7**
> The law of the Lord is perfect,
> reviving the soul;
> the testimony of the Lord is sure,
> making wise the simple...[1]

In Scripture, the Hebrew word chayah means "to live, vivify, or infuse life."[2] Likewise, our English word revival (re-vival) means to restore life or bring to life again.

A true revival is not defined by signs or wonders but by the restoration of life. And we have learned how God defines life. Remember the verses in Deuteronomy: *God will circumcise our hearts to love Him with all our heart and soul, so that we might live... Choose life by loving God, obeying His voice and living in union with Him.* Remember Jesus' exchange with the lawyer: *Love the Lord your God with all your heart, soul, mind and strength, and love your neighbor as yourself. Do this and you will live.* When God brings revival, He restores life by drawing us into union with Jesus and empowering us to love God with all our heart and soul. True revival restores the first command to first place. True revival sets people free from their own selfishness into the awesome love of God. True revival brings emotional healing to the heart and restores the capacity for love. This is why Scripture says that "the law of the Lord revives the soul." The power of revival is found in the glorious law of love.

The Glory Shall Cover the Whole Earth

Recently I talked with a man who was visiting from the north. God had given him a vision of the country.

"God showed me a picture of small fires appearing all over New Zealand. As I looked, I saw that each fire was a small group of people, represented by a burning candle. God connected these groups with threads of gold. The gold would weave into the hearts of people and then connect one group to another. From a distance it looked like New Zealand was covered by a net of fire and gold."

Fire represents the love of God in all its refining power and radiant glory.[3] Gold represents the love of God as the currency of greatest value. It is the love of God that burns within the heart and creates the perfect bond of unity.[4] Therefore the net that God is creating is made up of myriads of small groups that are founded on and knit together by love. Each of these groups will shine like a blazing light because of their love for one another. Each group in the net will be unique in expression and yet they will all share the same foundation. They will give to meet each other's needs. They will build each other up. They will equip and empower one another. They will be vulnerable, accepting and real with each other. They will love one another. This love will bring great glory to God and will effortlessly draw in non-believers. When non-believers come into these groups, they will be like fish caught in a strong net. And they will love it.

Not long after this meeting, I had an unexpected visit from a Korean man called David. God had been leading David all over the world to show him what He was doing in different countries. He asked about what God was doing in New Zealand. I shared about revival and the restoration of the Body of Christ into a wholehearted love for God. I shared about how God is bringing together small groups that are based on the first two commands. I shared about how these groups are connecting like a strong net which will hold the coming harvest. We talked for a long time, but there was almost nothing I shared with David that he did not already know.

"This is what God is doing all over the world. People call it different things. But everywhere God is gathering His people into small groups so they can love one another." He mentioned several countries where he had seen this recently: Israel, Korea, France, Australia, Indonesia and more.

Not long after this meeting, God showed me a vision of Tahiti. I saw a river of fire flowing down the side of a volcano. The river was consuming the jungle that had overgrown the ancient foundations and revealing a solid place to build the church: on love and unity with God. God is releasing His river of fire –an intense outpouring of His consuming love—over the islands of Polynesia, just as He is all over the world. **And He is releasing this fire of love through His people.** A few months after I received the vision, God told me to go to Tahiti. While there, I was taken to the home of a woman who was sick. Because of her illness, she spent her days in a chair, praying for Polynesia. As I arrived, the Holy Spirit spoke.

"This woman is like Simeon and Anna in the temple. Tell her that what she has been praying for has begun to come to pass."

I passed on the message and she was deeply encouraged.

"Can I ask what you have been praying for? What has begun to come to pass?" I asked.

"God has shown me a great move of His Spirit across the islands to restore His people into His love. But it will only happen in small groups," she replied.

All over the world God is bringing revival on His terms and in His way. He is reviving the Body of Christ by bringing us back into life as He designed. He is restoring us to love.

The Coming Harvest

Luke 5:4-7

And when he had finished speaking, he said to Simon, "Put out into the deep and let down your nets for a catch." And Simon answered, "Master, we toiled all night and took nothing! But at your word I will let down the nets." And when they had done this, they enclosed a large number of fish, and their nets were breaking. They signaled to their partners in the other boat to come and help them. And they came and filled both the boats, so that they began to sink.

When the disciples brought the net to the shore, the net was at breaking point. This is a picture of the coming revival. God is promising to fill the net to its breaking point. This means that as we inspire more people to become a part of the net, we help to set the stage for a greater revival.

Psalm 107:19-21

Then they cried to the LORD in their trouble,
and he delivered them from their distress.
He sent out his word and healed them,
and delivered them from their destruction.
Let them thank the LORD for his steadfast love,
for his wondrous works to the children of man!

Psalm 107 is a prophetic Psalm for this time in history. The Psalm looks at some of the ways God expresses His love for humanity by bringing us to the end of ourselves. When individuals and even nations become desperate, we turn to God in our distress and find deliverance and love. This is all to God's glory. It is His amazing, steadfast love in action.

We therefore need to see extreme times of need not as a curse but as an opportunity to love people and restore them to God. When the famine comes, we need to maintain our peace, knowing that the Father is drawing His prodigal children back home. We need to be there as living expressions of the Father, watching for the lost, ready to embrace the prodigal and lavish love without reserve.

Workers in the Harvest

> **Matthew 9:36-38** (NASB)
> Seeing the people, He felt compassion for them, because they were distressed and dispirited like sheep without a shepherd. Then He said to His disciples, "The harvest is plentiful, but the workers are few. Therefore beseech the Lord of the harvest to send out workers into His harvest."

When Jesus looked upon the harvest, He saw people who were distressed and dispirited. The harvest was ready. The people were at the end of themselves and yet the laborers were few. So Jesus called His disciples to pray for laborers to bring in the harvest.

The same is true for this time. The harvest is almost ready. We need to pray and ask God to prepare us as laborers for this harvest. Becoming a laborer does not mean that we will need to leave our jobs and go into full-time evangelism. We become laborers in the harvest simply by letting God weave us into His net. All we have to do is devote our lives to the first command and resolve to love one another. If we do this, God will connect us with other believers who also share His heart. As a group, God will then set us on fire and connect us to other groups by threads of love. Once our nets are mended, Jesus will then send us out fishing. And the catch will be great.

Next Step

If you would like to start a small group that is founded on the first two commands, talk to God about it and then talk to other people. Share this book with believers who you think would be open to laying a foundation of love. If people agree with the call of love, then ask if they would like to become a part of the net. All it takes is two or three people to get started.

Pray

Father, I love you. I thank you that you are restoring the greatest command to the highest place. I thank you that you are reviving your people and awakening your Bride. I thank you that we are about to witness an outpouring of your love that will exceed all imagination. I pray for people to be sent out to bring in this harvest. I pray for a multitude of laborers who are willing to share your love and truth with the world. I pray for multitudes to join together to form your net. Jesus, thank you that this is your work and you are doing it. I yield to your will. I pray that every hindrance to your love would be cut away from our lives. Break the chains of selfishness, pride, pain and unforgiveness. Tear down the strongholds. Let your people be healed and bound together by love. Please do whatever it takes to empower us to love one another. And may this be all to your eternal glory!

36 | Freely Give

Get Rich Quick

2 Corinthians 8:9

For you know the grace of our Lord Jesus Christ, that though he was rich, yet for your sake he became poor, so that you by his poverty might become rich.

I have a close friend called Donald who I have met with every few weeks for a number of years. Over that time, he devoted his life to the first and greatest command. One day I asked him a question:

"Imagine someone offered you one billion dollars. The only condition is that you have to give up on pursuing the first command and instead go back to your old Christian life. You can use the money to change the world, go into full-time ministry, or do anything you want, but you can't share the design of wholehearted love with anyone or pursue it yourself. Would you take the money?" Donald did not hesitate in his response.

"Absolutely not. This is who I am. This is at the heart of my identity. I could never sell this," he said with conviction.

"Doesn't it make you feel asset-rich?" I said. "You possess something worth more to you than a billion dollars." Donald smiled.

When we give our lives to the first command, we become rich beyond imagination. This spiritual wealth is only possible because Jesus became poor for our sake. He humbled Himself beyond measure so that we could partake of His nature and find the true, spiritual wealth of divine love. From this perspective of true wealth, I earnestly pray that this book has enriched your life.

Some people may wonder why this book is free.[1] Before I explain, I would like to write that I expect nothing in return for this book. Please be free from even the slightest sense of obligation or indebtedness. For me, this book is not a means of gain, but simply a way of multiplying the spiritual wealth that God has entrusted to me. So if you would like to help me build my treasure in heaven then please, *please,* take hold of your inheritance in the love of Christ and encourage others to do the same. Love God with all your heart and soul. Accept nothing less than your design of wholehearted love and unity with Jesus.

If God has moved your heart with these writings and you would like to give something back, then please start by sharing this book freely with others. If you would like to support our labor of love, then your support is welcome if it is given freely and gladly. The best thing to do is simply to ask the Holy Spirit. Ask Him if He wants to give through you. If you feel led by the Spirit to give, then we have four projects that you can give to:

Freeslaves.org

Freeslaves.org is a Pakistan-based project that we started in 2014. Our main focus is redeeming Christian families from bonded-labor slavery. We place the family in work and connect them with a local fellowship for discipleship. Oftentimes we can redeem enslaved people for as little as $100 each, though the average cost is $200 per person. We also run several schools for enslaved and very poor children. In addition, we provide aid and medical assistance to those in need as well as helping refugees who have fled persecution. We are also working to bring this message of love to the people of Pakistan and prepare His people for revival.

Acacia Media (www.acacia.media)

This project includes all our writing, media, printing, and translation work, including sites like onewithchrist.org and discoverjesus.today. Our vision is to establish Acacia Media with a specific focus on freely publishing media that honors God's design of love.

One Another Project (www.oneanother.net)

This is a website that provides resources and support for small groups that are founded on love. It also provides a way for people to connect to small groups in their area and to be woven into the net. If you have started a group or you would like to connect with group in your area, please feel free to visit www.oneanother.net

To give to any of these projects, please visit **acaciaprojects.org/donate**

Freely Receive, Freely Give

When I first started writing books 18 years ago, I applied the principle of *freely you have received, freely give.* I felt that God had given me a gift that I needed to freely share with others. Around five years ago, a friend dropped by, I think to encourage me.

"You know you're casting your pearls before swine by making the books free. People won't value them if they don't pay for them. What you're doing is stealing from your kids," he told me. I was unsure how to respond at the time. I did some research and found that what he was saying was true. Studies have found that people value and enjoy books more when they pay for them. I decided to talk to God about it.

"Lord, you sowed your seed on all types of ground. Can you tell me: Should we charge for the books or should we sow them freely?" I asked.

It was a warm spring day. As I walked outside, listening for the voice of the Spirit, I saw something I had never seen before. As high and as far as I could see in every direction, cotton-like seeds were floating through the air. The Spirit of God then spoke: *"Sow freely."*

I kept the books free online and found that people from poorer countries in Africa, Asia and South America were reading the books. These were people without credit cards who could not purchase books online. By making the books free, I was able to sow the material into many different countries and reach the poor with the good news. This was the initial reason I kept these books free of charge.

Beyond reaching the poor, this book is free simply because love gives freely. Love gives to meet need and demands nothing in return. As the Body of Christ, we desperately *need* to hear the truth and rediscover who we are in Jesus. We *need* to know what God is like and how we can come into His design of love. We *need* to learn how to return to our first love. We *need* to be inspired to embrace the cross and crucify our selfishness. We *need* to learn to live in covenant love with God and each other. We *need* to discover the unspeakable joy of living in unity with Jesus.

This book is my gift to the Body of Christ to try to meet some of these needs. It is my gift to you. I pray that it has been a blessing to you and that it produces the lasting fruit of love, intimacy, and unity with Jesus in your life. I pray that God would set you free from all legalism and that He would fill you with the strength to contend for love. May you be resolute in your devotion to the first command. May you know the awesome reality of a circumcised heart. May the Spirit of God fill every part of you so that your whole being radiates love for God. I pray that Jesus would weave you into His net of love with other believers. May His faith and love abound in you and may your whole life become a channel of His love. And may you be forever, one with Christ.

Get the Next Books!

First Love was written as the foundation for *Bride Arise* and *And He Will*. So, if you have been blessed by *First Love* then please know: **there is even greater blessing to be found in the next books.** These books have produced some incredible testimonies in people's lives, and I would love you to experience some more amazing encounters with Jesus. Both books are available for free at **onewithchrist.org**

Bride Arise

This book focuses on our journey into knowing Jesus as our Bridegroom. After reading *Bride Arise,* Sarah shared this testimony:

> "At the age of 17, I was sold into slavery. I spent seven years, bound by chains as a sex-slave in Pakistan. Just before my captor was going to kill me, God enabled me to escape and I fled the country. After six years in hiding, I was given a copy of *Bride Arise.* I devoted my life to loving Jesus with all my heart, and He became my Bridegroom! He is just so real to me. He keeps on filling me with love and joy and His love has completely healed me! I can no longer feel any pain in the memory of my slavery; neither is there any bitterness in my heart towards my captor. I am free and I am His bride!" – Sarah W, Asia

Read *Bride Arise* to hear more of this testimony and experience the same awesome love of Christ!

And He Will

This book focuses on our progression into covenant love. In it we learn how to access God's promise to circumcise our heart and bring us into the reality of wholehearted love and unity with Him. Some have said this is the best book of the series, so be sure to read it and experience a deeper realm of covenant love, purity, and unity with Jesus.

ONE WITH CHRIST

onewithchrist.org

Study Guide

As mentioned in the introduction, one of the goals of this book is to help the reader come into a deeper experience the love of God. This section contains questions and meditations to help you open your heart to His love. These can be used for personal or group study, and you are of course free to write your own questions or meditate on different Scriptures for each chapter.

Take your time with these reflections and do them with the Holy Spirit. It is His role to lead us into reality, so lean on Him for insight with the questions, and ask Him to inspire your imagination as you meditate on His word. Be sure that God is good; He wants to connect with you, to love you, and to be one with you. Invite Him to meet with you as you do the reflections and you can be certain He will come.

1. Revelation and Reality

Reflect

What is a promise that God has given to me?

Is that promise impressed on my heart?

How can I nurture that promise to reality?

Imagine

Psalm 23:1

The LORD is my Shepherd, I shall not want.

Take a verse or passage that the Spirit has been bringing to life lately. If no verse comes to mind, use Psalm 23:1. Take some time to meditate on the verse. Ask God to sanctify your imagination. Let Him bring life to your senses and emotions as you imagine what it would be like for that verse to be a reality in your life.

2. By Design

Why would God create anything?

Does everything have to have a purpose?

What things give me a lasting sense of satisfaction and fulfilment?

Are these things a part of God's design for me?

Imagine

Ecclesiastes 2:11

Then I considered all that my hands had done and the toil I had expended in doing it, and behold, all was vanity and a striving after wind, and there was nothing to be gained under the sun.

Imagine living without purpose and striving after the wind. Now imagine coming to know your true design and identity. What is that design? What does it look like? How does it feel to move from a place of vanity into a place of meaning and purpose?

3. First Things First

Reflect

Do I believe in my heart that it is possible to love God with my entire being?

If no, then why not? What does this suggest about God?

If yes, then how is it possible? Is the first command the top priority in my life?

Is there anywhere in the Bible that clearly says if it is possible for us to keep the first commandment?

Imagine

Luke 10:25-28

And behold, a lawyer stood up to put him to the test, saying, "Teacher, what shall I do to inherit eternal life?" He said to him, "What is written in the Law? How do you read it?" And he answered, "You shall love the Lord your God with all your heart and with all your soul and with all your strength and with all your mind, and your neighbor as yourself." And he said to him, "You have answered correctly; do this, and you will live."

Imagine approaching Jesus and asking Him, "What must I do to have eternal life?" Imagine Jesus looking you in the eyes and saying: "_____, just love God with all your heart, soul, mind and strength, and love your neighbor as yourself. Do this and you will live." Imagine what it feels like to hear Him speak those words personally to you.

4. Love in Union

Reflect

Have I been striving in my own strength to live a good life?

How can I come to a place of absolute surrender?

What does it mean to be yoked with Christ? How would that look?

Imagine

2 Corinthians 13:5b

...do you not realize this about yourselves, that Jesus Christ is in you?

Imagine the Spirit of Jesus filling your inner being with His presence. Imagine feeling His strength within you as He lifts away your burdens. Imagine Him pouring His love into every part of you. Imagine that love radiating back to God in wholehearted affection.

5. A Movement into Union

Reflect

What does it mean to believe into Jesus?

If I were to describe the gospel in terms of unity with Jesus, what would I say?

What would it look like to replace areas of striving in my life with surrender?

Imagine

1 Corinthians 6:17
But he who is joined to the Lord becomes one spirit with Him.

To really grasp the reality of being one spirit with Jesus takes an ongoing investment of faith-based imagination. Memorize this verse. Take some time to imagine yourself living in unity with Jesus. Imagine the Spirit of Jesus overwhelming your own spirit and making it one with Him. Imagine His love flowing through your heart and filling your soul and mind. Imagine Jesus sharing His feelings and thoughts with you. How does it feel?

6. What is Life?

Reflect

Do I want to love God more, hear His voice more, and live in greater unity with Him?

Do I want to choose life?

Is there a cost to choosing life?

Imagine

2 Corinthians 5:14-15

For the love of Christ controls us, because we have concluded this: that one has died for all, therefore all have died; and he died for all, that those who live might no longer live for themselves but for him who for their sake died and was raised.

Imagine Jesus approaching you with a gift. Imagine Him offering you the gift of a new life of eternal love. You know it will cost you your old life to accept the gift. You will no longer be able to live for yourself. It may cost you your reputation, your career, maybe even your family or friends. If you take hold of the gift, love will come to define you—you will forever live only for the love of God and others. Imagine looking into His eyes as He holds the gift out to you.

7. What is Love?

Reflect

Am I in the nest, am I falling, or am I flying?

Is there anything I need to let go of in order to learn to fly?

What is love to me?

Imagine

Deuteronomy 32:*11-12*

Like an eagle that stirs up its nest,
 that flutters over its young,
spreading out its wings, catching them,
 bearing them on its pinions,
the Lord alone guided him,
 no foreign god was with him.

Imagine a young eagle chick, leaving the nest for the first time. Imagine it falling through the air and then stretching its wings. Imagine what it would feel like for that eagle to discover flight for the first time.

God has prepared a life for you beyond your imagination. Imagine taking a step of faith into that life. Imagine the thrill of feeling the love of God fill your inner being and flow through you. Imagine Him stretching His wings within you and soaring with you towards the heights of love.

8. Love and Life

Reflect

Can I make myself more deserving of His love?

When was the last time I experienced the warmth that comes from showing love to someone?

Am I mixing selfishness with love?

How can I overcome my selfishness?

Imagine

1 John 3:18
Little children, let us not love in word or talk but in deed and in truth.

Imagine seeing someone in need. Imagine acting in love to meet their need. Imagine a sense of unity and peace flooding your being as you love. Imagine finding your identity in the act of love.

9. Circumcision of the Heart

Reflect

Do I want to choose life today?

Does God really want to circumcise my heart?

What would it be like to be free from selfishness?

If the Jesus asked me, "*What would you like me to give you today?*" What would I say?

Imagine

Deuteronomy 30:6 (NASB)
"Moreover the LORD your God will circumcise your heart and the heart of your descendants, to love the LORD your God with all your heart and with all your soul, in order that you may live."

To fully appreciate the promise of verse six, we need to engage our imagination. Spend a few minutes reading and re-reading this verse until you have it memorized. Once memorized, take ten minutes away from distraction and meditate only on this verse. Dwell on each phrase. Repeat the words. Receive the promise.

Imagine God speaking these words directly to you: _____, *I will circumcise your heart to love me with all your heart and with all your soul, so that you may live.* Imagine God fulfilling His promise. Imagine what it would feel like for God to cut out of your heart everything that resists His love. Imagine the Spirit filling you with His presence and love. Imagine your heart beating with love for God and your whole being resonating with love. Imagine being alive.

10. One Spirit

Reflect

What is my most valuable possession and who is my closest relationship?

Have I surrendered these to God?

What would life be like with a *shema* heart?

Am I abiding in the Spirit of God?

Imagine

Luke 3:16

John answered them all, saying, "I baptize you with water, but he who is mightier than I is coming, the strap of whose sandals I am not worthy to untie. He will baptize you with the Holy Spirit and fire."

Imagine waiting on God. Imagine just quietly worshipping God. Then imagine feeling a fire fall upon you. Imagine that fire slowly immersing you, but like the burning bush you are not hurt or consumed. Imagine that fire entering your inner being and washing your soul.[1] Imagine it consuming all your pain and brokenness. Imagine the fire blazing within your heart as an intense love for God.

Philippians 2:13

...for it is God who works in you, both to will and to work for his good pleasure.

Or take some time to memorize this verse. Spend some time dwelling on it. Imagine God filling you with His desires. Imagine His Spirit filling you with energy and enabling you to act on His desires. What desire is He placing in you? How does that look in action?

11. Higher Ways

Write

Matthew 20:32

And stopping, Jesus called them and said, "What do you want me to do for you?"

"What do you want me to do for you?" Jesus had heard the blind men call out for Him and so He stopped and offered them His help. What an incredible moment in time. The One for whom and through whom the whole universe was created—Jesus Christ Himself—stopped and asked these men, *"What do you want me to do for you?"* I often think about how I would respond to this question in different situations. But why wonder? Let us take a minute to share our thoughts with God. Quiet your heart and imagine Jesus approaching you and asking:

(Your name) _____, what do you want me to do for you?
Take a pen and paper or use this space, and write your response:

Now, let us turn the question back to God and believe that He will share His thoughts with us. Take some time and seek to write from the heart rather than the mind. Do not worry about the content of what you are writing right now—we will come back to it in the future and test what we hear or see. For now, just wait on God and ask Him to inspire your imagination. By faith take the thread of a quiet thought and see where it leads.

Now ask: Jesus, what do you want to do for me?

His response:

Reflect

How can I tell if what I have written is really God's voice or not?

Do I want to be able to hear God in this way?

Imagine

Exodus 33:11a

Thus the LORD used to speak to Moses face to face, as a man speaks to his friend.

Imagine that like Moses, you could have a two-way conversation with God and speak with Him like a friend. What would you talk about?

12. The Source of Thoughts

Reflect

Have I experienced thoughts that turned out to be from God?

Have I thought I heard God's voice, but it turned out to be something else?

Am I taking my thoughts captive?

Imagine

Psalm 40:5

You have multiplied, O Lord my God,
  your wondrous deeds and your thoughts toward us;
  none can compare with you!

Imagine God thinking wonderous thoughts of love towards you. Imagine Jesus thinking more thoughts about you than you could ever count with greater love than you could ever measure. Imagine leaning against Jesus' chest and listening as He whispers His thoughts to you.

Write

Jesus, is there a thought that you'd like to share with me today?

13. Testing Thoughts

Reflect

Is it possible that I have confused a religious spirit with the voice of God?

How can I know for sure that I am hearing the thoughts of God?

How can I practice hearing God's voice?

Imagine

John 16:13

When the Spirit of truth comes, he will guide you into all the truth, for he will not speak on his own authority, but whatever he hears he will speak, and he will declare to you the things that are to come.

As we learned earlier, the word *truth* here is the Greek word *aletheia,* which means "true to fact; reality."[2] The Holy Spirit is the Spirit of reality. He speaks the truth to us in order to take us into the reality of that truth.

Take some time to meditate on this verse. Imagine the Spirit of God speaking to you. Imagining Him exposing any lies you believe about God and teaching you the truth about His love. Imagine the Spirit teaching you how to recognize the sound of His voice. Imagine Him releasing life into you through every word and bringing you into reality.

Write

Lord, is there anyone that I could join with who would help me to practice hearing your voice?

14. Making Agreements

Reflect

What are some of the strongholds of my mind?

What lies are those strongholds built upon?

How can I build a stronghold of love?

Is the world truly full of God's love for me?

Write

Father, what are the agreements or strongholds in my life that you are breaking?

Imagine

Revelation 3:20
"Behold, I stand at the door and knock. If anyone hears my voice and opens the door, I will come in to him and eat with him, and he with me."

Imagine that Jesus is surveying your soul for a place to build His home. Imagine Him coming to the stronghold of your heart and calling your name. Will you open the gates to Him? Will you help Him to remove the rubble of your own self-defenses? Will you help Him to build a stronghold of love?

15. A New Identity

Reflect

Is it possible to put on the new self without putting off the old self?

Have I experienced the reality of being crucified with Christ?

How would my thinking change by adding *We*?

Imagine

Psalm 17:15 (BSB)
As for me, I will behold Your face in righteousness;
when I awake, I will be satisfied in Your presence.

Imagine waking up each morning in the presence of God. Imagine waking to see Jesus watching over you and waiting for you. Imagine Him present throughout your whole day, enjoying being with you and talking with you. Imagine Him sharing His thoughts with you and changing the way you think.

Write

Lord Jesus, what is one area of my life where you want me to start thinking "We"?

16. Identity in Love

Reflect

Is God really this good?

Does God really want to bless me with such extravagance?

What is keeping me from receiving the awesome love of God?

Imagine

Luke 15:20

"And he arose and came to his father. But while he was still a long way off, his father saw him and felt compassion, and ran and embraced him and kissed him."

Imagine returning to the Father. Imagine seeing the delight in the Father's eyes as He sees you. Imagine watching the Father run towards you with arms outstretched. Imagine feeling His embrace as He wraps His arms around you. Imagine feeling His love.

Write

Father, how much do you love me?

17. Prevailing Grace

Reflect

Am I more comfortable relating to God as my Father or as my Employer?

Have I tried to attain blessings through spiritual principles?

Are all the blessings of God truly mine in Christ Jesus?

Imagine

Luke 15:21-24

"And the son said to him, 'Father, I have sinned against heaven and before you. I am no longer worthy to be called your son.' But the father said to his servants, 'Bring quickly the best robe, and put it on him, and put a ring on his hand, and shoes on his feet. And bring the fattened calf and kill it, and let us eat and celebrate. For this my son was dead, and is alive again; he was lost, and is found.' And they began to celebrate."

Imagine coming before the Father. Imagine Him presenting you with a robe of glory. Imagine Him presenting you with a ring that signifies the highest authority in the universe. Imagine Him offering you shoes of humility for your feet. Do you feel worthy? What is your response? Would you like to try to earn these gifts?

Write

Father, is there any area in my life where I've been trying to earn your blessing?

18. Relationship and Religion

Reflect

Do I identify with the Pharisees in any way?

Do I delight in reading the word of God?

If legalism is a deception, how can I know if I am deceived or not?

Imagine

> **1 John 4:16**
> So we have come to know and to believe the love that God has for us.
> God is love, and whoever abides in love abides in God, and God abides
> in him.

Imagine coming into a true revelation of just how much God loves you.
Imagine truly believing in His limitless love for you. Imagine what it would
feel like to know that you never have to try to earn God's affection ever again.
How would your life be different?

Write

Father, how are you expressing your love and goodness towards me?

19. Life in Love

Imagine

Psalm 46:10a (NASB)

Cease striving and know that I am God.

Imagine coming before the presence of God. Imagine hearing Him say: *"Cease striving! Enough! Stop trying so hard. I love you more than you could ever know, for I am Love. Be still and know that I am God, that I love you, I like you, and I will always be with you. You are beautiful to me."*

Write

Write your own question for the Lord:

20. Breaking the Cycle

Reflect

Have I ever been caught in a cycle of striving and sin?

What has led me to sin in the past?

Is there still some brokenness in my heart that might lead me to sin?

If so, am I willing to let God heal my brokenness?

Write

Father is there any area in my heart that you want to heal?

Imagine

Matthew 11:28-29

Come to me, all who labor and are heavy laden, and I will give you rest. Take my yoke upon you, and learn from me, for I am gentle and lowly in heart, and you will find rest for your souls.

Imagine coming to Jesus. Imagine Him speaking these words to you:
"_____, *I want to give you rest. Let me take your burdens, your stress, your exhaustion, your pain, and your failure. In exchange, I will give you my yoke. Take it upon you and learn from me, for I am gentle and humble in heart. Together we will do my work and you will find rest for your soul. Let's be one together. I love you.*"

21. Crime and Punishment

Reflect

Is the judgment of God a good thing?

Do I ever need to fear being punished or making God angry?

Am I truly sick of my sin?

Write

Father, is it true that I have nothing to fear in you?

Imagine

Romans 8:15

For you did not receive the spirit of slavery to fall back into fear, but you have received the Spirit of adoption as sons, by whom we cry, "Abba! Father!"

Imagine the love of God filling your heart and soul. Imagine it expelling all fear and legalism from your life. Imagine being completely free to embrace the fullness of God's love for you.

22. Sin and Deception

Reflect

Have I been tolerating any sin in my life?

Am I carrying any unhealed scars of sin?

Have I been hiding any sin? If so, why?

Do I need to take some extreme measures against sin?

Write

Father, how do you see me?

Imagine

John 8:31-32, 36

So Jesus said to the Jews who had believed him, "If you abide in my word, you are truly my disciples, and you will know the truth, and the truth will set you free...So if the Son sets you free, you will be free indeed."

Imagine Jesus sharing the truth with you and breaking the chains of legalism and license from your heart and mind. Imagine Him cutting into your heart and taking away your selfishness and every instinct to sin. Imagine Him replacing it with His instinct of love. Imagine living a life that is energized by His love.

23. Teaching Grace

Reflect

Is the first command defining my vision for life?

Does it shape the way I view life?

Have I made my love for others conditional on their behavior?

How can I make my ordinary work an expression of love?

Do I want more discipline in my life?

Imagine

Deuteronomy 6:4

"Hear, O Israel: The LORD our God, the LORD is one! You shall love
the LORD your God with all your heart, with all your soul, and with
all your strength."

Take some time to memorize and meditate on this verse. What does it mean
to love God with all your heart? What does it mean to love with all your soul
and with all your strength? Imagine the love of God flowing into your heart
and soul and bringing life to your inner being. Imagine moving from being
a container of love to becoming a channel of God's love. Where will His love
flow to now?

Write

Father, how would you like to flow your love through me today?

24. Love in Eternity

Reflect

How can I prepare for eternity?

Does my history feel like it has been a long time?

How can I make the most of my future?

Am I willing to take a risk of love with Jesus?

Write

Father, what do you want to teach me about your love today?

Father, is there a risk that we can take together today?

Imagine

Psalm 144:4
Man is like a breath; his days are like a passing shadow.

Take some time to memorize this Scripture and write it on your heart. Then take a deep breath. Breathe out. *Man is like a breath.* Imagine the rest of your life passing in a moment of time. What happened in that moment?

Imagine falling to sleep and awakening in eternity. Imagine seeing yourself clothed in the glory of your love. Imagine seeing Jesus. Do you kneel? Do you fall down in worship? Or do you run to Him and embrace Him?

25. Multiplying Love

Reflect

What difference is there whether I use my gifts and abilities with love or without love?

Why does God let us use our spiritual gifts and natural talents without love?

What do I need from Jesus today?

Write

Write your own question to God and write His response. Then test what you have written.

Imagine

Revelation 3:18

I counsel you to buy from me gold refined by fire, so that you may be rich, and white garments so that you may clothe yourself and the shame of your nakedness may not be seen, and salve to anoint your eyes, so that you may see.

Imagine Jesus offering you gold refined in the fire. Imagine Him offering you white garments. Imagine being clothed in His glory. What will you do with the gold?

26. Love Like This

Reflect

How easy is it for me to be honest with God?

Do I want to be real with other people?

Am I am carrying an offence against anyone?[3]

What is the cost to God of a broken relationship?

Write

Father, is there someone I need to forgive? Or is there a relationship that needs repairing or refreshing?

Imagine

John 13:35

By this all people will know that you are my disciples, if you [continually] have love for one another.

Take a moment to memorize this verse. Imagine what it would be like to know people who deeply and selflessly love you. Imagine what it would feel like for the love of the Father to flow through you to His people. Imagine what your gatherings with those people would be like. How would the world be different if we became known for our intense love for God and for one another?

27. Loving and Giving

Reflect

How much am I loving God *through His people* right now?

Am I willing to embrace dependency on God so that our intimacy can grow?

How can I create a greater sense of dependency on God?

Is there someone I know who might be in need?

Imagine

Philippians 4:19
And my God will supply every need of yours according to his riches
in glory in Christ Jesus.

Love always meets need. Because God loves us, He promises to supply all our needs. So present any needs you have to God and leave them with Him. Imagine never having to worry about your own needs ever again. Imagine God providing for *all* your needs—financial, material, relational, emotional, and more. Imagine the joy and confidence of Christ filling you. Imagine the intimacy that would come as you see God meeting your need.

Now imagine the love of God flowing through you. Imagine seeing someone in need. Imagine looking into their eyes and seeing Jesus, living in need within them. What would you do to meet their need?

Write

Father, is there an area in my life that you are calling on me to depend on you?

Father, is there a need we can meet today?

28. Giving in Unity

Reflect

How can I help to create a culture of giving to meet needs in my fellowship?

Am I truly generous? Why? Or why not?

Am I giving in unity with Jesus?

Is giving risky?

Imagine

1 Peter 1:22

Since you have in obedience to the truth purified your souls for a sincere love of the brethren, fervently love one another from the heart...

Read over this verse a few times slowly. Imagine the blood of Christ purifying your soul for love. Imagine your soul being made completely clean and then being filled with the intense love of Christ. Imagine sharing that love with others. Imagine fervently loving others from your heart.

Write

Father, what have you given me to give away?

29. Love Discerns

Reflect

When I talk with people, do I spend more time talking or listening?

Do I listen to people to sense their heart and discover their need?

How can I grow in my discernment?

Are my emotions helping me to love others?

Write

Father, what do I need today?

Imagine

Philippians 1:9-11

And it is my prayer that your love may abound more and more, with knowledge and all discernment, so that you may approve what is excellent, and so be pure and blameless for the day of Christ, filled with the fruit of righteousness that comes through Jesus Christ, to the glory and praise of God.

May our love abound in knowledge and all discernment. Imagine training your powers of discernment through practice and developing detailed and accurate discernment. How would it change the way you love?

30. Will of God

Reflect

How good is God?

Is there anything in my heart that fears His will?

What is one of my greatest desires?

Does God share that desire with me?

Write

Father, here is one of my desires: I long for _____. What is your desire concerning this?

Imagine

James 1:17
Every good gift and every perfect gift is from above, coming down from the Father of lights, with whom there is no variation or shadow due to change.

Imagine coming before the Father and laying your desire down like a gift before Him. Imagine Him taking the gift and then drawing from His heart a desire of His own. Imagine Him carefully holding this desire like a precious jewel and then offering it to you. Imagine it entering your heart. How does it feel? What is the desire? How precious is that desire to you?

31. Founded in Love

Reflect

How can I simplify my life so I can love more?

Can I live according to my needs so that I can meet the needs of others?

How can I use what I have to love others?

How can I create more time for love?

Write

Father, are you giving me your grace to make a change in my life today?

Imagine

Psalm 1:1-3

Blessed is the man who walks not in the counsel of the wicked,
    nor stands in the way of sinners, nor sits in the seat of scoffers;
    but his delight is in the law of the Lord, and on his law he meditates
    day and night.
He is like a tree planted by streams of water that yields its fruit in its
    season, and its leaf does not wither.
In all that he does, he prospers.

Take some time to wait on God. Imagine your life like a tree. Imagine feeling your roots grow down and tap into living waters. Imagine your life flowing from a living foundation of love. How would a foundation of love change your life? How would it feel to have the love of Christ give direction and meaning to your life?

32.   All of You

Reflect

Am I loving people by calling them into their design of wholehearted love?

Do I have friends who are inspiring me to pursue my design of love?

Is love my primary goal when I meet with others?

How can I help to restructure my fellowship with other believers so that we build on a foundation of love together?

Write

Father, are you calling me to build a foundation of love with a few others?[4]

Imagine

Hebrews 10:24-25

And let us consider how to stir up one another to love and good works, not neglecting to meet together, as is the habit of some, but encouraging one another, and all the more as you see the Day drawing near.

This passage calls us to consider how we can stir one another up to love and good works. Take some time to write these verses on your heart. Imagine meeting with a few other believers and stirring each other up to keep the first and second commands of love. Imagine the Spirit of Jesus being present in those meetings. Imagine Him pouring out His love and wisdom as He interacts with each person. What would those meetings look like?

33. Infinite Love

Reflect

Do I really know or believe how much God loves me?

Do I know how much God loves the people around me?

Would the Father share His love for people with me?

Write

Father, do you really love me as much as you love Jesus? Is that even possible?

Imagine

John 17:22-23 (NLT)

I have given them the glory you gave me, so they may be one as we
are one. I am in them and you are in me. May they experience such
perfect unity that the world will know that you sent me and that you
love them as much as you love me."

If you skipped the imagination section, take some time now to focus on this
passage. Meditate on the Father's love for Jesus. Imagine being one with
Jesus. Imagine the Father loving you with the same love that He has for Jesus.
Imagine His love burning so powerfully within you that people around you
start to see the fire of His love in your eyes. Imagine sharing the love of God
with others.

34. The Simple Gospel

Reflect

Can I share the gospel with others if I'm not actually living in love?

Can I share the truth without love?

Am I willing to invest time in making disciples?

Imagine

Luke 14:23

"And the master said to the servant, 'Go out to the highways and hedges and compel people to come in, that my house may be filled.'"

Imagine being asked by the Father to call people to His great banquet. Imagine going to people and sharing the love of God with them. Imagine them responding to the call and falling in love with Jesus.

Write

Father, is there someone I can share your love with today? If so, how?

35. Revival Fire

Reflect

Do I want to be a laborer in this harvest?

What would it look like if the Spirit poured out revival in my life, my family, my community, my city or even my nation?

Have I reached the end of myself?

Write

Father, do you want to weave me into your net?

Imagine

Daniel 7:9-10 (NASB)
"I kept looking Until thrones were set up,
    And the Ancient of Days took His seat;
    His vesture was like white snow
    And the hair of His head like pure wool.
"His throne was ablaze with flames,
    Its wheels were a burning fire.
"A river of fire was flowing
    And coming out from before Him;
    Thousands upon thousands were attending Him,
    And myriads upon myriads were standing before Him;
    The court sat,
    And the books were opened."

Imagine seeing the river of fire flow from God's throne into your heart. Imagine the fire of God's love consuming every barrier to love. Imagine it burning within you. Imagine sharing that love with others.

36.   Freely Give

Reflect

How can I make others rich?

Is there anyone I can share this message of love with?

Pray

Father, thank you for your love! Please let your love be multiplied through me. Please let me share your love with others and help them to come into their design of love. Let us all become one with you in the glory of your eternal love.

Imagine

1 Corinthians 16:14
Let all that you do be done in love.

Imagine having a limitless supply of love. Imagine that love infusing every word you speak, everything you do, and everything you have. What would you do in your limited time with unlimited love?

Write

Father, how can I help to spread the gospel of love?

Would you like me to share this book with anyone?

Would you like me to support any of the projects mentioned in this book?

Would you like me to start reading the next book, Bride Arise?

Reference Notes

Introduction

[1] This question is taken from *The Little Book of Thunks: 260 Questions to Make Your Brain go Ouch!* by Ian Gilbert, Crown House Publishing, 2007.

1. Revelation and Reality

[2] In 1 Timothy 1:5, Scripture says that the goal of teaching is love from a pure heart. This book shares this goal and so if you do not experience God's love as you read *First Love*, then I have failed. So I humbly ask that you help me not to fail by opening your heart to love and investing time in connecting with God through the reflections. Your experience of love will be my reward.

[1] HELPS Word Study #225

[2] The Scriptures use parables, metaphors, symbols, types, and pictorial language devices (such as the imperfect aspect) deliberately to inspire the imagination.

[3] God knows how I like French baking, especially croissants. It was humbling to experience His love going beyond just meeting my basic need for food but blessing me with food that He knew I loved.

2. By Design

[1] The philosophy of selfishness is passed down to the next generation through our education systems. Western education teaches us that we evolved by chance through countless random changes to our genetic code. According to evolution, it is the "selfish gene" that is the driving force behind all life, motivating us to protect our own lives and pass our genes on to the next generation. Yet we cannot teach a creatorless evolution without exploring the impact of such a belief on our design, ethics, purpose, and value in life. Evolution values people according to the quality of their genes. If you are strong, beautiful, intelligent, or physically symmetrical then you are more valuable than other people. If you are weak, less attractive, homosexual, infertile, disabled, or less intelligent than others then you have less value to society. To the selfish gene, it is not personal. It is just the way it is: if you cannot contribute positively to the next generation then you have little or no value in the big picture of life.

Thankfully, the reality is that the universe did not create itself. It was created by a God of love with a specific design and purpose in mind. As part of His creation, God has said that all of us are fearfully and wonderfully made, and that each one of us is immensely valuable to Him. In order to experience the value that God has invested in us, we need to embrace His design for our lives.

3. First Things First

[1] Thayer's Greek Lexicon #1078

[2] Note that many commentators believe the term *genesis face* mentioned here refers to our state at our natural birth, being inherently sinful (Psalm 51:5). From this perspective, being a doer of the word would mean turning from sin and "putting aside all filthiness and all that remains of wickedness" (verse 21). This may well be true on one level for the Bible often describes the sin and selfishness that ravages the heart of humanity. But the Bible is so much more than a list of good and evil. It is a revelation of the God of love and His design for us. The principle of looking into the mirror of the word equally applies to the *genesis face* of our new birth in Christ. If we read the word of God and behold the image of Jesus and our life in Him, but we do not then act on that image, we are like people who stray from our true identity and forget who we really are. The message is clear: we need to abide in the word of God to discover the reality of who we are and then let the word of God change our identity and our actions.

[3] Matthew 5:48, Ephesians 4:2

[4] 1 Peter 1:22, 1 Thessalonians 5:17

4. Love in Union

[1] This parable is an invented story, not found in the Bible.

[2] When we try to do it alone, we draw on our own strength, break free from Christ's yoke, and quickly tire. But when we embrace our weakness and lean on Jesus as the source and power of our obedience, we find that His strength is limitless. Through our union with Jesus we discover the truth that God's grace is present and His power is perfected in our weakness (2 Corinthians 12:9-10).

[3] Matthew 23:4

[4] If we combine lexical entries from HELPS Word Study #10c (SN 1692) and the NAS Old Testament Hebrew Lexicon, we find that *davaq* means: to stick like glue, to be strongly connected by a strong bond, to become one with (in the sense of sexual union), to stay close, to stick with, follow closely, join to, overtake, catch.

5. A Movement into Union

[1] It is important to note that *eis* can change its meaning and nuance in different contexts. With this in mind, in John 3:16 and other places, it is not necessarily incorrect to translate *eis* with the word *in*, but by doing so the text loses the underlying sense of unity contained in the word *eis*.

[2] We will look more at the Law and what it means to enter into union with Jesus in the coming chapters.

[3] 1 Corinthians 1:30

[4] Psalm 139:17-18, 1 Corinthians 2:9-16, John 16:13. We will look more at sharing the thoughts of God in the coming chapters.

6. What is Life?

[1] It is noted that there is a significant difference in meaning between the Greek word *psyxē*, the Hebrew word *nephesh*, and the English word *soul*. See HELPS Word Study #5590 and #H5135 to explore the concept of the soul in Scripture.

[2] We can see this again in the way the sentence is constructed in the Greek. In both Greek and Hebrew, words that are emphasized are moved to the front of a phrase or sentence to give them focus. In this verse, the phrase *eternal life* is written as *life eternal* (*zoe aionion*). This puts the focus on life (that lasts forever) rather than on the eternal nature of life. Readers can discover the emphasis of the original Hebrew and Greek texts in *The Discovery Bible* (www.thediscoverybible.com).

[3] Because Jesus has conquered death and can never again die, when we are in union with Jesus, we cannot die even though our bodies expire. This is why Scripture speaks of physical death like sleeping—it is not the loss of life that we think it is, and it does nothing to diminish our love for God. After our bodies die, we will spend all of eternity living in the love and unity with Jesus that we have developed in this life.

7. What is Love?

[1] HELPS Word Study #25

[2] Analytical Lexicon of the Greek New Testament, Timothy Friberg, Barbara Friberg and Neva F. Mille. 2006, ἀγάπη.

[3] A Critical and Exegetical Commentary on the Epistle to the Galatians, Burton, Ernest DeWitt, p519

[4] Adam Clarke's Commentary, Matthew 22:37

[5] Thayer's Greek Lexicon, 25: ἀγαπάω

[6] An unnamed lexicon writer, quoted in Adam Clarke's Commentary, Matthew 22:37

8. Love and Life

[1] See *Born for Love: Why Empathy Is Essential--and Endangered,* by Bruce Perry and Maia Szalavitz, 2010 published by William Morrow (Harper Collins). See also work by Dr. Tiffany Fields at the Touch Research Centre at the University of Miami. Note that it is not only young babies that need love.

[2] *Loneliness and social isolation as risk factors for mortality: A meta-analytic review.* Perspectives on Psychological Science, 10, 227-237, Holt-Lunstad, J., Smith, T. B., Baker, M., Harris, T., & Stephenson, D. (2015).

[3] It should be noted that not all selfish actions give this sense of reward. Rather it is only those that we have attached reward to through the experience of previous pleasure or benefit.

The biochemistry of highs and addiction is complex and far beyond the scope of this material. Suffice to say that dopamine has a number of functions, one of which is to stimulate the reward center of the brain. This stimulation creates a high based upon the anticipated reward of an action. This then motivates a person to repeat a behavior for future reward. The more we feed this cycle, the more engrained it becomes until it reaches the point of addiction.

[4] These changes can be very small and easily missed by the "high" of selfishness but over time they culminate to create an atmosphere of lovelessness and death in a person's life. I wonder if the culture of selfishness is partially responsible for making depression such a prevalent heath issue in the modern world. I also wonder if part of an effective treatment for people on the downward spiral is to experience the effects of love by actively meeting the needs of others.

[5] Science confirms the devastating effects of ongoing stress on the brain and body. The body is beautifully designed to deal with short-term stress such as responding to emergencies. During a stressful situation, our bodies go into a kind of overdrive. The brain accelerates our physical function and ability by producing cortisol. Cortisol sets off a cascade of events within our bodies leading to raised glucose levels which enable the maximum amount of energy to be spent in responding to the stress or threat. Our hearts pump faster, our muscles have more strength, and we are able to perform at significantly higher levels. However, this all comes at a cost. This cost is minimal when the stress is momentary, but over time the constant presence of stress takes a damaging toll on the body and brain. God simply did not design us for a life of constant stress. He designed us for love, joy, freedom and peace.

[6] Again, the biochemistry of the brain is complex, and it is acknowledged that the treatment of both oxytocin and dopamine in this context is a simplification of the actual processes that occur in the brain.

[7] See https://en.wikipedia.org/wiki/Oxytocin for a brief overview of oxytocin.

[8] Colossians 3:14

[9] This is true for all people. God has given all of us—believers and unbelievers alike—the same inner-architecture which is designed to resonate with love. This is why whenever we give, receive, or witness love, we feel alive with a sense of wholeness, happiness, and lasting satisfaction. For this reason, many people are drawn to humanitarian and charity work. Finding fulfillment in loving others is a part of the universal human design. Yet Scripture defines real life as not just the love of others, but as the love of God. If we disconnect love from its source, we will only ever find a superficial experience of life. True life can only be found in the wholehearted *love of God.*

[10] We can often experience a sense of profound purpose and meaning in love, which can shape our whole outlook on identity and being. Rather than the philosophical *I think, therefore I am;* our whole sense of design as humans is found in loving others—*I love, therefore I am.*

9. Circumcision of the Heart

[1] 2 Timothy 3:2

[2] I am sure that some people will argue that we can love from selfish motives, saying that we love others because it feels good to us. Love certainly involves a lasting sense of self-fulfillment, but enjoying this sense of fulfillment is not selfish in the sense of gratifying the carnal or old self. The old self does not seek the true joy of love at all. It seeks gratification of its many lusts. Rather, the joy of love is sought after by the true self, what Scripture calls the "new self, which in the likeness of God has been created in righteousness and holiness of the truth." (Ephesians 4:24)

[3] To love God with all our strength means that all our energy, material wealth and all our resources are devoted to love. The short amount of time we have been given in this life is one of our greatest resources for love.

[4] Note that in Hebrew, the term *heart* (*lebab*) refers to the inner-aspects of a person, including their mind, will and emotions. The term *soul* (*nephesh*) refers to a person's entire being, including their spirit and body. It is essentially a person's entire identity, their whole self, which is created to exist in the love of God. For the purposes of this book, we generally use heart and soul in the same way. See HELPS Word Study #H5315 for more.

10. One Spirit

[1] Note that it is difficult to separate the Holy Spirit from Jesus and the Father. Together they are all one. For this reason, Scripture refers to the Holy Spirit as the Spirit of the Father (Matthew 10:30), the Spirit of Jesus (Galatians 4:6, Acts 16:7, Philippians 1:19) and simply the Spirit of God (Matthew 3:16, Romans 8:14). Both the Father and Son make their home within our hearts through the Holy Spirit (John 14:23. 1 John 2:24).

[2] Matthew 7:24-27

[3] HELPS Word Study #2309

[4] We look at this in more detail in the free book *Prepare a Place,* available at onewithchrist.org

[5] Song of Songs 8:6

[6] 2 Corinthians 5:14

11. Higher Ways

[7] See HELPS Word Study #4102*; Analytical Lexicon of the Greek New Testament,* Timothy Friberg, Barbara Friberg and Neva F. Mille. 2006; *Thayer's Greek-English Lexicon of the New Testament* (1889); *Vine's Complete Expository Dictionary of Old and New Testament Words* (1985).

[8] The Bible presents faith as a possession. Some people possess little faith and others possess great faith. In this sense, faith is like trust or confidence—it exists on a spectrum from little to great. We have little faith when our faith is merely a mild persuasion. When we possess great faith, we have an unshakeable conviction of the truth. Because faith exists as a measure of confidence, we always have the ability to grow our faith into a greater level of conviction.

[9] Romans 10:10

[10] 2 Corinthians 10:5-6

[11] HELPS Word Study #70b, referencing *Keil and Delitzsch Commentary on the Old Testament.*

12. The Source of Thoughts

[1] This is supported by the use of the indicative case in the Greek text.

13. Testing Thoughts

[1] John 6:63

[2] The "law and the prophets" is a phrase that is used to refer to the entire Old Testament.

[3] Romans 12:6

[4] The word *rhema* means a "spoken word, made from a living voice" (HELPS Word Studies #4487). When God speaks, we can ask Him to confirm His voice with two or three independent witnesses. For more on this, please see the free book, *For His Presence* available online at onewithchrist.org

[5] Romans 10:17

14. Making Agreements

[1] HELPS Word Study #3670

[2] Technically a filter of the mind can be thought of as a heuristic or a bias. A heuristic is a kind of shortcut that the brain uses to speed up decision making. Heuristics can create a cognitive bias or work to reinforce an existing bias.

[3] This is known as the *confirmation bias.*

[4] To fact check our assumptions requires great courage and vulnerability. It is not easy to say to someone *"When you did this, I thought or felt this… Was I getting the right message there?"* It is a challenge, but one that will bear fruit and help us to tear down our wrong strongholds.

15. A New Identity

[1] See *Prepare a Place,* where we look more at the cross in terms of the exchange of life. Through the cross, Jesus' flesh and blood become our nature and life and we become one with Christ.

[2] 1 Corinthians 6:17, Romans 8:11

[3] While we share our sense of identity with Jesus, it is important to note again that we do not become Jesus. God alone is God. We are neither more nor less than one with Christ.

[4] HELPS Word Study #3341. The first part of the word, *meta* introduces the sense that the change comes from being with something or someone. In terms of our relationship with God, our minds are changed after being with Jesus. Every moment we spend in prayer, worship or communing with Jesus brings about a greater level of repentance.

16. Identity in Love

[1] HELPS Word Studies #4698 and #4697

17. Prevailing Grace

1 When speaking of the Mosaic Law, the term *nomos* usually occurs with the Greek definite article and reads *The Law*. See HELPS Word Study #3551.

2 This is especially true where *nomos* occurs without the Greek definite article. See HELPS Word Study #3551.

3 The concept of a spiritual law can be more easily understood by looking at our natural laws. The law of gravity invisibly influences nearly every aspect of our physical life. Every day we make adjustments for gravity; we use it to our advantage and accept the consequences when we misuse it. The same principle is true spiritually. We all live within a system of spirituality, which affects almost every aspect of our spiritual life. Yet unlike the laws of physics, which we all have to yield to, we are able to choose which spiritual law we submit to in life. Scripture says that we have the choice to live under the law of sin and death (also called the "law of works") or under the law of the Spirit of life (also called the "law of faith").[3] Let us choose life so that we might live.

4 The ancient Greek language had no word for legalism but if it did Paul would have certainly used it.

5 Most of the religions of the world are based on a form of legalism, usually in the sense of "If your good works outweigh your bad works then you will go to paradise when you die (or enjoy a better life in your next reincarnation)." Many people also mistakenly apply this thinking to Christianity. However, Scripture is clear: it is only by God's grace that we are saved and made righteous through faith in Jesus Christ.

6 God intentionally makes it this way so that no one can boast in their own accomplishments. He deserves all the glory for our creation and our salvation and so He humbles us by removing any possibility for us to boast in our own works. Legalism works directly against this purpose of God, causing us to live in the bondage of spiritual pride instead of the freedom of humility.

18. Relationship and Religion

1 Galatians 3:24

2 Romans 10:17 Faith comes by hearing the *rhema* of Christ; *rhema* meaning a "spoken word from a living voice." See HELPS Word Study #4487

3 Romans 5:2—it is through faith that we access grace.

4 1 Corinthians 13:1-3

5 Romans 7:4-13, Romans 8:1-4, Galatians 5:1

6 Romans 7:12, James 1:25, 1 Timothy 1:8, Psalm 19:7

19. Life in Love

1 It is likely that many of these teachers were Pharisees who had converted to The Way. Circumcision was not the only focus. These teachers insisted that Jewish believers should still be subject to the Mosaic Law and should not associate with non-Jewish believers (Galatians 2:12). Paul was adamant that Christ has entirely fulfilled the Law and in Him we are made fully righteous. We are now only bound by the royal law of love—the single and greatest commandment of the Mosaic Law (Deuteronomy 6:1-5).

2 Note that as we learned earlier, the Hebrew word translated as *hold fast* is the word *davaq* meaning to cling, cleave to, or become one with. It is the same word that is used to describe a man *cleaving* to His wife to become one flesh with her (Genesis 2:24). Our call is to cling to God and to become one with Him.

3 2 Corinthians 11:1-4 shows how believers were being drawn away from the simplicity and purity of devotion to Christ. God's design of love for us is pure and simple, but it is often lost in the complexity and distractions of our modern teachings. I wonder if the greatest deception afflicting the present-day Church is the neglect of the first command as the first priority for every believer. What would the Church look like if she embraced the first command? I suspect she may look something like the Bride of Christ.

4 Mark 16:15

5 Note that the voice of legalism does not just come from within. Remember when Peter spoke against the will of God, Jesus said "Get behind me Satan!" Like Peter, there are lots of well-intentioned believers, even teachers, who will speak out the thoughts that a spirit of legalism has given them and try to sow the seeds of works into our minds.

6 Romans 7:4

7 Matthew 11:28-29

20. Breaking the Cycle

1 http://www.geoffbullock.com/Articles/goldenboy.html

21. Crime and Punishment

1 HELPS Word Study #6485

2 HELPS Word Study #3256

3 HELPS Word Study #7725

4 "Punish" from *The Oxford Living Dictionaries*, 2017 (online at https://en.oxforddictionaries.com/definition/punish)

[5] "Punish" from the *Cambridge Advanced Learner's Dictionary & Thesaurus* ©
Cambridge University Press 2017 (online at
http://dictionary.cambridge.org/dictionary/english/punish)

22. Sin and Deception

[1] Often sin is driven emotionally which means that we do not consciously deny the truth, rather we deny it on an emotional level. Regardless of whether it is a conscious or subconscious decision, when we sin, we enter into an agreement with the father of lies and give him permission to steal the truth from our hearts.

[2] 1 John 1:6-9

23. Teaching Grace

[1] See 2 Chronicles 34:25, Psalm 8:6, 28:5, 92:4, Proverbs 31:13, 31, Isaiah 59:6, Mark 6:2, Acts 7:41

24. Love in Eternity

[1] See Luke 12:33. The treasures of heaven are the spiritual treasures of His eternal love: wisdom, joy, hope, peace, zeal, passion, discernment, knowledge and so on. It is a great blessing and we do not need wait until we die to draw down on our spiritual inheritance. As we lay up a treasure such as joy, we can experience that treasure now in this life, as well as in eternity. We simply need to ask.

[2] Many of these testimonies can be found on the CBN channel on YouTube (https://www.youtube.com/user/CBNonline)

[3] If we have been slow to create a capacity for love, we can take heart in the thought that it is likely that in eternity our channel of love will always feel full, regardless of the capacity.

25. Multiplying Love

[1] Ezekiel 16:49

26. Love Like This

[1] HELPS Word Study #2531

[2] HELPS Word Study #2537

[3] As John later writes, this is not really a new commandment, but one which we have always had since the very beginning: that we love one another (2 John 1:5).

[4] Romans 5:5

27. Loving and Giving

[1] Not her real name.

[2] Michelle needed to release God from the blame she had put on Him, and to be restored back to his loving arms. She also needed help to forgive people from her past so she could be healed. While it was only a small start, after Michelle realized that Jesus shared her suffering, I dropped to my knees and asked for forgiveness on behalf of all the men who had ever hurt her. She wept and started to forgive and to release the pain. We all wept. All Michelle could say between the tears was, "Thank you. Thank you. Thank you." Love meets need and love heals.

[3] Romans 12:10, 1 Peter 1:22-23

[4] These were not her exact words.

[5] For the history of Elijah and the widow of Zarephath, read 1 Kings 17:8-16.

[6] Spoken in a talk given to Cornerstone Church, San Antonio, Texas on 29 April 2000.

28. Giving in Unity

[1] It is interesting to look at how the Early Church approached the subject of need. Written between 50 and 120AD, the Didache (pronounced dee-da-kay) is a letter that gives instructions to the churches on many aspects of church life. In terms of meeting need, the Didache reveals that the early Church did permit people to ask for their own needs but gave a warning that there would be a penalty if people requested help who were not in true need (Chapter One). This rule did not however apply to apostles or traveling ministers. Such people could ask for money on behalf of others in need, but if they requested money for themselves, they were judged to be false prophets (Chapter 11).

Note that the Didache is not in the same category of Scripture, but it is useful in giving us an insight into an early Church perspective on giving and receiving. It can be found online at: http://www.earlychristianwritings.com/text/didache-roberts.html

29. Love Discerns

[1] 2 Corinthians 4:13, James 2:14-17

[2] We can see this principle at work within families. When our children are young, we show them love by doing their washing and cooking their food. However, as they get older the expression of our love changes. We begin to show our love by teaching our children how to do their own washing and how to cook their own food. To keep doing this for them would only disempower them. There can come a time when what was once love is love no longer.

[3] Luke 20:18

[4] 2 Corinthians 1:3-4, Romans 12:15

[5] Hebrews 10:24, Matthew 16:24

[6] Matthew 23:37-39 reveals Jesus' emotional pain in being rejected by the people He longed to lavish with His love.

[7] Song of Songs 7:9

30. Will of God

[1] HELPS Word Study # 4336

[2] Just imagine what the world would be like if everyone acted to fulfill the prayers they prayed.

31. Founded in Love

[1] The word translated as *know* is the Greek word *ginosko,* meaning to know, especially through personal experience. See HELPS Word Study #1097.

[2] Matthew 7:13-14

32. All of You

[1] It is interesting that we never praise God for His predictability, so why would we expect the same predictable service whenever we meet together?

[2] This often happens when we praise God in song. God has designed our hearts to open up to love and to be united with those around us as we sing together. This occurs in spiritual and secular contexts. For example, in the military, companies of soldiers would sing together as they marched as a way of building unity. When we sing praises together, the Holy Spirit uses oxytocin to build unity between us. It is important to note however that we need to be able to hear others to experience this release of oxytocin. In many fellowships, the music drowns out the people and so prevents the oxytocin response. In such times of praise, a tangible sense of unity starts to build when the music stops but the people continue to sing and they can hear one another.

33. Infinite Love

[1] See Matthew 1:21. Jesus was named Jesus (meaning Yehovah or Yahweh saves) because He would save people from their sin. See also 1 Samuel 25:23-25 where Nabal is of one name and nature. To use a person's name in reference to their character and nature is still used in modern language, for example: 'They have a good name among the poor...'

[2] Romans 5:8

34. The Simple Gospel
[1] Matthew 7:24-27
[2] 1 Thessalonians 5:8, Galatians 5:6
[3] 1 John 3:11-23, James 2:14-26
[4] 1 Corinthians 13:1-3
[5] 1 Timothy 1:11
[6] HELPS Word Study #2098
[7] HELPS Word Study #2092
[8] At that stage in the conversation it would have been a distraction to talk about how all the other religions of the world try to earn their place in heaven through works. They strive to repay a debt that they cannot even begin to comprehend let alone pay back. In this sense, most of the world's religions work according to a principle of legalism, which can never attain righteousness in the sight of God. The whole world is in desperate need of the glorious gospel of love.

35. Revival Fire
[1] Note that the Hebrew word translated as *revive* in Psalm 19 is the word *shub* which literally means to turn back or change direction. In terms of revival, *shub* focuses on how the perfect law calls us to change direction and return to life.
[2] HELPS Word Study #2421a
[3] Song of Songs 8:6
[4] Colossians 3:14

36. Freely Give
[1] This book is part of the *One with Christ* series, which is available free online at onewithchrist.org. Note that some online stores do not let us list a book for free but may do a price-match if requested. While we are hoping to make the printed copies free to those in need, this may not be always possible in every case. Please contact us for more information.

Study Guide
[1] Isaiah 4:4
[2] HELPS Word Study #225
[3] If you are carrying an offense or there is broken relationship that needs mending, be brave and connect with that person.

4 Consider arranging a time to meet with one or two other people this week. Let love be your only agenda. Honor the people you meet with. Look them in the eye and take time to listen to them. Show your appreciation. Find out their needs. Affirm their identity in Christ and spur them on to the greatest command.

ONE WITH CHRIST

onewithchrist.org

Printed in Poland
by Amazon Fulfillment
Poland Sp. z o.o., Wrocław

60541480R00159